ROBERT BRIDGES

ROBERT BRIDGES

An Annotated Bibliography, 1873–1988

Lee Templin Hamilton

DELAWARE

Newark: University of Delaware Press
London and Toronto: Associated University Presses

Associated University Presses
440 Forsgate Drive
Cranbury, NJ 08512

Associated University Presses
25 Sicilian Avenue
London WC1A 2QH, England

Associated University Presses
P.O. Box 39, Clarkson Pstl. Stn.
Mississauga, Ontario
Canada L5J 3X9

The paper used in this publication meets the requirements
of the American National Standard for Permanence of Paper
for Printed Library Materials Z39.48-1984.

Library of Congress Cataloging-in-Publication Data

Hamilton, Lee Templin, 1950–
  Robert Bridges : an annotated bibliography, 1873–1988 / Lee
Templin Hamilton.
    p.   cm.
  ISBN 0-87413-364-5 (alk. paper)
  1. Bridges, Robert Seymour, 1844–1930—Bibliography.   I. Title.
Z8119.2.H36   1991
[PR4161.B6]
016.821'8—dc20   88-40577
                                                                       CIP

PRINTED IN THE UNITED STATES OF AMERICA

For my parents,
Robert and Marian

and my wife and children,
Dede, Courtney, and Blake

CONTENTS

ACKNOWLEDGMENTS

This bibliography, like all major research projects, could not have been completed without the cooperation and assistance of a great many people and organizations. Chief among these are the interlibrary loan departments of the Middleton Library at Louisiana State University and the Learning Resource Center at Pan American University. Their respective staff members provided invaluable assistance in acquiring much of the material for this bibliography.

When material was not available for loan, I relied on the support of Pan American University to travel to various collections. In this regard, I want to thank Ronald L. Applbaum, vice president for academic affairs, and Ernest J. Baca, dean of the College of Arts and Sciences, for financial assistance that allowed me to travel to the British Museum. I also want to express my deep appreciation for the personal and professional support given me by my department chairman, William L. Davis. His assistance in obtaining access to the departmental computers and his overall support for his faculty and their scholarly endeavors are exemplary.

I am also indebted to Jan Boney, Della Wissner, Edward Heckler, and Nicole McKelvy for their help in translating a number of the following articles and reviews. Rebecca W. Crump and Donald E. Stanford deserve special mention, for it was under their guidance that this project first began while I was at LSU. Their support and respective expertise in bibliography and Robert Bridges were essential in shaping this bibliography and bringing it to completion.

I also want to thank Morris Eaves and Michael Fischer for allowing me to work on the index to this bibliography during the summer I spent at the University of New Mexico participating in their NEH seminar. Their counsel and encouragement were greatly appreciated.

I owe a special debt of gratitude to Frieda Thompson and Brenda Gillard for their cheerful and willing assistance in putting the original manuscript of this bibliography into the departmental word processor and making the necessary editorial changes. Their handling of the technical matters regarding the production of the final copy of the manuscript was a demonstration of supreme professional skill.

Lauren Lepow and Brian MacDonald, both of Associated University Presses, deserve particular thanks for their patience, understanding, and professionalism in seeing this bibliography through to its completion. I am truly grateful for all they did for me.

Finally, I owe more than I can ever say to my parents and my wife. I owe the gifts of life and love of learning to my parents. To my wife, Dede, I owe the same gifts of love and life—our children, Courtney and Blake. Without the sacrifices and support of these people, this project would not have been possible.

INTRODUCTION

The life and work of Robert Bridges are not easily assessed. In neither his personal life nor his literary work does Bridges fit neatly into any predetermined category; both are characterized by a certain ambiguity and dichotomy. Born 23 October 1844 at Walmer in Kent, Bridges lived through the high tide and ebb of Victorian England. But he died 21 April 1930 during the first few months of the worldwide depression that was the interlude between the two world conflagrations that have marked the modern age and consciousness. Although it is generally recognized that the Victorian age is the spiritual and intellectual great-grandfather of the modern age, and that the Victorians themselves are more like us than unlike us, there are nevertheless attitudes, values, and world views that sharply distinguish the two periods. In this regard Robert Bridges embodies some characteristics that are distinctly and uniquely Victorian, and others that are entirely modern. Thus he cannot easily be placed into either period, but to say that he is merely a transitional figure between the two periods is inadequate and overlooks the diverse skills and achievements of this former poet laureate. It is this ambiguous dualism that pervades Bridges's life and work.

Only the bare outlines of Bridges's biography are known. He wanted no biography written about him and made a conscious effort to thwart any such attempt, his destruction of his letters to Gerard Manley Hopkins being the outstanding example of this. Bridges was the eighth of nine children. His parents were middle-class, and he seems to have had a rather idyllic mid-nineteenth-century childhood, growing up in the Kentish countryside. His father died in 1853 when Bridges was eight years old; and when his mother married the Reverend J. E. N. Molesworth the following year, the family moved to Rochdale in Lancashire. Typical of his class, Bridges attended Eton (1854–63) and Corpus Christi College, Oxford (1863–67), where he rowed for the Oxford team and earned a Second Class in Literara Humaniores. Although his educational background seems terribly middle-class, it belies two very different influences whose effects may be traced in Bridges's literary work.

At Eton Bridges became close friends with Digby Mackworth Dolben and came under the influence of the Tractarian movement. Later at Corpus Christi College he felt the influence of the Pre-Raphaelite movement, which pervaded the academic life of the university while he was there. These two movements, one inherently spiritual, the other essentially sensual, inform all of Bridges's work. In him the Tractarian emphasis upon tradition, authority, and orthodoxy combined with the Pre-Raphaelite quest for a romantic realism that blended matter and spirit. In addition to the Pre-Raphaelites, however, there was another even more profound influence at Oxford—Gerard Manley Hopkins. Of all of Bridges's friends, Hopkins stands preeminent in Bridges's life in his artistic and aesthetic influence on the future poet laureate. Although Hopkins's Catholic sentiments were not shared by Bridges, the two men did share a love of poetry and a desire to broaden its capacity to convey emotion and feeling through metrical experimentation. Whereas Hopkins pursued "sprung rhythm" while Bridges worked on syllabic verse, both were actually working on accentual verse. These two poets were two very different men of apparently antipodal world views and aesthetics; yet it is generally felt that each drew inspiration from the other and provided the necessary catalyst for one another's poetic experiments. Bridges provided restraint for Hopkins's lack of emotional discipline while Hopkins encouraged a broader expression of emotion in Bridges. Such poetic and aesthetic experiments are traditionally viewed as elements of the romantic tradition in art, not the classical tradition. Indeed, today nineteenth-century poets like Hopkins and Emily Dickinson are often regarded as precursors of modern poetry. Ironically, Bridges, who experimented with new meter virtually his whole life, is generally cast as a classicist, not as a romantic or a harbinger of modern poetry, so much of which is characterized by the kind of metrical and thematic innovation so typical of Bridges's art.

After Bridges graduated from Oxford, he traveled extensively in the Mediterranean and the Middle East. On returning to England in 1869, he began his medical studies at St. Bartholomew's Hospital, where he received his medical degree in 1874. This marks another of the many dichotomies already observed in Bridges's life and art. The man of letters, who had received his undergraduate degree at Oxford in humane letters, became a man of science. Two apparently contrary disciplines, the one essentially spiritual, the other exclusively material, combined in the same man and left their mark on all he did. After completing his medical studies, Bridges worked in the Casualty Department of St. Bartholomew's until 1878 when he was appointed assistant physician at the Hospital for Sick Children in Great Ormond Street. Later that same year he moved to the Great Northern Hospital in Holloway. In 1881 after a serious illness and a winter spent in Italy in order to recuperate, Bridges retired from medicine and devoted the rest of his life to literature. Bridges's literary career did not suddenly flower when he retired, however. In 1873, the year before he received his degree from St. Bartholomew's, Bridges published *Poems*, his first book of poetry. By 1881, the year he retired from medical practice, he had published a poem in Latin on St. Bartholomew's Hospital, two more anonymous series of poems, and an anonymous series of sonnets entitled *The Growth of Love*.

Between 1883 and 1895 Bridges wrote most of his plays, the most noteworthy being *Prometheus the Firegiver* (1883), *Nero, Part I* (1885), *Achilles in Scyros* (1890), and *The Return of Ulysses* (1894). Not all of Bridges's energy was focused on his work at this time, however. After he returned from Italy in 1881, Bridges moved to Yattendon to live with his mother while he recuperated from the illness that had forced him to abandon his medical practice. It was while he was in Yattendon that he met Monica Waterhouse, the daughter of Alfred Waterhouse, whom he later married in 1884.

Although much of Bridges's early poetry was primarily lyrical, there are several examples of his interest in prosody and metrical experimentation. These early poems, which show the influence of Hopkins and William J. Stone, include some of his most well-known verses, such as "London Snow," "On a Dead Child," and "Nightingales," all of which were written before 1900. Virtually all of the poetry Bridges wrote after 1900 retains the imprint of this period and illustrates his life-long interest and experimentation in prosody. From "Now in Wintry Delights" (1903) to the verses in *October and Other Poems* (1920) and *New Verse* (1925), Bridges's metrical innovation is continuous. All of the poems in these books prepare the way for the "loose alexandrines" of *The Testament of Beauty* (1929), his last major work.

These metrical experiments, however, were not always favored by the critics and were almost never read by the public. This may in part account for the lack of public recognition of Bridges's name when he was appointed poet laureate. Indeed his reputation might well be less than it currently is if in 1913 Prime Minister Asquith had not ignored popular sentiment, which favored the appointment of Kipling, and appointed Bridges to succeed Alfred Austin as the poet laureate of England, thus forcing Bridges and his poetry into the public spotlight. This attention was not welcomed by the new poet laureate, who found it all rather annoying and slightly embarrassing. Because he was so unknown, Bridges's appointment was generally greeted by bemused wonder in the English press. Those who already knew Bridges saw his appointment as a triumph for poetry and the laureateship. Here was a true poet who, unlike his predecessor, would bring honor and, above all, art to the office. Others who also knew Bridges knew of his strong sense of independence and realized he would not write on command and would not write the sort of occasional verse that was expected of the laureate. Both views were right.

During the war years Bridges was often criticized for not producing patriotic verses for the war effort. His critics expected the usual paeans to heroism and patriotism. Bridges chose another route. In 1916 he edited and published *The Spirit of Man,* an anthology of morally and spiritually uplifting verse drawn from ancient and modern sources of European culture. This volume was intended to give strength to the English people by reminding them of their cultural heritage and the principles for which they were fighting. But Bridges did not entirely ignore the more conventional duties of his office. When he did write poetry for the war, however, he published the poems individually and sporadically, without any fanfare, in papers and journals. It was not until 1920 that he collected and published his war poetry in *October and Other Poems.* Bridges's most important literary effort during the war years, some would say the most important literary effort of his entire career, was not related to the war at all, however. Rather it was a private memorial to a friend. In 1918 Bridges gave Gerard Manley Hopkins to the literary world in his edition of *Poems of Gerard Manley Hopkins.* This marked the beginning of Hopkins's literary reputation, a reputation that has, ironically, surpassed Bridges's own.

In 1924 Bridges visited America and taught at the University of Michigan during the spring semester. Prior to this period Bridges devoted much of his energy to further experiments in prosody and to the Society for Pure English, which he had founded in 1913 with Logan Pearsall Smith and Sir Walter Raleigh. The fruits of these experiments—what he called "Neo-Miltonic syllabics"—

appeared in *New Verse* (1925). These verses were the precursors to the "loose alexandrines," the twelve syllable lines, of *The Testament of Beauty* (1929), Bridges's last and, to some, greatest poem, published in October 1929, six months before his death.

The present bibliography is divided into three chapters, each arranged in chronological order. Chapter 1 contains Bridges's poetry, drama, and hymns. I have not attempted to trace the first publication of each of Bridges's poems, which were most often in magazines and journals of the day. Such an endeavor would have widened the scope of this project beyond my ability to complete it, given the onerous limitations of time, resources, and money that are inevitably imposed on all research. The first appearances of most of Bridges's poems may be fairly well traced by consulting McKay's *A Bibliography of Robert Bridges* (1933) and the bibliographical information found in the Oxford University Press's single-volume edition of *Poetical Works of Robert Bridges, with The Testament of Beauty, but Excluding the Eight Dramas* (1953). The first chapter of the present bibliography cites the published editions of Bridges's poetical works, including revised editions and reprints. I have attempted to note any changes that occur in the contents or texts of these later editions. There are, however, a few exceptions to this principle. Some of Bridges's poems were initially separately published and then collected in later editions of his poems. In such instances I have cited the separate publication of the poem. For example, "Now in Wintry Delights" was first published by the Daniel Press in 1903. The poem was later included in the Oxford University Press edition of the *Poetical Works of Robert Bridges, Excluding the Eight Dramas* (1912). In have included both entries, but there are only a handful of items like this. The dramas and hymns present no such problems. In each case I have cited the first publication of the plays. Unlike the plays, the hymns were always published in anthologies or separate editions, never individually.

Chapter 2 contains Bridges's prose: critical essays, introductions, memoirs, and letters. Unlike chapter 1, here I have attempted to cite the first appearances of the prose writings. When compared with the number of poems, the much smaller body of prose made this a much more feasible task. Bridges's essays and notes for the publications of the Society for Pure English present a minor problem, however. Many of the brief notes in the Society's Tracts are unsigned or else simply signed "Ed." It has been generally assumed by McKay, Nowell-Smith, and others that most of the unsigned material and the material signed "Ed." are by Bridges. I am not presently able to judge the accuracy of this assumption but have no reason to dispute it. However, I have taken a more conservative path and included only those essays signed by Bridges or known to have been written by him—for example, articles by "Matthew Barnes," a pseudonym employed by Bridges and his wife.

Many of the letters found in chapter 2 are taken from the newspapers. Letters found in secondary sources such as books, articles, and essays about Bridges are also included.

Chapter 3 is devoted to secondary sources: reviews, articles, essays, books, and other notes about Robert Bridges. Works in which Bridges is only mentioned once or twice are not included in the bibliography. For example, although the index of F. O. Matthiessen's *American Renaissance* indicates that Robert Bridges is mentioned on pages 585–87, a glance at those pages reveals that there is no critical discussion of Bridges or his work. His name appears only in regard to what he said about Hopkins's poetry. Because there is no evaluation of or comment about Bridges's criticism, the item is not included in this bibliography.

It has not been possible to search through all English and American newspapers for items on Bridges. Only the major papers with indices have been accessible. Smaller papers on both sides of the Atlantic, most without indices and many now defunct, have been unavoidably overlooked. American papers, such as *The Evening Mail* (New York), *The Evening Post* (New York), and *The Globe* (New York), and English papers, such as *The Daily Chronicle* (London), *The Morning Post* (London), and *The London Daily Mail*, are not generally included in the bibliography.

The names of Bridges and Hopkins are forever linked in English literary history. Although he was born in the same year as Bridges, Hopkins died forty years before his friend. Since then, his reputation has steadily grown and outstripped that of Bridges, who was responsible for first publishing Hopkins's poetry in 1918. The growing body of scholarship on Hopkins includes a good deal of discussion about Bridges and his relationship with Hopkins. To have researched thoroughly every item of Hopkins scholarship would have greatly protracted this project and very likely more than doubled the body of material to be obtained and consulted for the compilation of this bibliography. The major sources in Hopkins scholarship have been consulted; the minor sources have been passed over.

Finally, this chapter also includes anthologies that contain

Bridges's poetry. Given the vast number of anthologies already in existence and the number that are published each year, there are certain to be oversights in this area. The anthology citations reveal the trends in Bridges's popularity and the popularity of certain poems, those that have been most often anthologized. In general, there is a noticeable decline in the number of anthology entries between 1930 and 1960, which parallels a similar decline in scholarly interest in Bridges during the same period.

The critical reception of certain aspects of Bridges's art has been, on the whole, rather uniform. From the earliest review of *Poems* (1873), that by Andrew Lang in 1874, Bridges's lyric artistry and his refined emotional restraint have been acknowledged and praised. The delicate music of the lyrics and technical mastery of the meter have been consistently praised by the majority of critics over the years. His craftsmanship and strict adherence to form, all within the older traditions of poetic art, have led critics to classify him as a classicist. The large number of works on classical themes, especially in the dramatic works, lends credence to this view—a view that has dominated Bridges scholarship.

But there also has been a rather consistent dissenting view as well. Ironically, this dissent has grown out of what has been generally praised by other critics, that is, the technical mastery and emotional restraint of the verse. To some critics it has seemed that Bridges's careful attention to the technical side of his art has suffocated its emotional content. What has been praised as classical restraint by a majority of critics has been condemned by this second group who acknowledge the technical skill of the verse but lament its distinct lack of emotion. Faint stirrings of this view may be heard in Lang's review, but this view is more pronounced in the review of the second series of *Poems,* which appeared in *The Academy* in 1879. The author of this review praised the technical aspects of the poetry but also noted an emotional coolness in some of the poems.

Criticism in the same key marked the reception of *The Growth of Love,* which appeared earlier in 1876. Although this series of sonnets enjoyed a relative popularity among general readers, critics generally faulted it for not being a true sonnet sequence with a clearly delineated progression of emotion, and some critics even felt it had no genuine emotion at all. There was nevertheless a significant number who praised *The Growth of Love* as a classic sequence by a classical poet.

Throughout this early period prior to Bridges's experiments with classical prosody and English hexameters, most critics

praised the classical elements of Bridges's poetry, its form, technique, and restraint. Even those who criticized his verses for their
lack of emotion acknowledged his technical skill. The critics were
much less divided, however, regarding his experiments in classical
prosody; the critical reception was almost uniformly negative. For
most the cadence was jolting, and among critics with less understanding, some even wondered if Bridges had any ear at all for
sound or meter. Those critics who had criticized him earlier for
being more concerned with technique than emotion found further proof for their claim in these new experiments. To them
Bridges's experiments clearly showed his total absorption in technique and his utter disregard for emotional verity. The few critics
who commented favorably on the new verse generally found the
experiment interesting and felt that such poetry would improve
the general pronunciation of English, an end that was not altogether alien to Bridges's original intent.

Despite the critical attention given to his metrical experiments,
Bridges's plays received only minor attention in their day and are
still largely ignored today. Typical of much nineteenth-century
drama, the plays were primarily closet dramas that William Butler
Yeats recognized would have no commercial success, a judgment
seemingly borne out by the fact that the plays enjoyed only limited
production, and then generally only university productions. The
most highly regarded, as already noted, are *Prometheus the Firegiver* (1883), *Nero, Part I* (1885), *Achilles in Scyros* (1890), and *The
Return of Ulysses*. Taken together the plays on classical themes and
the experiments in classical prosody added further weight to the
critical perception of Bridges as a classicist. But some of the
criticism surrounding the plays is significant because it marks a
new vein in Bridges criticism. Several critics, most notably Yeats
and Arthur Symons, praised the subtle lyrics and the aesthetic of
delicate beauty that imbued the plays with emotion. These late
Romantics of the nineteenth century valued the delicately expressed beauty and emotion that they discerned in these plays.
They acknowledged the technical craftsmanship of the verse and
felt the emotion contained therein.

But the emotion they perceived was not the objective, dispassionate expression of feeling that was valued by critics of more
classical tastes. To these younger critics and poets, Bridges's expression of emotion was subjective and highly personal. This
critical perspective seems to fall between those critics who praised
the emotional restraint of his poetry and those who preferred
more spasmodic verse and who felt Bridges was devoid of genuine

emotion. In the opinion of the critics in this third category, Bridges felt life and passion on the pulses, recollected it in tranquillity, and transmuted it into what could in some instances be classified as Pre-Raphaelite poetry. Here again is the confluence of contending forces that marks Bridges's life and runs through his work.

The first Oxford edition of the *Poetical Works of Robert Bridges, Excluding the Eight Dramas* was published in 1912 and reprinted in 1913, the year of his appointment to the laureateship. This publication collected Bridges's poetry in a single volume for the first time and made it readily accessible to more people than ever before. The book was warmly received and even led one critic, John Baily, to suggest that Bridges should be the next poet laureate. Just as thirty-five years before, when Lang first reviewed Bridges's *Poems*, the lyrics in this collection were praised by the critics as the highest achievement of Bridges's art. This high regard for the lyrics perhaps made it impossible for any of the later poems, especially those in classical prosody and other experimental meters, to be fully appreciated or regarded on their own merit. Throughout the reviews of the later volumes of verse, *October and Other Poems* (1920) and *New Verse* (1925), there is general critical respect for the new poems and experiments, but there is also a recurring lament for the apparent loss of smoothness and beauty that distinguished the earlier lyrics. Many critics and reviewers seem to have given the new prosody only a cursory reading, and when they saw the poems were not like the early lyrics, they simply registered their disappointment and passed them off. This same sort of skewed critical vision marks much of the criticism of Bridges's prose writings.

When the Oxford University Press began to collect and publish Bridges's critical essays, it allowed Bridges to exercise his interest in spelling, pronunciation, and typographical reform by printing the essays in phonotype, following the poet's personal suggestions for pronunciation and using phonotype characters for spelling and printing. The reviews of these essays, almost without exception, focus more on the unusual typeface than on the content of the essays. As more new phonotype characters were added to each succeeding volume of the essays, the critics grew increasingly distressed and annoyed by what they felt was a needless encumbrance. As a result, the assessment of Bridges as a critic has been rather thin.

If the critics tended to ignore Bridges's criticism, they made up for their lack of attention when *The Testament of Beauty* was published in 1929. This poem was widely reviewed and highly praised, but praised for a wide variety of reasons. The largest segment of critical acclaim for the poem praised the poem as the distillation of knowledge and wisdom gained by the poet laureate over the long years of his life. A second, and similar, body of criticism was promulgated by a group of critics who seemed to praise the poem simply because they were astonished that such a long philosophical poem could be written by an eighty-five-year-old man. They praised the poem as much for the longevity of the poet as for the sheer length of the poem. The timing of the poem's publication—the fact that it appeared six months before Bridges died—may well have influenced these two groups of critics in their judgment and caused them to view the work with something less than critical acuity.

There were two other definable critical stances regarding *The Testament of Beauty,* and both were more critically significant in terms of assessing the poem than either of the two previous views. One group of critics looked at the philosophy of the poem and praised the manner in which Bridges had apparently combined philosophical idealism and scientific materialism. They felt Bridges had taken the history of Humanity and forged a new and transcendental vision of human history and destiny by taking the oldest intellectual traditions of the human race and combining them with the most recent scientific and technological knowledge. Opposed to this view of the poem was a group of critics who disapproved of the poem altogether. This minority of critics rejected *The Testament of Beauty* on precisely the same philosophical grounds the first group had praised it so highly—the linking of idealism and materialism. This second group felt the linking was forced and that Bridges had not made his argument in an intellectually or philosophically sound manner. They felt the optimism of the poem was too easily won and argued that the contentment and ease Bridges felt was too remote, too aloof, too complacent, and not consonant with the experiences of the majority of men. It did not deal with the harsh realities of life for those who were not as fortunate as Bridges himself. Although this view was decidedly the the minority view in 1930 when Bridges died, it has come to be more widely accepted since his death. The depression and war that followed in the decade after his death have done much to undermine Bridges's cool, aloof optimism and validate this second critical perspective.

One final issue has piqued critical debate since Bridges's death, and that is Bridges's role as editor of Hopkins's poetry. When

Bridges published Hopkins's poems in 1918, almost no mention was made of his role as editor. After his death in 1930 and the publication of the second edition of Hopkins's poetry that same year, critics began to assess that role. Critical opinion was initially against Bridges. He was seen as having delayed the publication of Hopkins's work and having been blinded by his own aesthetic and anti-Catholic prejudices. Later scholarship has altered this harsh judgment. There is currently no evidence that Bridges encouraged Hopkins to publish his poetry while the latter was still alive. After Hopkins's death Bridges himself published a few of Hopkins's poems in Alfred Henry Miles's *Poets and Poetry of the Century* (1893). Rather than seeing Bridges as a petty man who hid the poetry of a greater poet than himself, most modern critics regard Bridges as having held Hopkins's poetry back (if that is in fact what he did) until a proper and receptive climate existed for the introduction of his friend's verses. The creation of such a favorable climate seems largely attributable to the poetic experiments of Pound and Eliot. More recent studies of Hopkins's manuscripts also confirm Bridges's selection of poems for his edition of Hopkins's poetry. Critics now generally agree that Bridges, rather than being motivated by anti-Catholic prejudice to exclude certain poems from his edition of Hopkins' poems, exercised careful critical judgment in selecting poems for inclusion in his edition of his friend's work.

Such have been the major concerns and trends in the criticism and scholarship on Robert Bridges and his work. In general he has been labeled a classicist, and certainly there is ample, warrantable evidence for such labeling. The often conventional subject matter, the classical themes, the emphasis upon technical mastery and control, the restrained passion and emotion, the archaic diction—all are characteristic aspects of poetry in the classical tradition. But Bridges was influenced by the neoromanticism of the Pre-Raphaelite movement as well as the Tractarian movement. Although Bridges clearly exhibits classical and romantic tendencies, it is the classical element in his work that has been emphasized. The influence of romanticism has been largely ignored when critics have assessed Bridges's life and work.

Although it is fair to say that Bridges is more of a classicist than a romantic, the general view of him as such is a view that has been, in my view, overstated; and this is due in large part to the fact that the best critics of Bridges have themselves been classicists and have thus emphasized the classical elements of Bridges's art. In England this group of critics includes Francis Brett Young,

George Stuart Gordon, John Sparrow, and Simon Nowell-Smith. The best American critics form an unbroken critical tradition that can be traced directly from Yvor Winters to Albert J. Guerard, Jr., down to Donald E. Stanford, with these last two representing two of the best Bridges scholars today. Of all of these critics, Stanford takes the broadest view of Bridges and notes some of the romantic elements in his work. There is no doubt that the classical elements in Bridges's work are very strong, but the romantic elements are strong also. His constant innovation and experimentation in prosody are characteristic of a romantic dissatisfaction with old forms and a quest for new modes of expression. Similarly the aestheticism in his poetry, the worship of Beauty that was recognized by Symons and Yeats and then revealed in full in *The Testament of Beauty,* is a clear mark of romantic sensibilities. One need only consider Bridges's admiration for Keats and the similarity between his worship of Beauty and that of Shelley to see the extent of Bridges's romantic affinities.

In addition to the need for further study of the romantic elements in Bridges's work, there is also a major gap in our knowledge of Bridges's personal life. The full extent of his friendship with Hopkins and the influence of that friendship will probably never be fully understood as a consequence of Bridges's destruction of his correspondence with his friend. However, Donald E. Stanford's recent edition of Bridges's collected letters throws some light on Bridges's relationship with Hopkins and gives a much clearer picture of Bridges's other interests and his relationships with other literary figures of his day. These letters are a major step in the gradual process of filling in more of Bridges's biography. But it is the very absence of a definitive biography that is the second and most crucial aspect of Bridges scholarship that has been neglected.

Bridges insisted he wanted no biography written about him, and to this day his wish has been honored. Characteristically he wanted his poetry to stand on its own merits. He did not want his biography to cloud or color the reception of his verse. This is a legitimate fear that perhaps every writer feels, but it is a very narrow view of the role of biography in the evaluation of an artist. Knowledge of an artist's biography can sometimes reveal influences on the artist or the effect of those influences on the art itself. An understanding of anyone's biography contributes to the understanding of the whole person, and this includes the attitudes, ideas, values, and influences that shape the writer and affect all that he does. People are a part of all that they meet. It seems obvious that no thorough assessment of either Bridges or his work can be made without knowing more than is presently known about Bridges himself.

Bridges's career and reputation remain problematic. He was never universally or even widely popular, with the possible exception of the year in which he published *The Testament of Beauty.* His reputation seems to have peaked in 1930 and faded rapidly. The shift in modern poetic tastes, which is often associated with Pound and Eliot, coupled with the two world wars of this century, have made the quiet moods and delicate rhythms of Bridges's poetry seem quaint and unsuited for our time. It seems unlikely that he will ever be regarded as a major literary figure of our time. When he is compared with Yeats or Eliot, the reasons for his lack of popularity seem clear, but this is perhaps partly due to an unwarranted denigration or lack of appreciation of his artistic skills. It is not because his poetry has been overlooked and really is as fine as either Yeats's or Eliot's, but because he was a man of such wide and varied interests that most other men, not just poets, seem narrow and limited by comparison. No other man in this century, or perhaps any century since the Renaissance, has been so broadly interested in the literary arts or exhibited such a high degree of skill in so many areas of endeavor. Bridges was a poet, a dramatist, and a critic, true; but he was also a philologist in the broadest sense. He was actively interested in improving the pronunciation of English and advocated spelling reform as well. This interest in spelling reform carried over into his interest in typography. In addition to this he was a semanticist and a translator. It is perhaps an index of our age of specialization that few poets today are so diverse; and although some may object that these interests are the dabblings of an idle aristocracy, we should at least respect the broad learning and humanistic spirit that imbue the entire body of Robert Bridges's art.

ROBERT BRIDGES

1

POETRY AND DRAMA

1873

1. Bridges, Robert. *Poems.* London: [Basil Montague] Pickering, 1873.
   Fifty-two poems, including "Elegy: On a Lady," "Clear and gentle stream," and "I will not let thee go."

1876

1. Bridges, Robert. *Carmen Elegiacum de Noscomio Sti. Bartolomaei Londinensi.* London: Edward Bumpus, 1876.
   A poem on the history of the hospital.
2. [Bridges, Robert.] *The Growth of Love: A Poem in Twenty-four Sonnets.* London: Edward Bumpus, 1876.
   Includes "O Weary Pilgrims," "Rejoice Ye Dead," and "Tears of love, tears of joy."

1877

1. Bridges, Robert. *Carmen Elegiacum de Noscomio Sti. Bartolomaei Londinensi.* London: Edward Bumpus, 1877.
   Reprint of 1876.1. Lengthened by two lines.

1879

1. [Bridges, Robert.] *Poems: By the Author of "The Growth of Love."* London: Edward Bumpus, 1879.
   Includes "A Passer-By," "The Downs," and "There is a hill beside the silver Thames."

1880

1. [Bridges, Robert.] *Poems: By the Author of "The Growth of Love."* 3d Series. London: Edward Bumpus, 1880.
   Includes "London Snow," "On a Dead Child," and "The Ship."

1883

1. Bridges, Robert. *Prometheus the Firegiver*. Oxford: H[enry]
   Daniel Press, 1883.

1884

1. Bridges, Robert. *Poems*. Oxford: [Henry] Daniel Press, 1884.
     Includes selections from all previous series and adds
   seven new poems, including "Awake my heart to be loved"
   and "O youth whose hope is high."
2. Bridges, Robert. *Prometheus the Firegiver*. London: George Bell
   and Sons, 1884.
     Reprint of 1883.1.

1885

1. Bridges, Robert. *Eros and Psyche*. London: George Bell and
   Sons, 1885.
2. Bridges, Robert. *Nero, Part I*. London: George Bell and Sons,
   1885.
3. Bridges, Robert. *Prometheus the Firegiver*. London: George Bell
   and Sons, 1885.
     Reprint of 1883.1.

1888

1. Bridges, Robert. *The Humours of the Court*. [London:] George
   Bell and Sons, [1888.]
     Uniform with other Bell editions and paginated continu-
   ously throughout the series.

1889

1. Bridges, Robert. *The Feast of Bacchus*. Oxford: H[enry] Daniel
   Press, 1889.
2. [Bridges, Robert.] *The Growth of Love*. Oxford: H[enry] Daniel
   Press, 1889.
     Expanded and revised edition. Omits several sonnets
   from earlier editions and adds many more, including
   "Winter was not unkind because uncouth."

1890

1. Bridges, Robert. *Achilles in Scyros*. London: E[dward]
   Bumpus, 1890.

2. Bridges, Robert. *The Christian Captives*. London: Edward Bumpus, 1890.

3. [Bridges, Robert.] *The Growth of Love: A Poem in 79 Sonnets*. [Oxford: Henry Daniel, 1890.]
   Reprint of 1889.2.

4. Bridges, Robert. *Palicio*. London: Edward Bumpus, 1890.

5. Bridges, Robert. *The Return of Ulysses*. London: Edward Bumpus, 1890.

6. Bridges, Robert. *The Shorter Poems of Robert Bridges*. Four Books. London: George Bell and Sons, 1890.
   The poems in the first three books are reprinted from 1873.1, 1879.1, 1880.1, and 1884.1. The poems in the fourth book are new and include "I love all beauteous things," "The Wind-mill," and "The pinks along my garden walks."

1891

1. Bridges, Robert. *Eden: An Oratorio*. London: George Bell and Sons; New York: Novello, Ewer and Co., 1891.

2. Bridges, Robert. *Eden: An Oratorio*. New York: Novello, Ewer and Co., 1891.
   Includes full score with lyrics.

3. Bridges, Robert. *The Shorter Poems of Robert Bridges*. 2d ed. London: George Bell and Sons, 1891.
   Reprint of 1890.6.

4. Bridges, Robert. *The Shorter Poems of Robert Bridges*. 3d ed. London: George Bell and Sons, 1891.
   Reprint of 1890.6.

1892

1. Bridges, Robert. *Achilles in Scyros*. London: George Bell and Sons, 1892.
   Corrected reprint of 1890.1.

1893

1. [Bridges, Robert.] "Founder's Day: A Secular Ode on the Ninth Jubilee of Eton College." [Oxford: Henry Daniel, 1893.]

2. Bridges, Robert. *The Humours of the Court*. [London:] George Bell and Sons and J. & E. Bumpus, [1893].
   Reprint of 1888.1.

3. Bridges, Robert. *The Humours of the Court, and Other Poems*. London: George Bell and Sons; Boston: Macmillan, 1893.

 The "Other Poems" in this volume are Book 5 of *Shorter Poems*, here published for the first time, which include "The Garden in September," "So sweet love seemed," "Nightingales," and "I never shall love the snow again."

4. Bridges, Robert. *The Shorter Poems: Book I*. Oxford: Henry Daniel, 1893.

 Reprinted from 1890.6.

5. Bridges, Robert. *Shorter Poems: Book II*. Oxford: Henry Daniel, 1893.

 Reprinted from 1890.6.

6. Bridges, Robert. *Shorter Poems: Book V*. [Oxford: Henry Daniel, 1893.]

 The first Daniel edition of these poems. See 1893.3.

1894

1. Bridges, Robert. *Eros and Psyche*. Rev. ed. London: George Bell and Sons, 1894.

 Revised throughout with parts of first and second cantos rewritten.

2. Bridges, Robert. *The Feast of Bacchus*. London: George Bell and Sons and J. & E. Bumpus, 1894.

 Reprint of 1889.1.

3. Bridges, Robert. *The Growth of Love: A Poem in 79 Sonnets*. Portland, Maine: Thomas B. Mosher, 1894.

4. B[ridges], R[obert]. *Nero, Part II*. [London:] George Bell and sons and J. & E. Bumpus, Ltd., [1894].

 Adds a note on *Palicio*.

5. Bridges, Robert. *Shorter Poems: Book III*. Oxford: Henry Daniel, 1894.

 Reprinted from 1890.6.

6. Bridges, Robert. *Shorter Poems: Book IV*. Oxford: Henry Daniel, 1894.

 Reprinted from 1890.6.

7. Bridges, Robert. *Shorter Poems: Book V*. London: George Bell and Sons, 1894.

8. Bridges, Robert. *Shorter Poems*. Oxford: Henry Daniel, 1894.

 Contains all five books of *Shorter Poems*, each book separately paginated.

9. Bridges, Robert. *The Shorter Poems of Robert Bridges.* 4th ed. London: George Bell and Sons, 1894.

1895

1. Bridges, Robert. *Hymns in Four Parts.* Vol. 1. Oxford: Oxford University Press, 1895.
   Includes words and music.
2. Bridges, Robert. *Invocation to Music: An Ode.* London and New York: Novello, Ewer and Co., 1895.

1896

1. Bridges, Robert. *Ode for the Bicentenary Commemoration of Henry Purcell, with Other Poems.* London: Elkin Mathews; Chicago: Way and Williams, 1896.
   Includes "Ode to Music," "Winter Nightfall," and "The South Wind."
2. Bridges, Robert. *The Shorter Poems of Robert Bridges.* 5th ed. London: George Bell and Sons, 1896.
   Reprint of 1894.9.

1897

1. [Bridges, Robert, ed.] *Chants for the Psalter.* [Oxford: The Clarendon Press, 1897.]
   The title page of this book reads, "Yattendon 4-Part Chants."
2. Bridges, Robert. *Christmas Day, 1897.* Oxford: Henry Daniel, [1897.]
3. Bridges, Robert. *Hymns in Four Parts.* Vol. 2. Oxford: Oxford University Press, 1897.
4. Bridges, Robert. *Hymns in Four Parts.* Oxford: Oxford University Press, 1897.
   Combines vols. 1 and 2.

1898

1. Bridges, Robert. *Hymns in Four Parts.* Vol. 3. Oxford: Oxford University Press, 1898.
2. Bridges, Robert. *The Poetical Works of Robert Bridges.* Vol. 1. London: Smith, Elder and Co., 1898.
   Contains *Prometheus, Eros and Psyche,* and *The Growth of Love,* with new notes.

3. Bridges, Robert. *The Poetical Works of Robert Bridges*. Vol. 1. Oxford: The Clarendon Press, 1898.
   Reprints 1898.2.
4. Bridges, Robert. *A Song of Darkness and Light*. London: Novello, Ewer and Co.; New York: The H. W. Gray Co., 1898.
   Bridges's ode set to music by Hubert H. Parry.

1899

1. Bridges, Robert. *The Poetical Works of Robert Bridges*. Vol. 2. London: Smith, Elder and Co., 1899.
   Contains *Shorter Poems* and *New Poems*. The latter includes "Elegy: The Summer house on the mound" and "When Death to either shall come."
2. Bridges, Robert. *Shorter Poems, Book V*. London: George Bell and Sons, 1899.
   New edition of 1890.6 which adds a fifth book of *Shorter Poems*.
3. Bridges, Robert, ed. *Hymns*. Oxford: Henry Daniel, 1899.
   Adds new hymns to those previously published.
4. Bridges, Robert, ed. *Hymns in Four Parts*. Vol. 4. Oxford: Oxford University Press, 1899.
5. Bridges, Robert, ed. *Hymns in Four Parts*. Oxford: Oxford University Press, 1899.
   All four earlier volumes are here published in a single volume. See 1895.1, 1897.3, 1898.1, and 1899.4.
6. [Bridges, Robert, ed.] *The Small Hymn-Book*. London: Simpkin, Marshall, Hamilton, Kent and Co.; Oxford: B[asil] H. Blackwell, 1899.
   The words to the hymns of *The Yattendon Hymnal*. See 1899.7.
7. Bridges, Robert, and H[arry] Ellis Wooldridge, eds. *Hymns: The Yattendon Hymnal*. London: Oxford University Press, 1899.
   The same as 1899.5.

1900

1. [Bridges, Robert.] "Founder's Day." London: Novello and Co., Ltd.; New York: Novello, Ewer and Co., 1900.
   Reprint of 1893.1.

1901

1. Bridges, Robert. *The Poetical Works of Robert Bridges*. Vol. 3. London: Smith, Elder and Co., 1901.
   Contains *Nero, Part I* and *Achilles in Scyros*. Includes new notes on *Nero*.

1902

1. Bridges, Robert. *The Poetical Works of Robert Bridges*. Vol. 4. London: Smith, Elder and Co., 1902.
   Contains *Palicio* and *The Return of Ulysses*.
2. Bridges, Robert. *The Poetical Works of Robert Bridges*. Vol. 5. London: Smith, Elder and Co., 1902.
   Contains *The Christian Captives* and *The Humours of the Court*.

1903

1. Bridges, Robert. *Now in Wintry Delights*. Oxford: [Henry Daniel,] 1903.
2. B[ridges], R[obert]. *Peace Ode Written on the Conclusion of the Three Years War*. [Oxford: Henry Daniel,] 1903.
   The last publication of the Daniel Press.

1905

1. Bridges, Robert. *Demeter: A Mask*. Oxford: The Clarendon Press, 1905.
   Contains full score and lyrics. Music by W. H. Hadow.
2. Bridges, Robert. *Demeter: A Mask*. Oxford: The Clarendon Press, 1905.
   Contains only the lyrics and incidental music of the masque.
3. Bridges, Robert. *The Poetical Works of Robert Bridges*. Vol. 6. London: Smith, Elder and Co., 1905.
   Contains *The Feast of Bacchus* and *Nero, Part II*.

1907

1. Bridges, Robert. Poem. In *The Oxford Historical Pageant*, 13–15. Oxford: The Clarendon Press, 1907.
   Contains "An Invitation to the Oxford Pageant, July 1907."

2. Bridges, Robert. "Theobaldus Stampensis." In *The Oxford Historical Pageant,* 29–34. Oxford: Printed for the Pageant Committee, 1907.
   A one-act play on the founding of Oxford.

1908

1. Bridges, Robert. *Eton Memorial Ode.* London: Novello and Co.; New York: H. W. Gray Co., 1908.
   Bridges's ode set to music by C. Hubert H. Parry.

1909

1. Bridges, Robert. *Poems.* London: Smith, Elder and Co., 1909

1910

1. Bridges, Robert. *The Shorter Poems.* London: George Bell and Sons, 1910.
   Reprint of 1899.2. Reprinted again in 1913 and 1914.

1912

1. Bridges, Robert. *The Poetical Works of Robert Bridges, Excluding the Eight Dramas.* London: Oxford University Press, 1912.
   Contains all of Bridges's previously published poetry.
2. Bridges, Robert, trans. "Sonnet XLIV of Michaelangelo Buonarroti." N.p.: Privately printed, 1912.

1913

1. Bridges, Robert. *Achilles in Scyros.* London: George Bell and Sons, Ltd., 1913.
   Reprint of 1892.1.
2. Bridges, Robert. *The Growth of Love: A Poem in 79 Sonnets.* Portland, Maine: Thomas B. Mosher, 1913.
   Reprint of 1894.3.
3. Bridges, Robert. *The Poetical Works of Robert Bridges, Excluding the Eight Dramas.* London: Oxford University Press, 1913.
   Reprint of 1912.1.

1914

1. Bridges, Robert. "Hell and Hate." *Times Literary Supplement,* 24 September 1914, 432.

2. Bridges, Robert. *Poems Written in the Year MCMXIII*. Chelsea: The Ashendene Press, 1914.
   Includes "October," "Noel," "Narcissus," and "Flycatchers."

3. Bridges, Robert. *The Poetical Works of Robert Bridges, Excluding the Eight Dramas*. London: Oxford University Press, 1914.
   Reprint of 1912.1.

4. Bridges, Robert, and H[arry] Ellis Wooldridge, eds. *The Small Hymn-Book*. Oxford: B[asil] H. Blackwell, 1914.
   Reprint of 1899.6.

1916

1. Bridges, Robert. *The Chivalry of the Sea: Naval Ode*. London: Novello and Co.; New York: The H. W. Gray Co., 1916.
   Bridges's ode set to music by C. Hubert H. Parry.

2. Bridges, Robert. *Ibant Obscuri: An Experiment in Classical Hexameters*. Oxford: The Clarendon Press, 1916.
   Includes notes on Homer, translation, paraphrase, and Stone's prosody.

3. Bridges, Robert. "Lord Kitchener." London: Privately printed by Clement Shorter, 1916.

4. Bridges, Robert. *Ode on the Tercentenary Commemoration of Shakespeare*. [Oxford: Privately printed,] 1916.

5. [Bridges, Robert, ed.] *The Spirit of Man*. London: Longmans, Green and Co., 1916.

6. [Bridges, Robert, ed.] *The Spirit of Man*. London and New York: Longmans, Green and Co., 1916.
   Reprint of 1916.5 in a larger format.

1917

1. [Bridges, Robert, ed.] *The Spirit of Man*. London: Longmans, Green and Co., 1917.
   New impression of 1916.5.

1918

1. Bridges, Robert. *Britannia Victrix*. London: Oxford University Press, 1918.

2. [Bridges, Robert, ed.] *The Spirit of Man*. London: Longmans, Green and Co., 1918.
   Reprint of 1916.6.

1919

1. Bridges, Robert. *Britannia Victrix*. London: Oxford University Press, 1919.
   Reprint of 1918.1.
2. [Bridges, Robert, ed.] *The Spirit of Man*. London and New York: Longmans, Green and Co., 1919.
   Reprint of 1916.6.

1920

1. Bridges, Robert. *October and Other Poems*. London: William Heineman; New York: Alfred A. Knopf, 1920.
   Reprint of 1914.1 with the addition of new poems written since 1913. New poems include "The West Front," "Christmas Eve, 1917," and "Fortunatus Nimium."
2. Bridges, Robert, and H[arry] Ellis Wooldridge, eds. *The Small Hymn-Book*. London: Oxford University Press, 1920.
   A small-format reprint of 1899.6.
3. Bridges, Robert, and H[arry] Ellis Wooldridge, eds. *The Small Hymn-Book*. London: Oxford University Press, 1920.
   Reprint of 1899.6.

1921

1. Bridges, Robert, ed. *The Spirit of Man*. London and New York: Longmans, Green and Co., 1921.
   Reprint of 1916.6.

1922

1. Bridges, Robert. *October and Other Poems*. New York: Alfred A. Knopf, 1922.
   Reprint of 1920.1.

1923

1. [Bridges, Robert.] *Poor Poll*. [London: Oxford University Press, 1923.]

1925

1. Bridges, Robert. *New Verse*. Oxford: The Clarendon Press, 1925.
   Includes "Come se Quando" and "Low Barometer."

2. Bridges, Robert. *The Tapestry.* London: Privately printed by
   Stanley Morison, 1925.
   > Reprints selections from *October* and *New Verse.*

1926

1. Bridges, Robert. *New Verse.* Oxford: The Clarendon Press,
   1926.
   > Reprint of 1925.1.

1927

1. [Bridges, Robert, ed.] *The Spirit of Man.* London and New
   York: Oxford University Press, 1927.
   > Reprint of 1916.6.

1929

1. Bridges, Robert. *October and Other Poems.* London: Oxford
   University Press, 1929.
   > Reprint of 1920.1.
2. Bridges, Robert. *The Poetical Works of Robert Bridges.* 6 vols.
   Oxford: The Clarendon Press, 1929–33.
   > This six-volume edition is a reprint of the six-volume
   > Smith, Elder and Co. edition published from 1899 to 1905.
3. [Bridges, Robert, ed.] *The Spirit of Man.* London and New
   York: Oxford University Press, 1929.
   > Reprint of 1916.6.
4. Bridges, Robert. *The Testament of Beauty.* New York: Oxford
   University Press, 1929.
5. Bridges, Robert. *The Testament of Beauty.* Oxford: The Claren-
   don Press, 1929.
   > The limited issue edition of *The Testament of Beauty.*
6. Bridges, Robert. *The Testament of Beauty.* Oxford: The Clarendon Press, 1929.
   > The regular issue edition of *The Testament of Beauty.* The
   > poem went through nine impressions from 1929 to 1930.
7. Bridges, Robert. *The Testament of Beauty.* New York: Oxford
   University Press, 1929.
   > The first American edition of *The Testament of Beauty*

1930

1. Bridges, Robert. *On Receiving Trivia from the Author*. Stanford Dingley: The Mill House Press, 1930.
2. [Bridges, Robert, ed.] *The Spirit of Man*. London and New York: Longmans, Green and Co., 1930.
   A corrected reprint of 1916.6 with a new "Note to the Fourth Impression."
3. Bridges, Robert. *The Testament of Beauty*. New York: Oxford University Press; Oxford: The Clarendon Press, 1930.
4. Bridges, Robert. *The Testament of Beauty*. New York: Oxford University Press, 1930.
   Reprint of 1929.7.
5. Bridges, Robert. *The Testament of Beauty*. 2d ed. Oxford: The Clarendon Press, 1930.
   Corrected reprint of 1929.6.

1931

1. Bridges, Robert. *The Message of One of England's Greatest Poets to a Printer*. Edited by George W. Jones. London: The Sign of the Dolphin, 1931.
   Selected passages from *The Testament of Beauty*, excerpted by Monica Bridges, the poet's wife.
2. Bridges, Robert. *The Shorter Poems*. Oxford: The Clarendon Press, 1931.

1932

1. Bridges, Robert. *Verses Written for Mrs. Daniel*. Oxford: The Clarendon Press, 1932.
   Contains the title poem and "The Widow."

1933

1. Bridges, Robert. *The Poetical Works of Robert Bridges*. 6 vols. London: Oxford University Press, 1933.

1934

1. [Bridges, Robert, ed.] *The Spirit of Man*. London: Oxford University Press, 1934.
2. Bridges, Robert. *The Testament of Beauty*. Oxford: The Clarendon Press, 1934.
   Reprint of 1929.6.

1935

1. Bridges, Robert. *Eros and Psyche*. Newton, Wales: Gregynog Press, 1935.

    Illustrated with woodcuts designed by Burne-Jones.

1936

1. Bridges, Robert. *The Poetical Works of Robert Bridges*. 2d ed., enl. London: Oxford University Press, 1936.

    Updates 1912.1 by adding those poems written between 1913 and 1929, excluding *The Testament of Beauty*.

1937

1. [Bridges, Robert, ed.] *The Spirit of Man*. London: Oxford University Press, 1937.

    Reprint of 1916.6.
2. Bridges, Robert. *The Testament of Beauty*. Edited by Arundell Del Re. Tokyo: Hokuseido Press, 1937.

1938

1. Bridges, Robert. *The Testament of Beauty*. Oxford: The Clarendon Press, 1938.

    Reprint of 1930.3.

1940

1. [Bridges, Robert, ed.] *The Spirit of Man*. London and New York: Oxford University Press, 1940.

    Reprint of 1916.6.
2. Bridges, Robert. *The Testament of Beauty*. New York: Oxford University Press, 1940.

    Reprint of 1930.3.

1942

1. Bridges, Robert. *The Poetical Works of Robert Bridges, Excluding the Eight Dramas and The Testament of Beauty*. London: Oxford University Press, 1942.

    Reprint of 1936.1.

1943

1. Bridges, Robert. *Poems*. Oxford: Oxford University Press, 1943.

2. Bridges, Robert. *Robert Bridges.* [London:] Eyre and Spottiswoode, [1943].
   A paperback selection of poems.

1944

1. Bridges, Robert. *The Testament of Beauty.* Oxford: The Clarendon Press, 1944.
   Reprint of 1929.5.

1946

1. Bridges, Robert. *The Shorter Poems of Robert Bridges.* Oxford:
   The Clarendon Press, 1946.
   Reprint of 1931.2.

1947

1. Bridges, Robert. *The Poetical Works of Robert Bridges, Excluding
   the Eight Dramas and The Testament of Beauty.* London: Oxford University Press, 1947.
   Reprint of 1936.1.

1948

1. Bridges, Robert. *Poems.* Oxford: Oxford University Press,
   1948.

1949

1. Bridges, Robert. *The Testament of Beauty.* Edited by Arundell
   Del Re. Tokyo: Hokuseido Press, 1949.
   Reprint of 1937.2.

1953

1. Bridges, Robert. *The Poetical Works of Robert Bridges, with* The
   Testament of Beauty, but Excluding the Eight Dramas.
   London: Oxford University Press, 1953.
   Reprint of 1936.1 with addition of *The Testament of Beauty.*

1955

1. Bridges, Robert. *Robert Bridges: Poetry and Prose.* Edited by
   John Sparrow. Oxford: The Clarendon Press, 1955.
   Selections from all of Bridges's published poetry.

1959

1. Bridges, Robert. *The Poetical Works of Robert Bridges, with the Testament of Beauty, but Excluding the Eight Dramas.* London: Oxford University Press, 1959.
    Reprint of 1953.1.

1961

1. Bridges, Robert. *Poems.* Oxford: Oxford University Press, 1961.

1964

1. Bridges, Robert. *The Poetical Works of Robert Bridges, with The Testament of Beauty, but Excluding the Eight Dramas.* London: Oxford University Press, 1964.
    Reprint of 1953.1.

1970

1. Bridges, Robert. *Eden: An Oratorio.* New York: Readex Microprint, 1970. Microopaque.
    Microform reprint of 1891.1.
2. Bridges, Robert. *October and Other Poems.* Ann Arbor, Mich.: University Microfilms, 1970.
    Reprint of 1920.1.
3. [Bridges, Robert.] *Poems: By the Author of "The Growth of Love."* Chicago: Library Resources Inc., 1970. Microfiche.
    Reprint of 1879.1.
4. Bridges, Robert. *The Poetical Works of Robert Bridges.* 6 vols. Chicago: Library Resources Inc., 1970. Microfiche.
    Reprint of Smith, Elder and Co. volumes published from 1898 to 1905.

1971

1. Bridges, Robert. *The Poetical Works of Robert Bridges, with The Testament of Beauty, but Excluding the Eight Dramas.* London: Oxford University Press, 1971.
    Reprint of 1953.1.

1972

1. Bridges, Robert. *Demeter: A Mask.* Chicago: Library Resources Inc., 1972. Microfiche.
   Reprint of 1905.1.

2. Bridges, Robert. *Eros and Psyche.* Chicago: Library Resources Inc., 1972. Microfiche.
   Reprint of 1885.1.

3. Bridges, Robert. *The Feast of Bacchus.* Ann Arbor: University Microfilms, 1972. Photocopy.
   Reprint of 1889.1.

4. Bridges, Robert. *The Feast of Bacchus.* Chicago: Library Resources Inc., 1972. Microfiche.
   Reprint of 1889.1.

5. Bridges, Robert. *The Growth of Love.* Chicago: Library Resources Inc. 1972. Microfiche.
   Reprint of 1890.3.

6. Bridges, Robert. *The Growth of Love: A Poem in 79 Sonnets.* Chicago: Library Resources Inc., 1972. Microfiche.
   Reprint of 1890.3.

7. Bridges, Robert. *Poems.* Chicago: Library Resources Inc., 1972. Microfiche.
   Reprint of 1884.1.

8. Bridges, Robert. *Prometheus the Firegiver.* Chicago: Library Resources Inc., 1972. Microfiche.
   Reprint of 1883.1.

9. Bridges, Robert. *The Shorter Poems of Robert Bridges.* Chicago: Library Resources Inc., 1972. Microfiche.
   Reprint of 1890.6.

1974

1. Bridges, Robert. *Ibant Obscuri.* Ann Arbor, Mich.: University Microfilms, 1974.
   Reprint of 1916.2.

2. Bridges, Robert. *Robert Bridges: Selected Poems.* Edited by Donald E. Stanford. Cheshire, England: The Carcanet Press, Ltd., 1974.
   Selections from all of Bridges's major published poetry.

1975

1. Bridges, Robert. *Poetical Works of Robert Bridges, Excluding the Eight Dramas.* 2d ed. New York: AMS Press, 1975.
   Reprint of 1936.1.

1978

1. Bridges, Robert. *The Poetical Works of Robert Bridges.* 6 vols. Cambridge, Mass.: General Microfilm Co., 1978. Microfiche.
   Reprint of Smith, Elder and Co. volumes published from 1898 to 1905.
2. Bridges, Robert. *The Poetical Works of Robert Bridges, Excluding the Eight Dramas.* New York: AMS Press, 1978.
   Reprint of 1936.1.

1979

1. Bridges, Robert. *The Shorter Poems of Robert Bridges.* Westport, Conn.: Hyperion Press, 1979.
   Reprint of 1946.1.

2

PROSE

1876

1. Bridges, Robert. "A Severe Case of Rheumatic Fever Treated by Splints." *St. Bartholomew's Hospital Reports* 12 (1876): 175–81.
   Description of successful treatment of a patient with rheumatic fever.

1878

1. Bridges, Robert. "An Account of the Casualty Department." *St. Bartholomew's Hospital Reports* 14 (1878): 166–82.
   Review of work in the Casualty Department.

1887

1. [Bridges, Robert.] "On the Elements of Milton's Blank Verse in *Paradise Lost*." N.p.: Privately printed, 1887.
   Privately printed version of 1887.2.
2. Bridges, Robert. "On the Elements of Milton's Blank Verse in *Paradise Lost*." In *Milton's Paradise Lost, Book I*, edited by Rev. H. C. Beeching, 19–37. Oxford: The Clarendon Press, 1887.
   Reprint of 1887.1.

1889

1. Bridges, Robert. *On the Prosody of "Paradise Regained" and "Samson Agonistes."* Oxford: B. H. Blackwell, 1889.
   Supplement to "Milton's Blank Verse" in H. C. Beeching's *Paradise Lost, Book I*.
2. Bridges, Robert. *On the Prosody of "Paradise Regained" and "Samson Agonistes."* London: Simpkin, Marshall and Co.; Oxford: The Clarendon Press, 1889.
   Supplement to 1887.1.

1890

1. Bridges, Robert. "An Account of the Casualty Department."
   Charity Organization Review, August 1890.
       Reprint of 1878.1.

1893

1. Bridges, Robert. "Gerard Manley Hopkins." In *Robert Bridges
   and Contemporary Poets.* Vol. 8 of *The Poets and Poetry of the
   Century,* edited by Alfred H. Miles, 161–64. London:
   Hutchinson and Co., 1893.
       Introductory note to Hopkins's poetry.
2. Bridges, Robert. "Introduction." In *Milton's Prosody: An Examination of the Rules of Blank Verse in Milton's Later Poems,* 5–6.
   Oxford: The Clarendon Press, 1893.
       Essentially a reprint of 1887.1 with corrections.
3. Bridges, Robert. *Milton's Prosody: An Examination of the Rules of
   the Blank Verse in Milton's Later Poems.* Oxford: The Clarendon Press, 1893.
       The section on *Samson Agonistes* is reprinted from 1889.1
   but appendices now illustrate the text.

1894

1. Bridges, Robert. *Milton's Prosody.* Oxford: The Clarendon
   Press, 1894.
       Essentially a reprint of 1893.2, with minor changes and
   additions.

1895

1. Bridges, Robert. *John Keats: A Critical Essay.* London: Lawrence and Bullen, 1895.
       Originally written for 1896.1. Here separately published.
2. Bridges, Robert, ed. *Odes, Sonnets and Lyrics of John Keats.*
   Oxford: H[enry] Daniel, 1895.
       The preface indicates this selection of poems was guided
   by the recommendations found in 1895.1. The prospectus
   for this edition, however, indicates Bridges actually selected
   these poems.
3. Bridges, Robert. *Professorship of Poetry.* Oxford: Henry Daniel
   Press, 1895.
       Bridges's statement refusing the Oxford Chair of Poetry.
   Includes names of those who supported his nomination.

1896

1. Bridges, Robert. "Critical Introduction." In *The Poems of John Keats*, 2 vols., edited by G. Thorn Drury, 1:xiii–cv. London: Lawrence and Bullen; New York: Charles Scribner's Sons, 1896.
   Reprint of 1895.1.
2. Bridges, Robert. "Preface on the Musical Setting of Poetry." In *Ode for the Bicentenary Commemoration of Henry Purcell, with Other Poems*, 5–18. London: Elkin Mathews, 1896.

1897

1. Bridges, Robert. "A Case of Thickening of the Cranial Bones in an Infant, due to Congenital Syphillis." *Transactions of the Clinical Society of London* 12 (1897): 140–42.

1899

1. Bridges, Robert. "A Practical Discourse on Some Principles of Hymnology." *Journal of Theological Studies* 1 (1899): 40–63.

1900

1. Bridges, Robert. Letter. In *Memoirs and Correspondences of Coventry Patmore*, 2 vols., edited by Basil Champneys, 2:373–74. London: George Bell and Sons, 1900.
   A letter from Bridges to Patmore.

1901

1. Bridges, Robert. *Milton's Prosody*. Oxford: The Clarendon Press, 1901.
   Revises, enlarges, and expands 1889.1 and 1893.1 and adds William Johnson Stone's essay, "Classical Metres in English Verse."
2. Bridges, Robert. *A Practical Discourse on Some Principle of Hymn-Singing*. Oxford: B. H. Blackwell; London: Simpkin, Marshall, Hamilton, Kent and Co., 1901.
   Reprint of 1899.1.

1903

1. Bridges, Robert. "Dryden on Milton." *The Speaker* n.s. 9 (1903): 88–89.

2. Bridges, Robert. "Extraordinary." *The Athenaeum* 121 (1903): 93–94.

   A supplemental note on the pronunciation of "extraordinary" in line 1383 of *Samson Agonistes.*

3. Bridges, Robert. "Lord de Tabley's Poems." *The Speaker* n.s. 9 (1903): 272–73.

4. Bridges, Robert. "A Note on Prosody." In *Now in Wintry Delights*, 19–24. Oxford: [Henry Daniel,] 1903.

1904

1. Bridges, Robert. "The Causerie of the Week: Sir Thomas Browne." *The Speaker* n.s. 10 (1904): 163–64.

2. Bridges, Robert. "English Music: A Practical Scheme." *The Monthly Review* 16 (1904): 105–10.

3. Bridges, Robert. "Mr. Bradley on English." *The Speaker* n.s. 10 (1904): 228–30.

4. Bridges, Robert. "On the Pronunciation of English." *The Speaker* n.s. 10 (1904): 383–84.

5. Bridges, Robert. "The Pronunciation of Latin." *The Speaker* n.s. 10 (1904): 405–6.

1905

1. Bridges, Robert. "Bunyan's Pilgrim's Progress, I." *The Speaker* n.s. 11 (1905): 8–9.

2. Bridges, Robert. "Bunyan's Pilgrim's Progress, II." *The Speaker* n.s. 11 (1905): 31–32.

3. Bridges, Robert. "Memoir." In *The Last Poems of Richard Watson Dixon*, ix–xlv. Oxford: Henry Frowde, 1905.

4. Bridges, Robert, ed. *The Last Poems of Richard Watson Dixon.* Oxford: Henry Frowde, 1905.

1906

1. Bridges, Robert. "Gerard Hopkins." In *Robert Bridges and Contemporary Poets.* Vol. 7 of *The Poets and Poetry of the Nineteenth Century,* edited by Alfred Henry Miles, 179–82. London: George Routledge and Sons; New York: E. P. Dutton and Co., 1906.

2. Bridges, Robert. "Henry John Newbolt." In *Robert Bridges and Contemporary Poets.* Vol. 7 of *The Poets and Poetry in the Nineteenth Century,* edited by Alfred Henry Miles, 561–62.

London: George Routledge and Sons; New York: E. P. Dutton and Co., 1906.

3. Bridges, Robert. "Miss Beauchamp." *The Speaker* n.s. 14 (1906): 385–86.

4. Bridges, Robert. "Nepenthe." *The Academy* 36 (4 August 1906): 110–11.

1907

1. Bridges, Robert. "The Late Miss Coleridge and Stevenson." Letter. *Times Literary Supplement,* 7 November 1907, 339.
   This letter from Bridges corrects information in 1907.3.

2. Bridges, Robert. "On the Influence of the Audience." In *The Works of William Shakespeare,* 10 vols., edited by Arthur Henry Bullen, 10:321–34. Stratford-on-Avon: Shakespeare Head Press, 1907.

3. Bridges, Robert. "The Poems of Mary Coleridge." *The Cornhill Magazine* n.s. 23 (1907): 594–605.

4. [Bridges, Robert.] "Studies in Poetry." *Times Literary Supplement,* 21 November 1907, 356.

1908

1. Bridges, Robert. "George Darley." *Times Literary Supplement,* 6 March 1908.
   Reprint of 1906.4.

1909

1. [Bridges, Robert.] "Dante in English Literature." *Times Literary Supplement,* 24 June 1909, 235–36.

2. Bridges, Robert. "A Letter to a Musician on English Prosody." *The Musical Antiquary* 1 (1909): 15–29.

3. Bridges, Robert. "Memoir." In *Poems by the Late Rev. Richard Watson Dixon,* edited by Robert Bridges, i–xlvi. London: Smith, Elder and Co., 1909.
   Reprint of 1905.4.

4. [Bridges, Robert.] "The Springs of Helicon." *Times Literary Supplement,* 1 April 1909, 121–22.

5. Bridges, Robert, ed. *Poems by the Late Rev. Richard Watson Dixon.* London: Smith, Elder and Co., 1909.
   An expanded version of 1905.4.

1910

1. Bridges, Robert. "On the Present State of English Pronunciation." *Essays and Studies of the English Association* 1 (1910): 42–69.
2. [Bridges, Robert.] "Word-Books." *Times Literary Supplement*, 4 August 1910, 273–74.

1911

1. Bridges, Robert. "About Hymns." *Church Music Society* 11 (1911): 1–4.
   Extract of a letter from Bridges.
2. [Bridges, Robert.] "The Bible." *Times Literary Supplement*, 23 March 1911, 113–14.
3. Bridges, Robert. "English Chanting." *The Musical Antiquary* 2 (1911): 125–41.
4. Bridges, Robert. "Memoir." In *The Poems of Digby Mackworth Dolben,* edited by Robert Bridges, i–cxi. London: Oxford University Press, 1911.
5. [Bridges, Robert.] "The Poems of Emily Bronte." *Times Literary Supplement,* 12 January 1911, 9–10.
6. Bridges, Robert, ed. *The Poems of Digby Mackworth Dolben.* London: Oxford University Press, 1911.

1912

1. Bridges, Robert. "Anglican Chanting." *The Musical Antiquary* 3 (1912): 74–86.
   Argues that the style of Anglican chanting should be amended to reflect natural speech rhythm.
2. Bridges, Robert. "Chanting." In *The Prayer Book Dictionary.* London: Pitman, 1912.
   Combined and condensed version of 1911.3 and 1912.1.
3. [Bridges, Robert.] "The Glamour of Grammar." *Times Literary Supplement*, 30 May 1912, 221–22.
4. Bridges, Robert. "The Pronunciation of Latin: Arguments for Reform. *Times Educational Supplement,* 1 October 1912, 117–18.
5. Bridges, Robert. "The Pronunciation of Latin: Mr. Bridges on Reform." Letter. *The Times,* 20 September 1912, 8.
   A letter from Bridges urging improved teaching of Latin in the schools.

6. [Bridges, Robert.] "Wordsworth and Kipling." *Times Literary Supplement,* 25 February 1912, 81–82.

1913

1. Bridges, Robert. *On the Present State of English Pronunciation.* Oxford: The Clarendon Press, 1913.
   A reprint of 1910.1.
2. [Bridges, Robert.] "Prospectus." In *Society for Pure English.* Oxford: The Clarendon Press, 1913.
   Lists the fourteen charter members of the society.

1914

1. Bridges, Robert. "A Holy War." Letter. *The Times,* 3 September 1914, 9.
   A letter on the beginning of World War I.
2. Bridges, Robert. "A Letter to a Musician on English Prosody." *Poetry and Drama* 2 (1914): 255–71.
   Reprint of 1909.2.
3. Bridges, Robert. "Mr. Bridges on Football." Letter. *The Times,* 19 November 1914, 5.
   "It is high time that professional football should be discontinued."
4. Bridges, Robert. "Waste in Hotels." Letter. *The Times,* 9 September 1914, 9.
   A letter on waste in English hotels.

1915

1. Bridges, Robert. Brief Message in "The Cause and the Need." *The Times Recruiting Supplement,* 3 November 1915, 5.
   A patriotic message of hope and encouragement.
2. Bridges, Robert. "Memoir." In *The Poems of Digby Mackworth Dolben,* edited by Robert Bridges, i–cxi. London: Oxford University Press, 1915.
   Reprint of 1911.4.
3. Bridges, Robert, ed. *The Poems of Digby Mackworth Dolben.* London: Oxford University Press, 1915.
   Reprint of 1911.6.

1916

1. Bridges, Robert. *An Address to the Swindon Branch of the Workers' Education Association.* Oxford: The Clarendon Press, 1916.
2. Bridges, Robert. "Fight for Right." *Times Literary Supplement,* 6 April 1916, 162.
   Full text of Bridges's speech at Queen's Hall.
3. Bridges, Robert. "Introduction." In *The Star Fields, and Other Poems,* by Willoughby Weaving, vii–viii. Oxford: B. H. Blackwell, 1916.
4. Bridges, Robert. "John Keats: A Critical Essay." In *The Poetical Works of John Keats,* edited by Laurence Binyon, ix–li. London: Hodder and Stoughton, [1916].
   Revised reprint of 1895.1.
5. Bridges, Robert. "Preface." In *The Spirit of Man,* edited by Robert Bridges, n.p. London: Longmans, Green and Co., 1916.
6. Bridges, Robert. "Treatment of Prisoners." Letter. *The Times,* 19 July 1916, 9.
   A letter regarding prisoners of war.
7. Bridges, Robert, et al. "Perse School, Cambridge." Letter. *The Times Educational Supplement,* 7 December 1916, 234.
   A letter from Bridges and nine others.

1917

1. Bridges, Robert. "The Freedom of the Seas." Letter. *The Times,* 7 February 1917, 7.
   Bridges's letter includes a free translation of Fichte's account of Napoleon.
2. Bridges, Robert. "Speech." *Transactions of the Royal Society of Literature* 35 (1917): 23–27.
   Text of Bridges's speech at the Verhaeren Commemoration.
3. Bridges, Robert. "20,000,000,000!" Letter. *The Times,* 8 February 1917, 9.
   A letter concerning German war aims.

1918

1. "Books for Hospitals." *The Times,* 24 May 1918, 9.
   The text of Bridges's speech at the Sheldonian Theatre.

2. Bridges, Robert. *The Necessity of Poetry.* Oxford: The Clarendon Press, 1918.

3. Bridges, Robert. "Our Prisoners of War in Germany." *The Times,* 4 November 1918, 9.

4. Bridges, Robert. "Preface to Notes." In *Poems of Gerard Manley Hopkins,* edited by Robert Bridges, 94–101. London: Oxford University Press, 1918.

5. Bridges, Robert, ed. *Poems of Gerard Manley Hopkins.* London: Oxford University Press, 1918.

1919

1. Bridges, Robert. "On English Homophones." In *Society for Pure English: Tract No. 2,* 3–48. Oxford: The Clarendon Press, 1919.

2. [Bridges, Robert, and Logan Pearsall Smith.] "Preliminary Announcement and List of Members." In *Society for Pure English: Tract No. 1,* 3–15. Oxford: The Clarendon Press, 1919.

1920

1. B[ridges], R[obert]. "Correction to *Tract 2.*" In *Society for Pure English: Tract No. 4,* 36. Oxford: The Clarendon Press, 1920.

2. Bridges, Robert. "George Santayana." *The Dial* 69 (1920): 534–45.

3. Bridges, Robert. "George Santayana." *The London Mercury* 2 (1920): 411–19.

4. Bridges, Robert. "The Poet Laureate on Reconciliation." Letter. *The Times,* 27 October 1920, 13–14.

    Bridges's reply to critics of the Oxford Letter. See 1920.5.

5. Bridges, Robert. "Reconciliation: Oxford Letter to German Intellectuals." Letter. *The Times,* 18 October 1920, 13.

    Bridges appears to have been the prime mover behind this offer of reconciliation to the German intellectual community.

6. Bridges, Robert. "Report." In *Society for Pure English: Tract No. 4,* 43–44. Oxford: The Clarendon Press, 1920.

7. Bridges, Robert. "Some Lexical Matters." In *Society for Pure*

English: Tract No. 4, 36–42. Oxford: The Clarendon Press, 1920.

1921

1. Bridges, Robert. "Correspondence: Dialect Words." In *Society for Pure English: Tract No. 7*, 43. Oxford: The Clarendon Press, 1921.
2. Bridges, Robert. Dedication Speech made at the unveiling of a war memorial at the Newbury Grammar School on 12 July 1921. A broadsheet.
3. Bridges, Robert. "On the Dialectal Words in Edmund Blunden's Poems." In *Society for Pure English: Tract No. 5*, 23–32. Oxford: The Clarendon Press, 1921.
4. [Bridges, Robert.] "English Words in French." In *Society for Pure English: Tract No. 5*, 22. Oxford: The Clarendon Press, 1921.
5. Bridges, Robert. *Milton's Prosody.* Rev. final ed. Oxford: Oxford University Press, 1921.
6. Bridges, Robert. "A Note by Mr. Robert Bridges." *The Chapbook* 3.19 (January 1921): 22–24.
7. [Bridges, Robert.] "Notes." In *Society for Pure English: Tract No. 5*, 21. Oxford: The Clarendon Press, 1921.
8. Bridges, Robert. "Preface." In *The Historic Names of the Streets and Lanes of Oxford,* by H. E. Salter, 3–6. Oxford: The Clarendon Press, 1921.

1922

1. Barnes, Matthew [Robert Bridges]. "What is Pure French?" In *Society for Pure English: Tract No. 8*, 3–10. Oxford: The Clarendon Press, 1922.
2. Bridges, Robert. Essay. In *Keats: Poetry and Prose,* edited by Henry Ellershaw, 25–32. Oxford: The Clarendon Press, 1922.
   Excerpt from 1895.1.
3. Bridges, Robert. "Humdrum and Harum Scarum: A Lecture on Free Verse." *The London Mercury* 216 (1922): 647–58.
4. [Bridges, Robert.] "In or On a Ship." In *Society for Pure English: Tract No. 9*, 23–24. Oxford: The Clarendon Press, 1922.

5. Bridges, Robert. "Introduction." In *Society for Pure English: Tract No. 9*, 3. Oxford: The Clarendon Press, 1922.

6. [Bridges, Robert]. "Note on 'The Poverty of English Accidence.'" In *Society for Pure English: Tract No. 9*, 20–22. Oxford: The Clarendon Press, 1922.

7. B[ridges], R[obert]. "Notes and Correspondence." In *Society for Pure English: Tract No. 10*, 26. Oxford: The Clarendon Press, 1922.

8. Bridges, Robert. "A Paper on Free Verse." *The North American Review* 215 (1922): 647–58.

9. Bridges, Robert. "Report." In *Society for Pure English: Tract No. 10*, 3–8. Oxford: The Clarendon Press, 1922.

10. [Bridges, Robert, ed.] *Odes, Sonnets and Lyrics of John Keats.* Portland, Maine: Thomas Bird Mosher, 1922.
    Reprint of 1895.2.

11. Bridges, Robert, et al. "The American Invitation." In *Society for Pure English: Tract No. 11*, 21–22. Oxford: The Clarendon Press, 1922.

1923

1. B[ridges], R[obert]. "American Collaboration." In *Society for Pure English: Tract No. 14*, 25. Oxford: The Clarendon Press, 1923.

2. B[ridges], R[obert]. "Committee." In *Society for Pure English: Tract No. 15*, 24. Oxford: The Clarendon Press, 1923.

3. B[ridges], R[obert]. "Correspondence, etc." In *Society for Pure English: Tract No. 14*, 21–25. Oxford: The Clarendon Press, 1923.

4. [Bridges, Robert.] "Grammatical Inversions." In *Society for Pure English: Tract No. 13*, 29–33. Oxford: The Clarendon Press, 1923.

5. Bridges, Robert. *Milton's Prosody.* Rev. final ed. London: Oxford University Press, 1923.
    Reprint of 1921.5.

6. Bridges, Robert. "Pictorial, Picturesque, etc." In *Society for Pure English: Tract No. 15*, 3–24. Oxford: The Clarendon Press, 1923.

7. Bridges, Robert. "Poetic Diction in English." *The Forum* 69 (1923): 1536–43.

8. Bridges, Robert. "Two Essays." *The Forum* 69 (1923): 1649–51.
9. Bridges, Robert, and Henry Bradley. "On the Terms Briton, British, Britisher." In *Society for Pure English: Tract No. 14*, 3–25. Oxford: The Clarendon Press, 1923.

1924

1. Barnes, Matthew [Bridges, Robert.]. "Open Court on *Alright.*" In *Society for Pure English: Tract No. 18*, 14–16. Oxford: The Clarendon Press, 1924.
2. Bridges, Robert. "To the Donors of the Clavichord." [Oxford: Privately printed, 1924. 4 pp.]
3. B[ridges], R[obert]. "Erratum." In *Society for Pure English: Tract No. 16*, 38–39. Oxford: The Clarendon Press, 1924.
4. Bridges, Robert. "Grotesque." In *Society for Pure English: Tract No. 16*, 37–38. Oxford: The Clarendon Press, 1924.
5. Bridges, Robert. Letter. In *Poems Unpublished or Difficult to Obtain Easily,* edited by Walter Muir Whitehill. Boston: Athenaeum, 1924.
   A letter from Bridges to C. H. Daniel.
6. Bridges, Robert. "Mr. Bridges's Thanks." Letter. *The Times,* 11 November 1924, 15.
   Letter of thanks to the donors of the clavichord.
7. Bridges, Robert. "Poetry in Schools." In *Society for Pure English: Tract No. 18,* 9–14. Oxford: The Clarendon Press, 1924.
8. Bridges, Robert. "Report." In *Society for Pure English: Tract No. 18,* 24–26. Oxford: The Clarendon Press, 1924.
9. B[ridges], R[obert]. "SPE: Expenditure and Income Account." In *Society for Pure English: Tract No. 17*, 49. Oxford: The Clarendon Press, 1924.
10. Bridges, Robert, ed. *The Chilswell Book of English Poetry.* London: Longmans, Green and Co., 1924.

1925

1. Bridges, Robert. "Price of the Tracts." In *Society for Pure English: Tract No. 22*, 64–65. Oxford: The Clarendon Press, 1925.
2. Bridges, Robert. "Report." In *Society for Pure English: Tract No. 19,* 41–46. Oxford: The Clarendon Press, 1925.

3. Bridges, Robert. "Reviews and Miscellaneous Notes." In *Society for Pure English: Tract No. 22*, 55–65. Oxford: The Clarendon Press, 1925.

4. Bridges, Robert. "The Society's Work." *Society for Pure English: Tract No. 21*. Oxford: The Clarendon Press, 1925.

1926

1. Bridges, Robert. "Editorial." In *Society for Pure English: Tract No. 23*, 98–99. Oxford: The Clarendon Press, 1926.

2. B[ridges], R[obert]. "English Handwriting." In *Society for Pure English: Tract No. 23*, 71–78. Oxford: The Clarendon Press, 1926.

3. Bridges, Robert. *Henry Bradley: A Memoir*. Oxford: The Clarendon Press, 1926.

4. Bridges, Robert. *The Influence of the Audience*. Garden City, N.Y.: Doubleday, Page and Co., 1926.
   Reprint of 1907.2.

5. Bridges, Robert. "Note." In *An Account of the Scapa Society*, by Richardson Evans, 281–82. London: Constable and Co., Ltd., 1926.

6. Bridges, Robert, ed. *The Chilswell Book of English Poetry*. London: Longmans, Green and Co., 1926.
   A reprint of 1924.10.

1927

1. Bridges, Robert. *The Collected Essays, Papers, etc. of Robert Bridges*. Vol. 1. London: Oxford University Press, 1927.

2. B[ridges], R[obert]. "English Handwriting." In *Society for Pure English: Tract No. 28*, 223–51. Oxford: The Clarendon Press, 1927.

3. Bridges, Robert. "General Remarks." In *Society for Pure English: Tract No. 28*, 224–34. Oxford: The Clarendon Press, 1927.

4. B[ridges], R[obert]. "Introduction." In *Society for Pure English: Tract No. 26*, 175–80. Oxford: The Clarendon Press, 1927.

5. Bridges, Robert. "Introduction." In *Society for Pure English: Tract No. 28*, 223–24. Oxford: The Clarendon Press, 1927.

1928

1. Barnes, Matthew [Bridges, Robert]. "Words from the French, -e, -ee." In *Society for Pure English: Tract No. 30*, 298–305. Oxford: The Clarendon Press, 1928.

2. Bridges, Robert. "Broadcast English." Letter. *The Times*, 6 January 1928, 13.
   A letter in response to criticism of society suggestions for proper pronunciation of certain words by broadcasters.

3. Bridges, Robert. *The Collected Essays, Papers, etc. of Robert Bridges*. Vol. 2. London: Oxford University Press, 1928.

4. Bridges, Robert. Essay. In *Keats: Poetry and Prose*, edited by Henry Ellershaw, 25–32. Oxford: The Clarendon Press, 1928.
   Reprint of 1922.2

5. Bridges, Robert. "An Explanation." In *Society for Pure English: Tract No. 30*, 308–9. Oxford: The Clarendon Press, 1928.

6. Bridges, Robert. "Introduction." In *A Selection from the Letters of Sir Walter Raleigh, 1880–1922*, edited by Lady Raleigh, xix–xxi. London: Methuen and Co., [1928].

7. Bridges, Robert. "A Memoir." In *The Collected Papers of Henry Bradley*, 1–56. Oxford: The Clarendon Press, 1928.
   Reprint of 1926.3.

8. Bridges, Robert. "Pronunciation of Clothes, etc." In *Society for Pure English: Tract No. 30*, 305–8. Oxford: The Clarendon Press, 1928.

9. Bridges, Robert, ed. *The Collected Papers of Henry Bradley*. Oxford: The Clarendon Press, 1928.

1929

1. Bridges, Robert. "An Aerodome Near Oxford." Letter. *The Times*, 5 November 1929, 17.
   A letter protesting the building of an airport near Oxford.

2. Bridges, Robert. *The Collected Essays, Papers, etc. of Robert Bridges*. Vol. 3. London: Oxford University Press, 1929.

3. Bridges, Robert. "A National Theatre." Letter. *The Times*, 26 November 1929, 13.
   A letter to Sir Israel Gallancz supporting the establishment of a national theatre.

4. [Bridges, Robert]. "On the Scheme and Content of this Tract." In *Society for Pure English: Tract No. 32*, 339–40. Oxford: The Clarendon Press, 1929.

5. Bridges, Robert. *Poetry.* Cambridge: Cambridge University Press, 1929.
   Printed version of Bridges's poetry lecture on the BBC.

6. Bridges, Robert. "Poetry." *The Listener* 1 (1929): 269–70, 296–97.
   Edited reprint of Bridges's radio lecture. See 1929.5.

7. Bridges, Robert. "Poetry." *The Parents' Review* 40 (1929): 233–42.

8. Bridges, Robert. "Poetry." *Wessex*, 1.2 (1 June 1929).

9. Bridges, Robert, ed. "The B.B.C.'s Recommendations for Pronouncing Doubtful Words." In *Society for Pure English: Tract No. 32*, 5–20. Oxford: The Clarendon Press, 1929.

1930

1. Bridges, Robert. *The Collected Essays, Papers, etc. of Robert Bridges.* Vol. 5. London: Oxford University Press, 1930.

2. Bridges, Robert. "Preface to Notes." In *Poems of Gerard Manley Hopkins.* 2d ed. London: Oxford University Press, 1930.
   Reprint of 1918.3.

3. Bridges, Robert, and Charles Williams, eds. *Poems of Gerard Manley Hopkins.* 2d ed. London: Oxford University Press, 1930.
   Adds poems that were not published in 1918.[5]

1931

1. Bridges, Robert. Letter. In *The Message of One of England's Greatest Poets to a Printer,* edited by George W. Jones, n.p. London: The Sign of the Dolphin, [1931].
   A letter to George W. Jones on printing *The Testament of Beauty.*

2. Bridges, Robert. Letters. In "Robert Bridges: Recollections," by Logan Pearsall Smith. *The Society for Pure English* 35 (1931): 485–86.
   Three letters to Logan Pearsall Smith regarding Henry Bradley's membership and assistance in founding the society.

3. Bridges, Robert. *Milton's Prosody.* London and Oxford: Oxford University Press, 1931.
   Reprint of 1921.5.

1932

1. Bridges, Robert. *The Collected Essays, Papers, etc. of Robert Bridges.* Vol. 6. London: Oxford University Press, 1932.
2. Bridges, Robert. *The Collected Essays, Papers, etc. of Robert Bridges.* Vol. 7. London: Oxford University Press, 1932.
3. Bridges, Robert. Letter. In *Men and Memories: Recollections of William Rothenstein,* 2:299–301+. New York: Coward-McCann, 1932.
   A letter to Rothenstein regarding the inclusion of a poem by Tagore in Bridges's *Spirit of Man* and a letter from Tagore to Rothenstein expressing the former's reservations about the inclusion.
4. Bridges, Robert. *Three Friends.* London: Oxford University Press, 1932.
   Collects and reprints 1909.3, 1911.4, and 1926.3.

1933

1. Bridges, Robert. "Poetic Diction in English." In *English Critical Essays: Twentieth Century,* edited by Phyllis M. Jones, 1–10. London: Oxford University Press, 1933.
   Reprint of 1923.7.
2. Bridges, Robert, and Charles Williams, eds. *Poems of Gerard Manley Hopkins.* 2d ed. London: Oxford University Press, 1933.
   Reprint of 1930.3.

1934

1. Bridges, Robert. *The Collected Essays, Papers, etc. of Robert Bridges.* Vol. 8. London: Oxford University Press, 1934.
   Essay on "The Bible" printed complete for first time.
2. Bridges, Robert. *The Collected Essays, Papers, etc. of Robert Bridges.* Vol. 9. London: Oxford University Press, 1935.
   Includes a previously unprinted preface to a manuscript collection of psalms.

1935

1. Bridges, Robert, ed. *The Chilswell Book of English Poetry.* London: Longmans, Green, 1935.
2. Bridges, Robert. Letters. In *Men and Memories: Recollections of William Rothenstein,* 1:227–28, 297–98, 327–29, and passim. New York: Coward-McCann, 1935.

    Four letters and excerpts of letters to Rothenstein on subjects ranging from Rothenstein's *English Portraits* to journal contributions, Shakespearean criticism, and mutual friends.

1936

1. Bridges, Robert. *The Collected Essays, Papers, etc. of Robert Bridges.* Vol. 10. London: Oxford University Press, 1936.

1937

1. Bridges, Robert, and Charles Williams, eds. *Poems of Gerard Manley Hopkins.* 2d ed. London: Oxford University Press, 1937.

    Reprint of 1930.3.

1938

1. Bridges, Robert. *Three Friends.* London: Oxford University Press, 1938.

    Reprint of 1932.4.

1939

1. Bridges, Robert. Letters. In *Men and Memories: Recollections of William Rothenstein,* 3:31–33, 50–53, 109–10, and passim. London: Faber and Faber Ltd., 1939.

    Seven letters and excerpts of letters to Rothenstein on subjects ranging from Bridges's work on *The Testament of Beauty* to collecting handwriting samples. Also included is a reproduction of the note of thanks Bridges sent to all of the subscribers who contributed to the fund to buy him a clavichord for his eightieth birthday.
2. Bridges, Robert. Letter. In *The Pursuit of Poetry: A Book of Letters About Poetry Written by English Poets, 1550–1930,* edited by Desmond Flower, 270–71. London: Cassell, 1939.

    A letter from Bridges to Coventry Patmore discussing *The Unknown Eros.*

1940

1. Bridges, Robert. *Four Psalms Pointed in Speech-Rhythm.* London and Oxford: Oxford University Press, 1940.
   Written in 1918. Preface by Mary Monica Bridges.
2. Bridges, Robert. *On Hearing of the Death of Theodore Watts-Dunton.* Winchester: E. H. Blakeney, 1940.
3. Bridges, Robert. Letters. In *Correspondence of Robert Bridges and Henry Bradley, 1900–1923.* Oxford: The Clarendon Press, 1940.
   A total of eighty-five letters: seventy-one letters and postcards to Henry Bradley (most on technical philological matters), nine letters to Mrs. Bradley, and five letters to Bradley's sister-in-law.

1942

1. Bridges, Robert, ed. *The Spirit of Man.* London: Longmans, Green, 1942.

1943

1. Bridges, Robert, and Charles Williams, eds. *Poems of Gerard Manley Hopkins.* 2d ed. New York and London: Oxford University Press, 1943.
   Reprint of 1930.3.

1946

1. Bridges, Robert, ed. *The Spirit of Man.* London: Longmans, Green, 1946.

1947

1. Bridges, Robert. *Four Collects.* Stanford Dingley: The Mill House Press, 1947.
   Four prayers by Bridges.

1948

1. Bridges, Robert. "The Case against Free Verse." In *Writers on Writing,* edited by Walter Ernest Allen, 87–91. London: Phoenix House, 1948.
2. Bridges, Robert. Essay. In *Keats: Poetry and Prose,* edited by Henry Ellershaw, 25–32. Oxford: The Clarendon Press, 1948.

Reprint of 1922.2.

3. Bridges, Robert. "Preface to Notes." In *Poems of Gerard Manley Hopkins,* 3d ed., edited by Robert Bridges and W. H. Gardner, 2–5. New York: Oxford University Press, 1948.
    Reprint of 1918.4.

4. Bridges, Robert, and W. H. Gardner, eds. *Poems of Gerard Manley Hopkins.* 3d ed. enl. London: Oxford University Press, 1948.

5. Bridges, Robert, and W. H. Gardner, eds. *Poems of Gerard Manley Hopkins.* 3d ed. New York: Oxford University Press, 1948.
    First American edition.

1949

1. Bridges, Robert. "The Case against Free Verse." In *The Writer on His Art,* edited by Walter Ernest Allen, 87–91. New York: Whittlesey House, 1949.
    Reprint of 1948.1.

2. Bridges, Robert. "The Case against Free Verse." In *Writers on Writing,* edited by Walter Ernest Allen, 87–91. New York: E. P. Dutton, 1949.
    Reprint of 1948.1.

3. Bridges, Robert, ed. *Poems of Gerard Manley Hopkins.* New York: Peter Pauper Press, [1949].
    "The arrangement is essentially that of Robert Bridges, the friend and first editor of the poet."

1951

1. Bridges, Robert. Letters. In "Three Poets Discuss New Verse Forms," by Derek Patmore. *The Month* n.s. 6 (1951): 71–73, 77–78.
    Three letters on "new prosody" to Coventry Patmore. Bridges says, "I shall never write on prosody myself." Several comments on Hopkins and his poetry.

1955

1. Bridges, Robert. Letters. In *XXI Letters: A Correspondence between Robert Bridges and R. C. Trevelyan on "New Verse" and*

"The Testament of Beauty." Stanford Dingley: The Mill House Press, 1955.

2. Bridges, Robert. Prose. In *Robert Bridges: Poetry and Prose,* edited by John Sparrow, 104–57. Oxford: The Clarendon Press, 1955.

   Selections from Bridges's major prose works, including excerpts from essays on Dolben, Dixon, Keats, Emily Bronte, Poetry, and Poetic Diction.

1956

1. Bridges, Robert, and Charles Williams, eds. *Poems of Gerard Manley Hopkins.* 3d ed. London: Oxford University Press, 1956.

1957

1. Bridges, Robert. Letters. In "Bridges, Hopkins and Dr. Daniel," by Simon Nowell-Smith. *Times Literary Supplement,* 13 December 1957, 764.

   Excerpts from eight letters (six to Dr. Daniel, two to Hopkins's mother) regarding the publication of Hopkins's poems.

2. Bridges, Robert. Letters. In *XXI Letters: A Correspondence between Robert Bridges and R. C. Trevelyan on "New Verse" and "The Testament of Beauty."* Stanford Dingley: The Millhouse Press, 1957.

1958

1. Bridges, Robert. "The Case against Free Verse." In *Writers on Writing,* edited by Walter Ernest Allen, 87–91. Boston: The Writer; London: Phoenix House, 1959.

   Reprint of 1948.1.

2. Bridges, Robert. Letter. In "A New Letter of Robert Bridges to Coventry Patmore," by David Bonnell Green. *Modern Philology* 55 (1958): 198–99.

   Bridges discusses *Nero, Eros and Psyche, Ulysses, Bacchus, The Christian Captives,* the poor sales of his works, printing, and his friendship for Hopkins.

1959

1. Bridges, Robert. "The Case against Free Verse." In *Writers on Writing*, edited by Walter Ernest Allen, 87–91. New York: E. P. Dutton, 1959.
2. Bridges, Robert. Letters. In "Housman Inscriptions," by Simon Nowell-Smith. *Times Literary Supplement*, 6 November 1959, 643.

   Excerpts of two letters to Housman asking his assistance in writing a Latin inscription for Bridges's edition of Hopkins's poems.

1960

1. Bridges, Robert. "The Case against Free Verse." In *Writers on Writing*, edited by Walter Ernest Allen, 87–91. Boston: The Writer, 1960.
2. Bridges, Robert. Essay. In *Keats: Poetry and Prose*, edited by Henry Ellershaw, 25–32. Oxford: The Clarendon Press, 1960.

   Reprint of 1922.2.

1961

1. Bridges, Robert, and W. H. Gardner, eds. *Poems of Gerard Manley Hopkins*. 3d ed. enl. New York: Oxford University Press, 1961.

   Reprinted with additions and corrections to 1948.5.

1965

1. Bridges, Robert. *Milton's Prosody*. Oxford: The Clarendon Press, 1965.

   Reprint of 1921.5.

1966

1. Bridges, Robert. *The Influence of the Audience*. New York: Haskell House Publishers, 1966.

   Reprint of 1907.2.

1967

1. Bridges, Robert. *Milton's Prosody*. Oxford: The Clarendon Press, 1967.

   Reprint of 1921.5.

2. Bridges, Robert. "The Oddities of Genius." In *Hopkins: A Collection of Critical Essays*, edited by Geoffrey Hartman, 71–75. Englewood Cliffs, N.J.: Prentice-Hall, 1966.
    Reprint of Bridges's "Preface" to his edition of Hopkins. See 1918.3.

1968

1. Bridges, Robert. Letters. In *The Correspondence of Robert Bridges and Henry Bradley, 1900–1923*. Ann Arbor, Mich.: University Microfilms, 1968. Microfilm.
    Reprint of 1940.3.

1969

1. Bridges, Robert. *The Necessity of Poetry*. Folcroft, Penn.: Folcroft Press, 1969.
    Reprint of 1918.1.
2. Bridges, Robert. "Preface to Notes on Poems of Gerard Manley Hopkins." In *The Poets and Their Critics: Arnold to Auden*. Vol. 3 of *The Poets and Their Critics*, edited by James Reeves, 80–82. London: Hutchinson and Co., 1969.
    Reprint of 1918.3.

1970

1. Bridges, Robert. *The Collected Essays, Papers, etc. of Robert Bridges*. 10 vols. Folcroft, Penn.: Folcroft Press, 1970.
    Reprint of 1927–36 Oxford University Press edition.
2. Bridges, Robert, ed. *The Collected Papers of Henry Bradley*. Oxford: University Microfilms, 1970.
    Reprint of 1928.9.
3. Bridges, Robert. *Influence of the Audience on Shakespeare's Drama*. Studies in Shakespeare, No. 24. Brooklyn, N.Y.: Haskell Booksellers, Inc., 1970.
    Reprint of 1907.2.
4. Bridges, Robert. Letters. In *The Printer and the Poet*, edited by Nicholas Barker. Cambridge: Cambridge University Press, 1970.
    Fourteen letters to Stanley Morison.
5. Bridges, Robert. "A Memoir." In *The Collected Papers of Henry Bradley*, 1–56. Oxford: University Microfilms, 1970.
    Reprint of 1928.7.

6. Bridges, Robert. *Milton's Prosody.* Rev. final ed. Folcroft, Penn.: Folcroft Press, 1970.
   Reprint of 1921.5.

1971

1. Bridges, Robert. "The Case against Free Verse." In *Writers on Writing,* edited by Walter Ernest Allen, 87–91. London: Dent, 1971.
2. Bridges, Robert. Letters. In "Robert Bridges and Samuel Butler on Shakespeare's Sonnets: An Exchange of Letters," by Donald E. Stanford. *Shakespeare Quarterly* 22 (1971): 329–35.
   Two letters to Butler in which Bridges agrees with Butler's interpretation of a reference to the Spanish Armada and an early dating of the entire sonnet sequence. Bridges disagrees with Butler's view that William Hughes is the "W. H." of the sonnets, and rejects the idea that the sonnets are not an organic whole.
3. Bridges, Robert. Letters. In "Robert Bridges on His Poems and Plays," by Donald E. Stanford. *Philological Quarterly* 50 (1971): 283–91.
   Five letters to Samuel Butler regarding *Eros and Psyche, Prometheus, Nero, Ulysses, The Humours of the Court, Bacchus,* and the essay on Keats.
4. Bridges, Robert, ed. *The Chilswell Book of English Poetry.* Freeport, N.Y.: Books for Libraries, 1971.

1972

1. Bridges, Robert. *The Collected Essays, Papers, etc. of Robert Bridges.* Hildesheim, N.Y.: G. Olms, 1972.
   Reprint of the 1927–36 Oxford University Press edition.
2. Bridges, Robert. *John Keats.* Studies in Keats, No. 19. Brooklyn, N.Y.: Haskell Booksellers, Inc., 1972.
   Reprint of 1895.1.
3. Bridges, Robert. Letters. In *Stanley Morison,* edited by Nicolas Barker, 252–66 and passim. Cambridge: Harvard University Press, 1972.
   Seven letters and excerpts of letters to Morison, primarily regarding the printing of Bridges's work.
4. Bridges, Robert. *Milton's Prosody.* Rev. final ed. Folcroft, Penn.:

Folcroft Library Editions, 1972.
Reprint of 1921.5.

5. Bridges, Robert, ed. *Poems of Gerard Manley Hopkins*. Chicago: Library Resources Inc., 1972. Microfiche.
Reprint of 1918.3.

6. Bridges, Robert, and W. H. Gardner, eds. *Poems of Gerard Manley Hopkins*. Chicago: Library Resources Inc., 1972.
Reprint of 1948.5.

1973

1. Bridges, Robert. *Influence of the Audience on Shakespeare's Drama*. Folcroft, Penn.: Folcroft Library Editions, 1973.
Reprint of 1907.2.

2. Bridges, Robert. Letters. In *The Correspondence of Robert Bridges and Henry Bradley, 1900–1923*. Ann Arbor, Mich.: University Microfilms, 1973. Microfilm.
Reprint of 1940.3.

3. Bridges, Robert. Letters. In *XXI Letters: A Correspondence between Robert Bridges and R. C. Trevelyan*. Folcroft, Penn.: Folcroft Library Editions, 1973.

4. Bridges, Robert, ed. *The Spirit of Man*. Introduction by W. H. Auden. London: Longmans, Green, 1973.

1974

1. Bridges, Robert. *The Collected Essays, Papers, etc., of Robert Bridges*. 10 vols. Folcroft, Penn.: Folcroft Library Editions, 1974.
Reprint of 1927–36 edition printed by Oxford University Press.

2. Bridges, Robert. *The Influence of the Audience*. Folcroft, Penn.: Folcroft Library Editions, 1974.
Reprint of 1907.2.

3. Bridges, Robert. Letters. In *XXI Letters: A Correspondence between Robert Bridges and R. C. Trevelyan*. Folcroft, Penn.: Folcroft Library Editions, 1974.

4. Bridges, Robert, ed. *The Chilswell Book of English Poetry*. Arno, 1974.
Reprint of 1924.10.

1975

1. Bridges, Robert. *A Critical Introduction to Keats.* Folcroft, Penn.: Folcroft Library Editions, 1975.
2. Bridges, Robert. Letters. In *XXI Letters: A Correspondence between Robert Bridges and R. C. Trevelyan.* Norwood, Penn.: Norwood Editions, 1975.
3. Bridges, Robert. *Three Friends.* Westport, Conn.: Greenwood Press, 1975.
    Reprint of 1932.4.

1976

1. Bridges, Robert. Letters. In *XXI Letters: A Correspondence between Robert Bridges and R. C. Trevelyan.* Norwood, Penn.: Norwood Editions, 1976.
2. Bridges, Robert. *Milton's Prosody.* Norwood, Penn.: Norwood Editions, 1976.
    Reprint of 1921.5.
3. Bridges, Robert. *The Necessity of Poetry.* Folcroft, Penn.: Folcroft Library Editions, 1976.
    Reprint of 1918.1.

1977

1. Bridges, Robert. *The Collected Essays, Papers, etc. of Robert Bridges.* 10 vols. Norwood, Penn.: Norwood Editions, 1977.
    Reprint of the 1927–36 Oxford University Press edition.
2. Bridges, Robert. *Influence of the Audience.* Norwood, Penn.: Norwood Editions, 1977.
    Reprint of 1907.2.
3. Bridges, Robert. Letters. In *The Correspondence of Robert Bridges and W. B. Yeats,* edited by Richard J. Finneran. London: Macmillan, 1977.
    These annotated letters span the duration of the friendship of the two poets, from 1896 to 1930, and include twenty-seven letters from Bridges to Yeats.
4. Bridges, Robert. Letters. In *Letters to W. B. Yeats,* 2 vols., edited by Richard J. Finneran, et al., 1:27, 30, 52, 82, 265; 2:313, 319, 499. New York: Columbia University Press, 1977.
    Eight letters to Yeats on various subjects.
5. Bridges, Robert. Letters. In *XXI Letters: A Correspondence be-*

tween Robert Bridges and R. C. Trevelyan. Philadelphia:
R. West, 1977.

6. Bridges, Robert. *The Necessity of Poetry.* Folcroft, Penn.:
   Folcroft Library Editions, 1977.
   Reprint of 1918.1.

7. Bridges, Robert. *The Necessity of Poetry.* New York: Haskell
   House Publishers, 1977.
   Reprint of 1918.1.

8. Bridges, Robert. *The Necessity of Poetry.* Norwood, Penn.: Norwood Editions, 1977.
   Reprint of 1918.1.

1978

1. Bridges, Robert. *A Critical Introduction to Keats.* Norwood,
   Penn.: Norwood Editions, 1978.

1979

1. Bridges, Robert. Letter. In "Robert Bridges on English Quantitative Verse: An Unpublished Letter," by Peter Godman.
   Notes and Queries n.s. 26 (1979): 335–36.
   Bridges thanks W. M. Lindsay for his approving remarks
   regarding *Ibant Obscuri.* Although he gets great pleasure
   from reading the hexameters aloud, Bridges is "not in love
   with this English quantitative verse" and says he only wrote
   them "to keep a hasty promise to a young friend who died."

2. Bridges, Robert. *Society for Pure English.* Vol. 1. Edited by
   H. Steele Commanger. New York: Garland Publishing,
   1979.

3. Bridges, Robert, ed. *The Chilswell Book of English Poetry.* Great
   Neck, N.Y.: Granger Book Co., 1979.
   Reprint of 1924.10.

4. Bridges, Robert. *Society for Pure English.* Vol. 3. New York:
   Garland Publishing, 1979.

1980

1. Bridges, Robert, ed. *The Poems of Digby Mackworth Dolben.*
   Louisville, Ky.: Lost Cause Press, 1980. Microfiche.
   Reprint of 1915.3.

1982

1. Bridges, Robert. Letters. In *The Correspondence of Robert Bridges and Henry Bradley, 1900–1923*. Oxford: The Clarendon Press, 1982.
    Reprint of 1940.3.

1983

1. Bridges, Robert. Letters. In *The Selected Letters of Robert Bridges,* vol. 1, edited by Donald E. Stanford. Newark: University of Delaware Press, 1983.
    This volume and its companion (1984.2) contain more than a thousand letters and are only a part of Bridges's extant correspondence. Included are all the extant letters to Hopkins and to members of Hopkins's family.

1984

1. Bridges, Robert, ed. *The Collected Papers of Henry Bradley.* Ann Arbor, Mich.: University of Michigan Photoduplication Service, 1984.
    Reprint of 1928.9.
2. Bridges, Robert. Letters. In *The Selected Letters of Robert Bridges,* vol. 2, edited by Donald E. Stanford. Newark: University of Delaware Press, 1984.
3. Bridges, Robert. "A Memoir." In *The Collected Papers of Henry Bradley*, 1–56. Ann Arbor, Mich.: University of Michigan Photoduplication Service, 1984. Microfilm.

3
REVIEWS, CRITICISM, AND ANTHOLOGIES

1874

1. Lang, Andrew. Review of *Poems* [by Robert Bridges]. *The Academy* 5 (1874): 53–54.

    In this volume "a music long silent is revived." The lyrics are "plain, and dally with the innocence of love; they show at once true feeling and reticence." The sonnets and rondeaus are technically good but less satisfactory. These charming verses have a novel and simple artistic aim.

1879

1. Review of *Poems, by the Author of the Growth of Love* [by Robert Bridges]. *The Academy* 15 (1879): 299.

    The author has not "fully digested his own powers"; although there are some blemishes, there is hardly one of these poems "which is not remarkable for metre, language, or thought, and generally for all combined."

1881

1. [Bridges, Robert.] Poem. In *The Garland of Rachel*, 25–27. Oxford: H[enry] Daniel Press, 1881.

    Contains "Press thy hands and crow."

2. Review of *Poems,* 3d Series [by Robert Bridges]. *The Academy* 19 (1881): 352.

    The author should publish his work in a more convenient and accessible form because such superior poetry ought to be readily available and the author known. The poems in new prosody are annoying and seem to be reducible to the older forms.

1884

1. Mackail, J. W. Review of *Prometheus the Firegiver,* by Robert Bridges. *The Academy* 26 (1884): 334–35.

    There is nothing closer to the Greek spirit in English literature since Milton. Bridges is a scholar who knows how to write blank verse and "dares to be natural." His verse is singularly free of echoes of modern Poets. "This is the very touch of Virgil; and, when that is said, there is not further praise."

1885

1. Patmore, Coventry. "Mr. Robert Bridges's *Eros and Psyche.*" Review of *Eros and Psyche,* by Robert Bridges. *St. James's Gazette* 11 (1885): 7–8.

    Bridges's version of Apuleius's myth "will probably be the standard transcript" for future writers because he "takes the story as it stands." The writing is equal, vigorous, astute, and controlled. "Mr. Bridges writes neither above nor below himself."

2. Patmore, Coventry. "Mr. Robert Bridges's *Prometheus the Firegiver.*" Review of *Prometheus the Firegiver,* by Robert Bridges. *St. James's Gazette* 10 (1885): 607.

    Bridges is not generally popular because his work is too "perfect"—that is, a perfection "which bears little or no sign of work." He treats the myth in a straightforward manner and never attempts to imbue it with secondary meaning; yet "multiple meanings unveil themselves in proportion to the deserts and capacity of the beholder." Prometheus, "like nature, is full of symbolism and innocent of conscious intention." No other English drama so closely approximates the Greek model.

3. Review of *Prometheus the Firegiver,* by Robert Bridges. *The Athenaeum* 85 (1885): 115.

    This has the usual finenesses and faults of an English translation of Greek, but some of the metrical slips are unforgivable because so much attention has obviously been paid to the poem. The human characters lack emotion.

1886

1. "Dr. Bridges's Poems." Review of *Nero* and *Eros and Psyche,* by Robert Bridges. *The Spectator* 59 (1886): 421–22.

Nero fails because it seems little more than history put into the form of dialogue; however, *Eros and Psyche* is "a very tasteful and genuinely poetical piece of work."

1889

1. Lang, Andrew. "II. Of Modern English Poetry." In *Letters on Literature*, 24–28. London: Longmans, Green and Co., 1889.

    After giving a brief publishing history of Bridges's work, Lang praises the poetry of *Poems* (1873) for "a certain austere and indifferent beauty of diction and a memory of the old English poets," and also lauds the blank verse of *Prometheus* and *Nero I.*

1890

1. Review of *The Shorter Poems of Robert Bridges. The Saturday Review* 70 (1890): 484–85.

    Bridges's best poems are the shorter poems; they have no unnecessary words, are not overburdened by thought, and are written in a clear style. The experiments in "New Prosody" are best ignored.

2. Watson, William. Review of *The Shorter Poems of Robert Bridges. The Academy* 38 (1890): 496–97.

    Here are "strong and passionate" lyrics and "tenderly fanciful nature-pieces." The "Elegy on a Lady" is the pinnacle of Bridges's lyric achievement. He is at times too restrained and seems to have written these primarily for himself, not the public.

1891

1. *"Achilles in Scyros."* Review of *Achilles in Scyros,* by Robert Bridges. *The Spectator* 66 (1891): 382–83.

    Here is "dignified and sonorous verse" on a theme absolutely suited to Bridges. The music of the diction conveys "dignity, wholesomeness, and manliness."

2. Beeching, H[enry] C. "The Shorter Poems of Robert Bridges." Review of *Shorter Poems,* by Robert Bridges. *Murray's Magazine* 10 (1891): 280–90.

    Bridges is a metrical technician who shows no Victorian influence in his writing, a little Romantic influence, and a great many sixteenth-century and Miltonic influences. "On a Dead Child" and "London Snow" are the best of the "new prosody." His poems show increasing musical skill, but his chief creative gift is dramatic.

3. Johnson, Lionel. "The Poems of Mr. Bridges: A Brief and General Consideration." *The Century Guild Hobby Horse* 6 (1891): 148–60.

   The duty of the poet is to revere past and present masters. Bridges's poetry is modeled on the masters but not slavishly so. Throughout his poetry "substance is congruous with form." The lyrics of *Shorter Poems* (1890) and *The Growth of Love* (1890) are meditative, gracious, and restrained, though at times too concise and compact. *Bacchus, Eden,* and *Achilles* best illustrate Bridges's metrical achievements. There is "limited charm" in Bridges's poetry, a charm "too dainty for common use"; this is the hallmark of great poetry. The great poets are all contemporaries, and Bridges is "the most admirable in recent times."

4. Review of *The Shorter Poems of Robert Bridges. The Athenaeum* 97 (1891): 239–40.

   These poems show a "tendency . . . toward an Elizabethan quaintness, and the increase of a tendency toward translation-like versification." Some poems have no recognizable meter, and the elegies do not seem to be imbued with profound melancholy. "Mr. Bridges oftenest adopts the simplest and most natural forms of English verse."

1892

1. Bridges, Robert. Poem. In *Songs of Sundry Natures,* edited by William Byrd and G. E. P. Arkwright, 19, 53–56. London: James Parker and Co., 1892.

   Contains "November." This poem results from Bridges being asked to write new words for an old song.

2. "The Poetry of To-Day—and To-Morrow." Review of *The Shorter Poems of Robert Bridges. The Church Quarterly Review* 35 (1892): 201–17.

   Although not a poet of great force or originality, in taste, craftsmanship, delicacy of observation, and refinement of expression, Bridges is without living peer. He represents the best in the modern age's desire to look back. In him careful, conscious art has replaced spontaneous art. His ear for meter, however, is deficient.

3. Review of *Achilles in Scyros*, by Robert Bridges. *The Bookman* (London) 2 (1892): 183.

There is dramatic power evident in the conception of the characters of this play, but there is little action. Although the blank verse is "dignified and full-sounding," the meter does not always seem to fit English speech.

4. "Two Notable Poets." Review of *Ode for the Bicentenary Commemoration of Henry Purcell*, by Robert Bridges. *Spectator* 76 (1892): 635–36.

Bridges "seems . . . to delight in introducing words which are almost conundrums" in the flow of thought. His poetry is "an elaboration of the mind, not of the heart."

1893

1. Bailey, John C. "The Poems of Robert Bridges." *Eclectic Magazine* 124 (1893): 446–56.

Bridges's poetry reflects a contemplative rural life; this rural withdrawal accounts for the weaknesses in his poetry. *Achilles* is a poor play but contains much good poetry. Bridges's insight into nature and his ability to interpret nature echoes Wordsworth, Keats, and Milton. *Shorter Poems* exhibit a freer rein of the imagination, and Bridges seems more in his element, but none of the poetry here is as fine as that found in *Achilles*. "What he chiefly seems to need for the attainment of complete success is more life and flow and freedom, a more absolute surrender to the mood of inspiration."

2. Bailey, John C. "The Poems of Robert Bridges." *Littell's Living Age* 199 (1893): 556–63.

Reprint of 1893.1.

3. Bailey, John C. "The Poems of Robert Bridges." *Temple Bar* 99 (1893): 225–35.

Reprint of 1893.1.

4. Bridges, Robert. Poems. In *Robert Bridges and Contemporary Poets*. Vol. 8 of *The Poets and Poetry of the Century*, edited by Alfred Henry Miles, 114–22. London: Hutchinson and Co., 1893.

Includes "I have loved flowers that fade," "On a Dead Child," "I love all beauteous things," and excerpts from *Eros and Psyche, Palicio, The Christian Captives*, and *Achilles in Scyros*.

5. Lang, Andrew. "II. Of Modern English Poetry." In *Letters on Literature*,20–24. London: Longmans, Green and Co., 1893.

Reprint of 1889.1.

6. Warren, Thomas Herbert. "Robert Bridges." In *Robert Bridges and Contemporary Poets*. Vol. 8 of *The Poets and Poetry of the Century,* edited by Alfred Henry Miles, 113–22. London: Hutchinson and Co., 1893.

A brief biography and publishing history of Bridges's work. The lyrics stand on their own merit. Bridges is "no haphazard writer of occasional verse, but a careful and practised artist" who combines "grace and gravity." *The Growth of Love* is his "most remarkable work, reaching the highest height, the deepest depth in thought and in expression of all his writings."

1894

1. Binyon, Laurence. Review of *Milton's Prosody,* by Robert Bridges. *The Academy* 46 (1894): 202–3.

This book should correct many false notions about poetry and establish a "right standard." "Certainly, if we are to develop and extend English prosody . . . this seems the right path to strike."

2. Dowden, Edward. "The Poetry of Robert Bridges." *The Fortnightly Review* 62 (1894): 44–60.

Bridges is "not a poet with a mission." "All he has to tell is that he loves beauty and loves love." He is a craftsman who "has published nothing that is not carefully considered, and wrought to such excellence as can be conferred on it by studious and delicate workmanship." There is nothing revolutionary in his metrical experiments; they are "little more than nicely calculated variations of stress." Bridges's lyrics are "charged with fine and tender human sentiment," and his dramas reveal the strengths and weaknesses of his art.

3. Dowden, Edward. "The Poetry of Robert Bridges." *Littell's Living Age* 202 (1894): 451–62.

Reprint of 1894.2.

4. Johnson, Lionel. "The Poems of Mr. Bridges." In *The Growth of Love: A Poem in 76 Sonnets,* by Robert Bridges, xi–xxxvii. Portland, Maine: Thomas B. Mosher, 1894.

Reprint of 1891.3.

5. Kingsland, William G. "London Literaria." *Poet Lore* 6 (1894): 222–23.

Bridges has "no special 'message'" to give the world, but he has the distinctive note of a "true poet." Although it is unlikely he will ever become popular, his poetry has "the unmistakable ring of genius," full of subtle music and irresistable charm.

6. Payne, William Morton. "Recent Books of Poetry." Review of *The Humours of the Court, and Other Poems*, by Robert Bridges. *The Dial* 16 (1894): 83.

The play and poems are faintly Elizabethan in spirit and treatment.

7. P[orter, Charlotte]. "Old Friends and New Faces." Review of *The Growth of Love*, by Robert Bridges. *Poet Lore* 6 (1894): 639–41.

These sonnets, which were written "in a realm of pure aspiration," celebrate the growing purification of the poet's love for eternal beauty and infuse the love of the past with the wisdom of the present. "The flaw of these sonnets is of the sort that proceeds from learned observation of metrical secrets."

8. Review of *Milton's Prosody*, by Robert Bridges. *The Athenaeum* 103 (1894): 372–74.

Between the Pre-Raphaelite Brotherhood and the present, Bridges is preeminent in culture and artistic endowment; however, his terminology seems needlessly pedantic.

9. "Mr. Robert Bridges' New Poems." Review of *Shorter Poems of Robert Bridges, Book V; Plays by Robert Bridges; The Humours of the Court, and Other Poems*, by Robert Bridges. *Spectator* 72 (1894): 236–37.

Bridges has found "his own note" in these poems and "strikes it more firmly and sustainedly" than before. His rhythms are new but not as difficult as in early endeavors. His muse is proud and shy but has a heart. *Humours of the Court* is imbued with the philosophy of love and adds to the range but not the rank of the poet.

1895

1. Bridges, Robert. Poem. In *A Book of Christmas Verse*, 159. London: Methuen and Co., 1895.

Contains "Winter was not unkind because uncouth."

2. Bridges, Robert. Poems. In *Lyra Sacra,* 317–22. London: Methuen and Co., 1895.

 > Seven poems by Bridges.

3. Bridges, Robert. Poems. In *A Victorian Anthology, 1847–1895,* edited by Edmund Clarence Stedman, 437–40. Boston and New York: Houghton, Mifflin and Co.; Boston: The Riverside Press, 1895.

 > This anthology includes "Poore Withered Rose," "I will not let thee go," "A Passer-By," "Awake, My Heart," and "So sweet love seem'd."

4. Daniel, Henry. "Notes on the Bibliography of Robert Bridges." *The Oxford Magazine* 13 (1894–95): 446–47.

 > A bibliography of Bridges's published works, dating from 1873 to 1895. Also mentions the number of copies printed of those works printed by the Daniel Press.

5. Dowden, Edward. "Preface." In *New Studies in Literature,* i–xi. London: Kegan Paul, Trench, Trubner and Co., Ltd., 1895.

 > The article on Bridges is "an aperçu rather than . . . an appreciation," and seeks "only to extend the circle of those who enjoy [his] fine work."

6. Dowden, Edward. "Robert Bridges." In *New Studies in Literature,* 61–89. London: Kegan Paul, Trench, Trubner and Co., Ltd., 1895.

 > A reprint of 1894.2 which adds a paragraph on *Nero II.*

7. M., A. "Eros & Psyche." Review of *Eros and Psyche,* by Robert Bridges. *The Bookman* (London) 7 (1895): 116.

 > The work of a fastidious, "occasionaly finnicking," craftsman, *Eros and Psyche* preserves the original and adds vivid new touches. Though perhaps a bit lacking in humanity, there is "not a fault anywhere against delicacy and grace."

8. "Mr. Bridges' *Eros and Psyche.*" Review of *Eros and Psyche,* by Robert Bridges. *The Saturday Review* 79 (1895): 41–42.

 > Of the three modern renderings of this myth (Pater, Morris, and Bridges), Bridges's version is told most sparely. His is more Hellenic and less modern, but it is flawed by the imposition of moral doctrine.

9. Yeats, William Butler. *A Book of Irish Verse,* 250–52. London: Methuen and Co., 1895.

 > In condemning Thomas Moore's loose and vague poetry, Yeats quotes Bridges's rendering of Gautier's translation of

Moore's *The Epicurean* to illustrate the superiority of precise versification and concrete imagery.

1896

1. Bridges, Robert. Poems. In *Ode for the Bicentenary Commemoration of Henry Purcell,* by Robert Bridges. London: Elkin Mathews, 1896.

     Includes the title poem, "November," and "The South Wind."

2. LeGallienne, Richard. *Retrospective Reviews.* 2 vols. London: The Bodley Head; New York: Dodd and Mead, 1896. 2:61–66.

     A review of *Shorter Poems, Book V.* Bridges's poetry reflects a "dilettantism" that "can never make any general appeal." The "archaic and affected forms" in which his works appear are "outward expressions of the characteristics of his work." Great poets blend the temperaments of both the prophet and the artist, but Bridges seldom appeals to any sense other than the artistic. His love lyrics "breathe no passion."

3. Lewis, E. H. Review of *Milton's Prosody,* by Robert Bridges. *The School Review* 4 (1896): 553–54.

     Bridges brings the "ear of a poet" to the study of Milton's prosody and solves many questions for teachers. His theory of Miltonic elision clarifies many problems of pronunciation, "but there is danger that the theory involved may be made to account for too much." Bridges ignores the question of blank verse stanzas.

4. Review of *Ode for the Bicentenary Commemoration of Henry Purcell, with Other Poems,* by Robert Bridges. *The Athenaeum* 108 (1896): 411–12.

     This is a "mechanical structure" of "unexceptional sentiments" expressing a tame and prosaic argument. The poem is on a "crawling level" throughout. "We read without interest what has been written without impulse . . . and find a radical lack of vital heat throughout the entire composition."

5. "Two Notable Poets." Review of *Ode for the Bicentenary Commemoration of Henry Purcell, with Other Poems,* by Robert Bridges. *The Spectator* 76 (1896): 635–36.

     The "Ode to Music" is fraught with "willful obscurity."

Bridges seems "to delight in introducing words which are almost conundrums where they actually stand, into the flow of his thought.

6. Watson, H. B. Marriott. "Five Books of Verse." Review of *Ode for the Bicentenary Commemoration of Henry Purcell,* by Robert Bridges. *The Bookman* (London) 10 (1896): 84.

Bridges is a great poet whose talent is here wasted on a poetically unprofitable theme.

1897

1. Yeats, William Butler. "Mr. Robert Bridges." *The Bookman* (London) 12 (1897): 63–65.

The Return of Ulysses is "written . . . in what is practically the classic manner." It is "perfect after its kind" and has "admirable beauty" because the play's "classical gravity of speech subdues all passions into lyrical and meditative ecstasies." The climax is "not the climax of an excitement of nerves, but of that unearthly excitement which has wisdom for fruit." Bridges's slavish attention to the unities of time and place compels a logical rather than an instinctive procession of events.

1898

1. "Mr. Bridges's Poems." Review of *Poetical Works of Robert Bridges,* vol. 1. *The Bookman* (London) 15 (1898): 79–80.

Bridges "is not essentially a lyric poet" because his reticence inhibits the revelation of emotion. It is his refined art rather than a lack of emotion that chills his poetry. In *Eros and Psyche* form and plan are perfectly wedded to theme. *Prometheus* links an austere form with a didactic temper. Bridges "is more than an excellent craftsman; though distant and discreet, he speaks to the heart as well as to the aesthetic senses."

2. Mr. Robert Bridges." Review of *Poetical Works of Robert Bridges,* vol. 1. *The Academy* 55 (1898): 467.

The strengths of Bridges's poetry are its directness and sparseness of imagery. Its weaknesses are excessive thoughtfulness, gravity, and choiceness of style. Precision of meter and vocabulary distinguish his style. He is less successful, however, in the ardent lyrical vein than in quieter lyrical moods.

3. "The Poetry of Robert Bridges." Review of *Poetical Works of Robert Bridges*. *The Academy* 53 (1898): 155–56.

   The critical silence around Bridges is surprising. He is a master of meter who stands aside from the turmoil of the world to write with a wide range of feeling about Nature and Love. This is "the poetry of a scholar and a recluse" who has perfect mastery of his medium. His lyrics are his best work.

4. Review of *The Poetical Works of Robert Bridges*. *The Spectator* 81 (1898): 688–89.

   Prometheus is "ingenious and beautiful rather than felt." One may read *Eros and Psyche* with extreme pleasure and never desire to reread it. *The Growth of Love* has beautiful poetry but no apparent connecting idea. "The whole book suggests the temperament of one who thinks rather than acts, meditates rather than dreams; it shows great clearness of mind allied to a certain weakness of artistic purpose."

5. Yeats, William Butler. "The Autumn of the Flesh." *The Dublin Daily Express*, 3 December 1898, sect. 1, n.p., col. 2.

   Bridges and the delicate rhythm of his poetry are a part of a growing tradition of subtle poetry that illuminates "the little inner world which alone seeks more than amusement in the arts."

1899

1. Binyon, Laurence. "Mr. Bridges' *Prometheus* and Poetic Drama." *The Dome* NS 2 (1899): 199–206.

   The current critical practice of hasty reviews hurts artists like Bridges whose subtle beauty inheres deep within the entire body of his work and lies in its unity of imagery and rhythm flowing organically from its subject matter. Bridges, who carries on the lyric art of Shelley, is the "sure master of all that he attempts."

2. "A Poet of Content." Review of *The Shorter Poems of Robert Bridges*. *The Academy* 56 (1899): 454–55.

   Bridges's poetry is content; it does not speak in fashionable plaintive terms. He writes on popular subjects but remains unpopular because he is austere, classical, precise, and reticent.

3. Review of *The Shorter Poems of Robert Bridges*. *The Spectator* 82 (1899): 888.

This is the poetry of "a man whose poetry is always accomplished and finely wrought"; yet it leaves the reader cold. Despite Bridges's mastery of poetic style, "we do not see in him any mastery of metre, still less any mastery of emotion."

4. Yeats, William Butler. "The Autumn of the Flesh." In *Literary Ideals in Ireland,* edited by John Eglington, et al., 69–75. London: T. Fisher Unwin, 1899.
   Reprint of 1898.5.

5. Yeats, William Butler. "The Theatre." *Beltaine* 1 (1899): 20–23.
   The Return of Ulysses is "one of the most beautiful and . . . dramatic of modern plays" but would have no success in commercial theater.

6. Yeats, William Butler. "The Theatre." *The Dome,* April 1899.
   Reprint of 1899.5.

1900

1. Gosse, Edmund. "Mr. Bridges's Poems." *The Independent* 52 (1900): 105–8.
   Bridges's poetry "does not present aspects of magnitude"; its greatness lies in his mastery of meter and language. He is an "untiring experimentalist" whose isolation has encouraged a certain indifference to public reading taste. "He pushes restraints to the point of dryness." Regardless, he is "one of the most original of recent English poets."

2. Gosse, Edmund. "Mr. Robert Bridges's Poems." *Current Literature* 28 (1900): 36–37.
   Condensed version of 1900.1.

3. Patmore, Coventry. Letters. In *Memoirs and Correspondence of Coventry Patmore,* 2 vols., edited by Basil Champneys, 2:246–52. London: George Bell and Sons, 1900.
   Twelve letters to Bridges, covering the period from 1884 to 1895, discussing Hopkins's poetry and Bridges's work on Keats and *Prometheus.*

1901

1. Bridges, Robert. Poem. In *Through Human Eyes,* by A[lice] [Mary] Buckton, ix–xi. Oxford: The Daniel Press, 1901.
   Contains "Introductory."

2. Bridges, Robert. Poem. In *Through Human Eyes,* by A[lice] [Mary] Buckton, ix–xi. London: Mathews, Elkins and Co., 1901.

    Reprint of 1901.1 with the addition of a new first line.

3. Symons, Arthur. "Robert Bridges." *The Monthly Review* 4 (1901): 114–27.

    Bridges's art contains nothing gratuitous; "everything exists for the sake of poetry." His poetry, "more than almost any in English, is art for art's sake." The lyrics reveal "equable sensitiveness to fine emotions." The dramas, however, exhibit only beauty of detail rather than structural beauty and therefore "remain, for the most part, interesting experiments, not achievements." The sonnets in *The Growth of Love* are technically beautiful but sterile, generalized, and trite. Nevertheless, "no one in our time has written verse more consciously and more learnedly." Bridges is "the wisest of living poets, as he is artistically the most faultless."

1902

1. [Bridges, Robert.] Poem. In *The Garland of Rachel,* 25–27. Portland, Maine: Thomas Bird Mosher, 1902.

    Reprint of 1881.1.

2. Bridges, Robert. Poem. In *A Volunteer Haversack,* 23. Edinburgh: Printed for the Brigade, 1902.

    Contains "Matres Dolorosae."

3. Clerke, A. M. Review of *The Return of Ulysses,* by Robert Bridges. *The Edinburgh Review* 196 (1902): 85.

    The play contains much fine speech, feeling, and conduct; however, it has no mass appeal and seems better suited to the closet.

4. MacDonell, A. "Another Ulysses." Review of *Poetical Works of Robert Bridges,* vol. 4. *The Bookman* (London) 21 (1902): 209–10.

    Compared with Stephen Phillips's *Ulysses,* Bridges's *Return of Ulysses* is more narrowly focused, more sober in manner, more barbaric in action, and less dramatic in exposition.

5. Newbolt, Henry. "On the Line." Review of *The Poetical Works of Robert Bridges,* vol. 4. *Monthly Review* 6 (March 1902): 12–16.

    Although Bridges's *Return of Ulysses* is not as well known

as Stephen Phillips's recent version of the same myth, Bridges's play has been praised by prominent critics. Bridges and Phillips seek the same goal; however, Bridges's ideal is of the past and future whereas Phillips's ideal is of the present.

6. "The Return of Ulysses." Review of *The Poetical Works of Robert Bridges*, vol. 4. *The Academy* 62 (1902): 187–88.

    Bridges's version of the Ulysses myth is more in the Greek spirit than is Stephen Phillips's. Bridges's work combines Attic and Shakespearean elements, controlled by the twofold unity of character and action, told in "dignified, restrained and admirably varied blank verse."

7. Review of *Poetical Works of Robert Bridges*, vol. 3. *The Athenaeum* 119 (1902): 40.

    Nero is the most dramatic of Bridges's plays. *Achilles* is too contrived. "[Bridges] will live by his lyrics, not by his plays."

8. Review of *Poetical Works of Robert Bridges*, vols. 4 and 5. *The Athenaeum* 120 (1902): 646.

    "Mr. Bridges is not a dramatist, but he writes plays which can be read with something like uneager absorption." *Ulysses* is fine poetry, but it is not drama. *Palicio* and *The Humours of the Court* have no substance, no human interest; and *The Christian Captives* depicts a remote, romantic life. Bridges can only achieve intensity in the lyric.

9. Thompson, Francis. "Mr. Bridges and Metre." Review of *Milton's Prosody*, by Robert Bridges. *The Academy* 62 (1902): 85.

    Bridges's work is excellent for the poetical student, though whether it will be of use to the general reader of poetry is another question." Verse based on quantity without accent will not sound like verse to English ears.

10. "Two Books on English Prosody." Review of *Milton's Prosody*, by Robert Bridges. *The Nation* 74 (1902): 370–71.

    Bridges's use of the word "fiction" to describe elision is not satisfactory, neither is his distinction between syllabic and stress verse, nor his ideas about natural stress rhythm. This is nevertheless a thorough and sympathetic study of Milton's verse, with a keen insight and appreciation for delicate feelings and shades in Milton's poetry.

1903

1. Bridges, Robert. Poems. In *Lyra Sacra,* 358–63. London: Methuen and Co., 1903.

   Six poems by Bridges.

2. Dam, B. A. P. van. "Metrik." Review of *Milton's Prosody,* by Robert Bridges. In *Englische Studien,* 98–110. Leipzig: O. R. Reisland, 1903.

   In failing to define "elision" and "contraction," Bridges inconsistently applies his own dubious metrics. His understanding of stress is "crude." "If he had made it his business to investigate the practice of other poets in analogous cases, he would very soon have found out the futility of his reasonings."

3. Gilde, Alfred. "Die dramatische Behandlung der Rueckkehr des Odysseus bei Nicholas Rowe, Robert Bridges und Stephen Phillips." Ph.D. Diss., Königsberg, 1903.

4. "Quantity and Accent: Mr. Robert Bridges's New Poem." Review of *Now in Wintry Delights,* by Robert Bridges. *Times Literary Supplement,* 10 April 1903, 109–10.

   This brief survey of man's place in the universe "reads somewhat as though Horace had been reading 'de Rerum Natura' and had written to tell Maecenas his impressions." The prosody, which is the quantitative hexameters of classical poetry, will assist in the improved pronunciation of English.

5. Yeats, William Butler. "The Autumn of the Body." In *Ideas of Good and Evil,* 299. London: A. H. Bullen; New York: Macmillan, 1903.

   A reprint of 1898.5.

6. Yeats, William Butler. "The Return of Ulysses." In *Ideas of Good and Evil,* 312–19. London: A. H. Bullen; New York: Macmillan, 1903.

   Reprint of 1897.1.

1904

1. Bridges, Robert. Poem. In the Program of the Reception at Queen's Hall, London, 16 May 1904.

   A sonnet, "To Joseph Joachim," celebrating the Diamond Jubilee of Joachim's first performance in London in 1844.

2. Bridges, Robert. Poem. In *Wayfarer's Love,* edited by the Duchess of Sutherland, 66. Westminster [London]: Archibald

Constable and Co, 1904.
Contains "The Portrait of a Grandfather."

3. Symons, Arthur. "Robert Bridges." In *Studies in Prose and Verse*, 207–23. London: J. M. Dent and Co., 1904.
Reprint of 1901.3.

1905

1. "A Daughter of Dreams." Review of *Demeter,* by Robert Bridges. *Saturday Review* (London) 100 (8 July 1905): 57–58.

Bridges's telling of the Demeter myth "will not greatly enhance his well-won poetic reputation." The versification flows easily, and the diction is graceful and worthy. Unfortunately, the beauty of the myth is overlaid with cliched philosophising. His eccentricities of scansion, spelling, and phonetics suit neither the subject nor the occasion.

2. "Keats." Review of *The Poems of John Keats,* edited by G. Thorn Drury. Introduction by Robert Bridges. *Times Literary Supplement,* 14 April 1905, 117.

Bridges's essay is probably "the best thing that has been written on the art of Keats." Regrettably, Bridges has misunderstood the plan of *Hyperion.* The fragment ends pointing the way toward rebirth, not decay, as Bridges says.

3. "Mr. Bridges' *Demeter.*" Review of *Demeter,* by Robert Bridges. *Times Literary Supplement,* 16 June 1905, 189–90.

One feels the "luxury of an aristocratic repose and quietness" in reading Bridges. His is not the voice of Milton. He is "content to possess his own soul, think his own thoughts, and live his own life apart." *Demeter* contains the "same scholarly severity of manner" and "utter refusal of all cheap triumphs of effect over emotion" that are typical of Bridges's work. Although he has put his heart and mind into the mask, the "metrical experiments and pedantries of orthography" are regrettable. Bridges's version of the myth contains more than was conceived by the Greek mind and less.

4. "Mr. Robert Bridges's 'Demeter.'" Review of *Demeter,* by Robert Bridges. *The Athenaeum* 126 (1905): 6.

Demeter is full of "graceful thought and sober meditation," and written in simple, easy, adequate blank verse. Like all of Bridges's dramas, this one lacks vital heat.

Bridges's lyrics are his best work, while his metrical experiments are more unfortunate.

5. "Mr. Robert Bridges's 'Demeter.'" Review of *Demeter,* by Robert Bridges. *Littell's Living Age* 246 (1905): 506–8. Reprint of 1905.4.

6. "Mr. Robert Bridges's Mask." Review of *Demeter,* by Robert Bridges. *The Academy* 68 (1905): 607–8.

Bridges has written a version of the myth that can be enjoyed by the modern world. Demeter's emotions, however, seem intellectualized and inconsistent. Bridges's blank verse is as current as Fletcher and as self conscious as Tennyson; yet, it is spoiled by his use of accent, which seems to conflict with the rhythm of the lines. The lyrics are clever and experimental, but they are not his best verse.

1906

1. Bridges, Robert. Poems. In *Robert Bridges and Contemporary Poets.* Vol. 7 of *The Poets and Poetry of the Nineteenth Century,* edited by Alfred Henry Miles, 113–24. London: George Routledge and Sons, 1906.

Essentially a reprint of 1893.4, with the addition of "Nightingales" and excerpts from the English hexameters and *Demeter.*

2. Roberts, J. Slingsby. "Nero in Modern Drama." *The Fortnightly Review* 85 (1906): 92–95.

Bridges's *Nero* is generally lifeless but has good dialogues. There is much that is modern in the self-analyzing psychology of the protagonist.

3. Warren, Thomas Herbert. "Robert Bridges." In *Robert Bridges and Contemporary Poets.* Vol. 7 of *The Poets and Poetry of the Nineteenth Century,* edited by Alfred Henry Miles, 113–24. London: George Routledge and Sons, Ltd., 1906.

An updated reprint of the 1892–97 edition. Warren notes the publication of the fifth book of *Shorter Poems* and *Demeter,* and comments on W. J. Stone's influence on Bridges's Latin verse.

1907

1. Omond, T. S. "New Prosody." In *English Metrists: 18th and 19th Centuries,* 201–7. London: Oxford University Press, 1907.

The "laws" that Bridges adduces in *Milton's Prosody* "are sometimes too absolute." His insistence that verse stresses be constant is questionable. Bridges's verse as well as his prose "must be taken into account in dealing with English prosody."

1908

1. Saintsburg, George. "Milton." In *From Shakespeare to Crabbe.* Vol. 2 of *A History of English Prosody,* 257–59. London: Macmillan, 1908.

   Bridges is "the most important and the most thoroughgoing" of the recent students of Milton's prosody; however, his theory is inadequate.

1910

1. Bridges, Robert. Poems. In *In Praise of Gardens,* edited by Temple Scott, 134–36. New York: Baker and Taylor Co., 1910.

   This anthology includes "The Garden in September" and "The pinks along my garden walks."
2. Muhlbach, E. "Die Englische Nerodramen des XVII Jahrhunderts insonderheit Lees Nero." Ph.D. Diss., Leipzig, 1910.
3. Saintsbury, George. "The Later English Hexameter." In *From Blake to Swinburne.* Vol. 3 of *A History of English Prosody,* 434–36. London: Macmillan, 1910.

   Although the modern revival of classical verses is due in large measure to the "ingenious audacity" of Robert Bridges, his experiments with classical hexameters are unsatisfactory.
4. Symons, Arthur. "Robert Bridges." In *Studies in Prose and Verse,* 207–23. London: J. M. Dent and Co., 1910.

   Reprint of 1901.3.

1912

1. Abercrombie, Lascelles. "Robert Bridges." *The Manchester Guardian,* no. 20682, 19 November 1912, 7.

   Bridges's poetry is literary art of the highest order. It radiates depth of mood, imagination, and intellect. "As a master of blank verse he must be put as high as anyone who has written since Milton."
2. Bridges, Robert. Poems. In *The Oxford Book of Victorian Verse,*

edited by Arthur Quiller-Couch, 697–707. Oxford: The Clarendon Press, 1912.

Includes "Awake, my heart to be loved," "A Passer-By," and "Nightingales."

3. Figgis, Darrell. "Mr. Robert Bridges." In *Studies and Appreciations,* 155–68. London: J. M. Dent and Sons, 1912.

Art is ritual and ritual is disguised ecstasy, but Bridges has managed to "purge" all ecstasy from his art. "One has to search for his moments of inspiration among his lyrics, for they are not many." This same lack of emotion affects his dramas. "Mr. Bridges is too contemplative and meditative for those explosive emotions that go to make great drama." His mood is "best adapted to dramas conceived in the Greek manner." *Demeter,* his best drama, is "the loveliest treatment in English of the loveliest legend of the Greeks."

4. Newbolt, Henry. "Six Living Poets." *The Poetry Review* 12 (1912): 154–56.

Bridges is classical in every sense, but he is also very English and very modern. He penetrates deeply into such moods as joy, sorrow, and love. His poetry is vital and personal, not cool and objective.

5. Review of *The Poetical Works of Robert Bridges. The Bookman* (London) 43 (1912): 24.

Bridges has never had a large following owing to his classical form and diction. His verses are delicate and are characterized by their exquisite restraint of emotional intensity. *The Growth of Love* ranks among the greatest modern poems. Includes a portrait.

1913

1. Abercrombie, Lascelles. "Robert Bridges." *Poetry and Drama* 1 (1913): 313–18.

Bridges "is the greatest of living poets"; "his work belongs to the canon of great English poetry"; therefore, his ascension to the laureateship is "the only tolerable appointment." The inaccessible and expensive nature of his works has caused him to be little known. His long poems are as important as his lyrics; both have profoundly moving passions but not the exhilaration of new insight or discovery. His dramas are generally closet dramas.

2. Bailey, John. "The Poetry of Robert Bridges." Review of *Poetical Works of Robert Bridges, Excluding the Eight Dramas* and

Poetical Works of Robert Bridges, 6 vols. *The Quarterly Review* 219 (1913): 231–55.

Bridges's plays, masques, and metrical experiments are important only insofar as they shed light on his lyrics, which are what his fame will ultimately rest on. Though Bridges is only a minor poet, the lyrics are of an invariably fine quality and blend "philosophy and fact." He is a superb poet of nature and landscape, and only Tennyson "can compare with him in his knowledge of the scientific movement of his day." "In Mr. Bridges the scholar, the artist, the thinker, contend on less unequal terms with the poet." He should be the next poet laureate.

3. Bailey, John. "The Poetry of Robert Bridges." *Littell's Living Age* 218 (1913): 515–29.

Reprint of 1913.2.

4. Braithwaite, William Stanley. "The Lyrical Poetry of the New Laureate." *The Forum* 50 (1913): 877–90.

Although there is nothing in his style that is strikingly original, Bridges is within the best tradition of English poetry. His art is highly self-conscious and restrained in emotion. Some of his lyrics, the best of which are about nature, are without peer in English poetry. *The Growth of Love* ranks second only to Bridges's lyrics and is comparable with the great sonnet sequences of the nineteenth century.

5. "Bridges Third on List of Poets." *New York Times,* 3 August 1913, sect. 3, p. 4, col. 2.

Bridges finished third behind Kipling and Watson in a contest sponsored by the *Journal of Education* to determine the greatest living English poet.

6. Bronner, Milton. "Robert Bridges as Lyricist." *The Bookman* (New York) 38 (1913–1914): 42–45.

Bridges is a supreme individualist whose timeless lyrics are indifferent to modern problems and questionings. His poetry is marked by exquisite simplicity, tender beauty, and unforced music, but it also lacks emotion. Bridges will never be generally popular because he is too detached from the modern world.

7. "Decaying English Pronunciation." *The Literary Digest* 47 (1913): 174.

Excerpts from the *Times Literary Supplement* review of Bridges's "On the Present State of English Pronunciation."

8. De la Mare, Walter. "The Poetry of Robert Bridges." Review of *The Poetical Works of Robert Bridges, Excluding the Eight Dramas. Saturday Westminster Gazette*, 30 August 1913.

   Bridges is "a poet's poet" whose artistic "aim has always been essentially poetry, and only indirectly ethical, dialectic, circumstantial." He is a scholar and a poet whose poetic tendency is toward "the impersonal and academic." Although the inspiration of his verse is clear, the passion is sometimes wanting. His primary themes are love and happiness. "It is as a writer of lyrics that Mr. Bridges will live."

9. "Dr. Robert Bridges New Poet Laureate." *New York Times*, 17 July 1913, p. 3, col. 3.

   Bridges has a cold, formal style, which exhibits purity, delicacy, and precision of expression. He has the courage of his opinions. His primary interest in English prosody is with natural speech rhythms and stress. Excerpts from "Elegy" and *Demeter.*

10. "England's Content with Her Laureate." *The Literary Digest* 47 (1913): 286–87.

    Excerpts from British papers regarding Bridges's appointment to the laureateship.

11. Hewlett, Maurice. "To the Poet Laureate." *Current Opinion* 55 (1913): 200.

    A poem to Bridges.

12. Hewlett, Maurice. "To the Poet Laureate." *Westminster Gazette* (1913).

    Same as 1913.11.

13. "Hymns of the Poet Laureate." *The Literary Digest* 476 (1913): 529–30.

    Excerpts of an article praising Bridges's skill as a hymn writer.

14. "Interesting but a Disappointment." *New York Times,* 25 December 1913, p. 8, col. 5.

    Bridges's "Queer Christmas poem" has more than a little interest, but why should he waste time producing relics of the past?

15. Kilmer, Joyce. "Robert Bridges, England's New Poet Laureate." *New York Times,* 20 July 1913, sect. 5, p. 10, col. 1.

    Bridges's devotion to abstruse technical matters has narrowed his appeal. His study of music is reflected in verse that exhibits a "calm rapture." "The Laureateship could go to no poet more devoted to his art." Quotes extensively from Symons's essay. See 1901.3.

16. "Kipling's Popularity." *New York Times,* 10 August 1913, sect. 2, p. 2, col. 8.

   The criticism in the English press of Bridges's appointment to the laureateship reveals the immense popularity of Rudyard Kipling.

17. "The Laureate and His Work." *The Independent* 75 (1913): 259–60.

   Summarizes Bridges's life and his major works. Includes "Millicent," "The Iron Ship," "Elegy: To H.E.W.," and "The Woodchopper."

18. "Laureate's Bays." *Poetry and Drama* 1 (1913): 270.

   Bridges "is a true representative of poetry, of beauty as revealed in poetry." His appointment to the laureateship is entirely nonpolitical and brings honor to the office, but since officialdom and poetry are incompatible, he is not likely to write ceremonial odes or official verse.

19. "Laureate's First Poem for the King." *New York Times,* 24 December 1913, p. 4, col. 4.

   Bridges has revived the ancient custom of presenting the monarch with a poem on the occasion of a religious holiday. Reprints "Christmas Eve, 1913."

20. M., B. "Poet Laureate's Verse." Letter. *New York Times,* 23 July 1913, p. 6, col. 5.

   Cites "I have loved flowers that fade" as "the most significant of all [the verses] contained in [Poetical Works]."

21. "The New Laureate." *The Literary Digest* 47 (1913): 174–75.

   Excerpts from American papers regarding Bridges's appointment to the laureateship.

22. "The New Laureate." *The Nation* 97 (1913): 73–74.

   Bridges is deeply rooted in the great tradition of English poetry and possesses genuine poetic feelings. His dramas are weak, but his lyrics are truly great. He is not likely to celebrate patriotic occasions.

23. "The New Laureate." *New York Evening Post,* 1913.
   Reprint of 1913.22.

24. "The New Poet Laureate." *The Educational Review* (London) 46 (1913): 322–24.

   Bridges's artistic passion for Beauty is a pure motive,

which places him above politics, party, and patriotism. "The honor paid to Mr. Bridges is an honor paid to poetry."

25. "News Notes." *The Bookman* (London) 44 (1913): 187.

Bridges is a scholarly poet whose poetry is marked by dignity, beauty, and technical finish. Although his verse is sometimes "lacking in fire and emotion," his poetry will restore distinction to the laureateship.

26. "Notes and Gleanings." *New York Times*, 21 December 1913, sect.3, p. 4, col. 1.

The current edition of the *Simplified Spelling Bulletin* contains examples of Bridges's recommendations for simplified spelling.

27. Osborn, E. B. "The Art of Robert Bridges." *Morning Post*, 1 August 1913, 11.

Bridges is an impeccable craftsman who, as laureate, will stand above politics. Although his Latin metrical experiments sometimes fail, his lyrics are "his title-deeds to immortality."

28. "An Oxford Poet." Review of *Poetical Works of Robert Bridges*. *The Nation* 96 (1913): 83–84.

Bridges lacks intellectual and self-critical powers, but his refinement, sense of beauty, sincerity, and modesty of self-confession serve him well. The poems in classical prosody are failures. The "dreamy languor" of some of his poetry associates him with the romance of Oxford.

29. "The Poet Laureate." *New York Times*, 18 July 1913, p. 8, col. 4.

Although he writes "fine and thoughtful verse," Bridges is an obscure gentleman whose appointment is a compromise that relieves the government of having to choose from among better and more popular poets.

30. "The Poetical Works of the New Poet Laureate." Review of *Poetical Works of Robert Bridges, Excluding the Eight Dramas*. *The Contemporary Review* 104 (1913): 284–86.

Bridges's appointment is literary, not political or social. Influenced by Milton, Spenser, Shelley, and Keats, he is "a poet's poet." His poetry combines strength with "deep philosophic and spiritual force."

31. "The Poetry of Robert Bridges." *The Literary Digest* 47 (1913): 185–88.

Bridges is a thoroughgoing artist who has never catered

to public opinion. He writes more sympathetically of love and death than of love and life. Includes "A Passer-By," "Elegy," "Matres Dolorosae," "Peace Ode," "When Death to either shall come," and "I have loved flowers that fade."

32. "To Restore 'Pure English.'" *New York Times,* 7 December 1913, sect. 8, p. 3, col. 4.

    Bridges announces the formation of the Society for Pure English.

33. "Robert Bridges." *The Outlook* 104 (1913): 594–95.

    Bridges should be made laureate because he possesses the art and imagination of a true poet, although he lacks the passion and range of great poets. His appointment "would once more identify an ancient office with high standards and distinguished achievement." Reprints "A Passer-By."

34. "Robert Bridges at 70 Still has the Enthusiasm of 20." *New York Times,* 26 October 1913, sect. 7, p. 5, col. 1.

    Bridges escorted the interviewer on a lively and spirited tour of Oxford and related anecdotes of his undergraduate days there. Although annoyed by the publicity and attention that goes with his new position, he hopes to restore to the laureateship much of its "lost dignity and power."

35. "Robert Bridges' Literary Alphabet." *The Independent* 76 (1913): 131.

    Summarizes Bridges's views on modifying the spelling and printing of English and prints an example of the sorts of changes he desires. Includes a portrait.

36. "Robert Bridges, Poet Laureate." *The Dial* 55 (1913): 69–71.

    Bridges is an admirable choice for the laureateship. "No English poet now living carries on the great tradition of English song . . . with a finer sense of the poet's mission . . . than does this modest man of science and accomplished classical scholar."

37. Taylor, Edward Robeson. Letter. In *The Nation* 97 (1913): 141–42.

    Bridges needs no apologies to wear the laurels of the laureate; he is above being damned with faint praise. Irrational modern prejudice against sonnets has damned *The Growth of Love,* whose sonnets share the form and substance of Shakespeare's sonnets.

38. "Topics of the Week." *New York Times,* 3 August 1913, sect. 4, p. 420, col. 2.

Mentions the lukewarm approval *The Times* (London) gave Bridges's appointment to the laureateship.

39. "The Two Supreme Notes on Robert Bridges' Genius." *Current Opinion* 55 (1913): 198–200.

Excerpts from several articles on Bridges. The two great themes in Bridges's work are Love and Religion. Includes a portrait.

40. Warren, Thomas Herbert. *Robert Bridges, Poet Laureate.* Oxford: The Clarendon Press, 1913.

Bridges is "a laureate, in the true English line of English poetry, of Chaucer and Spenser, of Milton and Gray, of Wordsworth and Tennyson." Bridges's poetry echoes his childhood at Walmer; school days at Eton and Oxford; travels to Egypt, Italy, and Greece; athletic endeavors; and experiences at St. Bartholomew's and the Children's Hospital. Bridges's prose works, especially his critical studies, "should be remembered by anyone who wishes to study his poetry with thoroughness, and to understand his art and its development completely."

1914

1. "Bridges Praises Burns." *New York Times,* 24 January 1914, p. 3, col. 2.

Reprints Bridges's poem on Burns, which he wrote for the Greencock Burns Club.

2. Bridges, Robert. "Thou Careless, Awake!" *Times Literary Supplement,* 13 August 1914, 381.

3. Douglass, E. J. "The Poet Laureate's 'Effusions.'" Letter. *New York Times,* 17 August 1914, p. 6, col. 5.

"Ye careless, awake!" is a regrettable effusion.

4. Gray, William Forbes. "Alfred Austin." In *The Poets Laureate of England: Their History and Their Odes,* 287. London: Sir Isaac Pitman and Sons, Ltd., 1914.

Mentions Bridges's accession to the laureateship and quotes "Christmas Eve," his first official poem.

5. Groom, Bernard. "Contemporary Literature." In *A Literary History of England,* 365. London: Longmans, Green and Co., 1914.

Bridges is a poet of "flawless taste" whose "verbal music," descriptive phrases, and simple language appeal to deep and subtle emotions. He is a poet of "Beauty and Joy" who is devoted "to the highest ideals of his art."

6. "The Laureate's Christmas Song." *The Outlook* 106 (1914): 5–6.

    Bridges's poems show careful workmanship, a classical spirit, and a distinctly individual voice, one that "is entirely free from the commonplaces of his predecessor." Excerpts verses from "Christmas Eve."

7. "The Laureate's New Effort." *The Literary Digest* 48 (1914): 20.

    Excerpts from papers expressing doubts about the efforts of Bridges and the Society for Pure English to reform English pronunciation.

8. "Poet Laureate Sings." *New York Times*, 26 March 1914, p. 4, col. 4.

    An eight-line excerpt from *Narcissus*.

9. "Poet Laureate's Call." *New York Times*, 9 August 1914, sect. 2, p. 3, col. 5.

    Reprints "Thou careless, awake!" from *TLS* (see 1914.2).

10. "The Poets and Peace." *New York Times*, 10 August 1914, p. 6, col. 2.

    Bridges's poem "Ye careless, awake!" is doggerel.

11. "Robert Bridges." Review of *Poetical Works of Robert Bridges, Excluding the Eight Dramas*. *New York Times*, 22 February 1914, sect. 6, p. 84, col. 1.

    Here are the works of a writer "whom every intelligent reader should know." These poems are neither coldly classical nor didactic. Bridges shows us that pleasure comes when we simply open our hearts to the beauty of the world and life.

12. Young, Francis E. Brett. *Robert Bridges: A Critical Study.* London: Martin Secker, 1914.

    The expression of beauty is the aim of the art of Robert Bridges. However, Bridges is unwilling to involve himself in "the complex and the intense" and is therefore not to be ranked with the greatest poets in our language. His art is in the tradition of the great Romantics. "There is that in his work which has not been heard in English poetry since Shelley died—the note of joy." Like Keats, Bridges loves the principle of beauty in all things, as is manifested in *The Growth of Love;* but it is not the sensual love of Keats. Rather it is "more nearly love according to the Book of Common

Prayer." *The Shorter Poems* contain "the flower of Bridges' work" and "the finest product of English genius." Bridges's sincerity, graceful diction, charm, and skillful use of stress-prosody are admirable. "The whole of Bridges' achievement in stress-prosody is to enforce the idea of regularity in line-length while avoiding suggestion of a recurrent bar-beat." The dramas have been overpraised, and the later poems are "inconsiderable."

1915

1. Bridges, Robert. Poems. In *The Country Life Anthology of Verse*, 51–52. London: Country Life and George Newnes; New York: Charles Scribner's Sons, 1915.

    Contains "An Invitation" and "Spring's Children."

2. Davis, Cora. "Robert Bridges' *Narcissus*." *The Forum* 53 (1915): 386–92.

    Bridges's *Narcissus* is the product of a scholar who maintains the old traditions. It shows the influences of Shakespeare, Milton, Ovid, Platonism, and Pantheism.

3. Gray, William Forbes. "Alfred Austin." In *The Poets Laureate of England: Their History and Their Odes*, 287. New York: E. P. Dutton and Co., 1915.

    Reprint of 1914.4.

4. Kellett, E. E. "The Poems of Robert Bridges." *The London Quarterly Review* 124 (1915): 232–48.

    Bridges is "an Oxford poet," and the Oxonian spirit of restraint permeates his work, alike for good and for ill. He is a critic first and a poet second; thus, his poems seem to have been written to exemplify his ideas and theories, "rather than because an irresistible impulse had come over him compelling him to express himself or die." Although Bridges is "too often conscious of his art," he is "at his best in lyric poetry, in which, as a rule, spontaneity is everything."

5. Miles, Louis Wardlaw. "The Poetry of Robert Bridges." *The Sewanee Review* 23 (1915): 129–39.

    Bridges's aristocratic temper will prevent him from being widely popular. He is a classical poet with a weakness in creative power and personal expression. *Prometheus* and *Demeter* are pedestrian classicism. *Eros and Psyche* reveals a poet of form and substance. *The Growth of Love* is a series of more or less connected personal experiences with no discernible progression. Bridges's fame will rest on *Shorter Poems*. His reticent treatment of love, philosophy, and religion lead to the erroneous charge that he has no passion or emotion in his verse. He is not a good choice for laureate because his occasional verse is broad, abstract, and platitudinous.

6. Noguchi, Yone. "Robert Bridges: A Japanese Impression of the Poet Laureate." *The Nation* 101 (1915): 465–66.

Recounts an overnight visit and afternoon stroll with Bridges.

7. Waugh, Arthur. "Some Movements in Victorian Poetry: The Example of Mr. Robert Bridges." In *Reticence in Literature*, 84–85. New York: E. P. Dutton and Co., 1915.

Bridges's work exemplifies "the aristocracy of art." "His work is at once simple and subtle, undemonstrative, and of flowing charm." In an age hostile to classical simplicity, he has sustained the classical spirit.

1916

1. Bridges, Robert. "The Chivalry of the Sea." *New York Times*, 28 August 1916, p. 16, col. 3.

Reprint of "The Chivalry of the Sea."

2. Bridges, Robert. "Ode on the Tercentenary Commemoration of Shakespeare." In *Shakespeare's England*, 2 vols., edited by Sir Walter Raleigh, 1:xxi–xxiv. Oxford: The Clarendon Press, 1916.

3. [De la Mare, Walter.] *"The Spirit of Man."* Review of *The Spirit of Man*, by Robert Bridges. *Times Literary Supplement*, 3 February 1916, 49–50.

This anthology reveals the mind of the writer; it shows "a serene solitude of the spirit, yet of a spirit not aloof from the hideous storm and terror of these days, but above it; not unmoved by it, but its master."

4. Freeman, John. "Robert Bridges." In *The Moderns: Essays in Literary Criticism*. 319–41. London: Robert Scott, 1916.

While Bridges's poetry often resembles common speech, it exhibits a continual modification of rhythm, which is the distinguishing feature of all poetry. Bridges's dramas "are full of human feeling, full of wise speech upon near and dear things; and . . . the natural free rhythm of unmistakable, spontaneous poetry." The sonnets of *The Growth of Love* show "little evidence of the 'growth of love'"; rather they show "love as the natural fulfillment of human life." Two main features of Bridges's work are his love of England and his love of Love. His poetry depicts the "essential joyousness of life," and "all his art is offered as tribute to ideal beauty."

5. "The Growth of Man's Soul through the Ages." Review of *The Spirit of Man*, by Robert Bridges. *New York Times*, 26 March 1916, sect. 7, p. 105, col. 1.

   This anthology, which reveals Bridges's exquisite artistry, and his commitment to noble ideals and the highest principles of creative endeavor, teaches us that spirituality is the basis of human life. Bridges's harsh indictment of the Germans in the introduction, however, detracts from the Poet Laureate's reputation and undermines the larger purpose of the anthology.

6. Hearn, Lafcadio. "Robert Bridges." In *Appreciations of Poetry*, edited by John Erskine. 385–402. London: William Heinemann, 1916.

   Bridges is "one of the greatest of the English minor poets of our time" and "one of the least known." He is relatively unknown because his poetry has "no philosophy, no originality, no passion." "Eros" is the touchstone of Bridges's ideas. He is a supreme poet of childhood and women. He "ranks next to Rossetti as a love poet" and is comparable with Browning in his feelings for "the deeper and nobler qualities of love."

7. Martindale, C. C. "Anthologia Laureate." Review of *The Spirit of Man*, by Robert Bridges. *The Dublin Review* 158 (1916): 259–65.

   This anthology, which should have been a tonic to the modern soul, is tainted with "that sapping subjectivism which, when all is said and done, contributes an element of poision . . . to a book which should have been all health and wholesomeness."

8. Review of *The Spirit of Man*, by Robert Bridges. *Catholic World* 103 (1916): 394–95.

   This anthology is "a symphony . . . of poetry" that strikes "a grand chord of moral and spiritual nobility."

9. Review of *The Spirit of Man*, by Robert Bridges. *The Living Age* 289 (1916): 295–300.

   Reprint of 1916.3.

10. Review of *The Spirit of Man,* by Robert Bridges. *The New Statesman* 6 (1916): 427–28.

The anthologized passages are juxtaposed with great art. Reading them in order reveals more clearly what Bridges saw to admire in each and allows the reader to interpret human destiny as Bridges believes it to be.

11. "A Sonnet to Kitchener." *New York Times,* 13 June 1916, p. 11, col. 4.

Reprints Bridges's "Sonnet to Kitchener."

1917

1. Bridges, Robert. "Christmas Eve, 1917." *Times Literary Supplement,* 27 December 1917, 641.

2. Bridges, Robert. "To the United States of America." *Times Literary Supplement,* 3 May 1917, 211.

3. "British Poet Laureate Acclaims U.S. in Verse." *New York Times,* 1 May 1917, p. 13, col. 4.

Excerpts from "Brothers in blood! They who this wrong began."

4. Colum, Padriac. "Robert Bridges and Thomas Hardy." *The New Republic* 12 (1917): 47–49.

Bridges, whose "thrilling lyricism" has widened the scope and variety of English literature, stands for half of English life: culture and court. Hardy represents the other half. Bridges traces the flow of the river, whereas Hardy examines the swirls.

5. Drinkwater, John. "Robert Bridges on Keats." Review of *The Poetical Works of John Keats,* edited by Laurence Binyon, with an introduction by Robert Bridges. *The Bookman* (London) 51 (1917): 175–76.

Bridges's remarks on Keats are those of a genius, but his imperfect understanding of Elizabethan genius is apparent when he criticizes Elizabethan influences on Keats.

6. "An Experiment in Quantity." Review of *Ibant Obscuri,* by Robert Bridges. *Saturday Review Supplement* (London) 123 (31 March 1917): iv–v.

There seems to be little reason why any more hexameter verse should be written in English; "the measure is, and remains, an exotic one." The hexameters are neither intolerable nor pleasing, only tolerable.

7. "Hexameters in English." Review of *Ibant Obscuri*, by Robert Bridges. *Times Literary Supplement*, 8 March 1917, 114.

   Bridges has written quantitative hexameters like no one else in English; he is "as fully quantitative as Horace." However, he has more hypermetric lines than Virgil, and his reading of long and short vowels is inconsistent. It remains to be seen whether the public will accept such experiments.

8. "Laureate Writes Christmas Poem." *New York Times*, 25 December 1917, p. 2, col. 2.

   Reprints "Christmas Eve, 1917."

9. "At Least He Was 'Sincere.'" *New York Times*, 26 December 1917, p. 8, col. 4.

   The "clumsy dullness" of "Christmas Eve, 1917" surpasses the worst any poet laureate ever wrote, even Alfred Austin.

10. "The Poet Laureate on Vulgarity." Review of *The Improvement of the Educational Condition of the Working Classes*, by Robert Bridges. *Times Literary Supplement*, 4 January 1917, 6.

    The vulgar tastes Bridges deplores among the lower classes are shared by the upper classes. He is correct, however, to attribute this degradation of taste to an irrational democratic fear of anything that smacks of superiority or high culture.

11. "Quantitative Hexameters in English." Review of *Ibant Obscuri*, by Robert Bridges. *The Nation* 105 (1917): 147–48.

    Bridges's metrical experiment is built on a misconception of Greek and Latin stress. Those acquainted with Virgil may find some of Bridges's experiments agreeable, but "verse-patterns that no one can make out who is not familiar with Virgil can never be 'congenial to English speech.'"

1918

1. Binyon, Laurence. "Robert Bridges and the Poetic Art." *The Bookman* (London) 54 (1918): 144–47.

   Bridges expresses the human need for poetry. His poetry is redolent of fine, delicate emotions presented in elusively simple lyrics. *Shorter Poems* avoids Victorian moralizing. All modern poets owe a debt of liberation to Bridges, who should be seen as a "fruitful innovator," not as an old-fashioned conservative.

2. Binyon, Laurence. "Robert Bridges and the Poetic Art." *The Living Age* 299 (1918): 155–60.

    Reprint of 1918.1.

3. "Books for the Forces." *The Times*, 23 May 1918, 9.

    Reports Bridges's speech at the Sheldonian Theatre urging the donation of books to hospitals for wounded soldiers.

4. Bridges, Robert. "To Australia." *The Times*, 14 October 1918, 9.

5. Bridges, Robert. "England to India." *The Times*, 20 December 1918, 3.

6. Bridges, Robert. "Harvest Home." *The Times*, 28 November 1918, 7.

7. "To President Wilson." *New York Times*, 12 September 1918, p. 10, col. 8.

    Reprints "To President Wilson" from *The Times* (London).

8. Williams, Harold. "Poets of the Transition." In *Modern English Writers*, 29–31. London: Sidgwick and Jackson, 1918.

    In content, thought, and imaginative power, Bridges's work does not claim a distinctive place. "He has never felt with sufficient intensity to be a great poet." His later work suffers from metrical experimentation and "laboured accentuation." Bridges's fame will rest on *The Growth of Love* and the five books of *Shorter Poems*.

1919

1. Bridges, Robert. Poem. In *Poems of the Great War*, edited by J. W. Cunliffe, 31. New York: Macmillan, 1919.

    The anthology contains "Lord Kitchener."

2. Bridges, Robert. Poems. In *The Oxford Book of English Verse, 1250–1918,* edited by Sir Arthur Quiller-Couch, 1014–24. Oxford: The Clarendon Press, 1919.

    Includes "My Delight and Thy Delight," "Nightingales," and "Pater Filio."

3. "Commons Jests on Silent Laureate." *New York Times,* 3 August 1919, sect. 2, p. 1, col. 7.

    Noting that Bridges had not produced any peace ode celebrating the end of the war, Horatio Bottomley, member of Parliament, suggested a cask of wine might inspire the poet laureate. When asked to comment on the incident, Bridges replied, "I don't care a damn."

4. "Criticism Seemingly Justified." *New York Times,* 1 August 1919, p. 10, col. 5.

    The criticism of Bridges's lack of official verse seems justified. There is no excuse for him not to be writing more appropriate verse; it is his duty.

5. "Gerard Hopkins." Review of *Poems of Gerard Manley Hopkins,* by Robert Bridges. *Times Literary Supplement,* 9 January 1919, 19.

    Bridges's notes to the poems are helpful; he is to be congratulated for giving Hopkins to the world.

6. "It's Easy to Shine as Laureates." *New York Times,* 1 August 1919, sect. 3, p. 1, col. 7.

    Bridges should not hesitate to write for fear of sounding inadequate. He is certainly a better poet than most of his predecessors, who were generally unexceptional.

7. "The Laureate's 'Damn.'" *The Literary Digest* 62 (1919): 23.

    Excerpts reactions in several New York papers to Bridges's "I don't care a damn" reply to reports of Parliament's pique at his poetic silence.

8. Newbolt, Henry. "Poetry and Rhythm." In *A New Study of Poetry,* 37–51 and passim. New York: E. P. Dutton and Co., 1919.

    Bridges's "Recollections in Solitude" exemplifies the elevating, transcendent power of poetry. It refines thought by intensifying emotion and fusing thought with sense. Bridges is the first poet to employ rhythm properly in stress prosody. He is correct in asserting the need for science and literature in education as a means of showing the relationship between disparate disciplines.

9. "Poet Laureate." *House of Commons Debates.* Vol. 118 of *The Parliamentary Debates: Official Report,* 5th series, 2104. London: His Majesty's Stationery Office.

    Horatio Bottomley, member of Parliament, suggests Bridges be paid in Canary wine, "on the off-chance of his [Bridges] getting inspiration."

10. "Poet Laureate." *House of Commons Debates.* Vol. 119 of *The Parliamentary Debates: Official Report,* 5th series, 355–56. London: His Majesty's Stationery Office.

    Several members of the House of Commons wonder if the laureateship is "a silent sinecure."

11. Williams, Harold. "Poets of the Transition." In *Modern English Writers,* 29–31. London: Sidgwick and Jackson; New York:

A. A. Knopf, 1919.
Reprint of 1918.8.

1920

1. "Ask Who Inspired Unknown's Burial." *New York Times,* 10 December 1920, p. 13, col. 3.

    Horatio Bottomley, member of Parliament, asked Lloyd George to appoint a new poet laureate. George declined.

2. Bickley, Frances. "October." Review of *October and Other Poems,* by Robert Bridges. *The Bookman* (London) 58 (1920): 177–78.

    The poems in this volume are disappointment to Bridges's admirers and the average readers who long for the grace and smoothness of *Shorter Poems.* The war poems are inadequate; he's not the equal of Laurence Binyon. Bridges is too prone to "mechanical optimism."

3. Braithwaite, William S. "Poet Crowned with Laurel." *The Boston Transcript,* 28 August 1920, 4.

4. Bridges, Robert. Poems. In *Modern British Poetry,* edited by Louis Untermeyer, 5–7. New York: Harcourt, Brace and Co., 1920.

    This anthology includes "Winter Nightfall" and "Nightingales."

5. Gorman, Herbert. "Poets Who Recall Glowing Verse of the Nineties." Review of *October and Other Poems,* by Robert Bridges. *New York Times,* 29 August 1920, sect. 3, p. 13, col. 1.

    These poems by the greatest authority on meter and prosody in England form a coherent whole and show that Bridges is temperamentally suited to the laureateship. Although the verse "lacks fire" and Bridges himself seems more interested in form than substance, these poems are consistently elevated and genuinely inspired. Unfortunately, this volume of verse "does not bring anything particularly new to bear on Mr. Bridges's poetry."

6. "His Sorrow Should Be Gladness." *New York Times,* 11 December 1920, p. 12, col. 5.

    "Of Dr. Bridges, the present laureate, it cannot be said, indeed, that anything he writes is likely either to give offense or to excite ridicule." Poets should write only when they feel moved. If Bridges feels unmoved, then it is just as well—doggerel verse is thus avoided.

7. Monro, Harold. "A Glance Backward." In *Some Contemporary Poets,* 34–35. London: Leonard Parsons, 1920.

Bridges is among the six most important living poets of the "older generation" and should be praised for the fact that he accepted the laureateship on his own terms and refused to write occasional and ceremonial verse. "He has restored much dignity to the office, besides adding a significance which it had not previously possessed."

8. M[urray], J[ohn] M[iddleton]. "The Dignity of Poetry." Review of *October and Other Poems,* by Robert Bridges. *The Athenaeum,* 9 April 1920, 472–74.

Bridges's mastery of language and rhythm make him the most accomplished living English metrist, "a true artist." Although there is nothing here which compares with his earlier sonnets and lyrics, "nothing he writes, be the occasion never so official or the inspiration tenuous, is marred by a touch of the shoddy; the dignity of poetry is safe in his hands."

9. Perry, Bliss. "Rhythm and Meter." In *A Study of Poetry,* 123, 170–71. New York: Houghton Mifflin Co., 1920.

Cites Bridges as an example of a poet risking the total effect of a poetic passage upon a mere catalog of euphonious proper names. Also quotes some of Bridges's quantitative hexameters to illustrate "non-English rhythm."

10. "Poet Laureate." *House of Commons Debates.* Vol. 135 of *The Parliamentary Debates: Official Report,* 5th series, 2411–12. London: His Majesty's Stationery Office.

Horatio Bottomley asked the Prime Minister to remove Bridges from the laureateship and appoint a new poet laureate due to Bridges's apparent poetic silence on the events of the Great War.

11. "The Poet Laureate's Apologia." *The Times,* 27 October 1920, 13.

Bridges has had a rather sudden change of heart regarding his attitude toward Germany.

12. Rothenstein, William. "Robert Bridges." In *Twenty-Four Portraits,* n.p. New York: Harcourt, Brace and Co., 1920.

Bridges is "a distinguished master of his chosen style and a bold and fruitful innovator." His *Shorter Poems* "reached out to a novel and unsuspected range of music in English verse" and "opened the ears of a new generation." He is a master of English landscape poetry.

13. Squire, John C. "Robert Bridges's Lyrical Poems." *The London Mercury* 1 (1920): 708–17.

Content is never subordinated to form in Bridges's lyrics; "words and music are always inseparable." His taste is "flawless"; "he knows the ways of lovers' hearts," and he is always "self-controlled and never shouts." He is partly ignored because his doctrines are common, not foreign. "A reader who went to him for knowledge of how to live would certainly not be led on the rocks."

14. Untermeyer, Louis. "Robert Bridges." In *Modern British Poetry*, 5. New York: Harcourt, Brace and Co., 1920.

Bridges's plays and poems "are classical in tone as well as treatment." Rhythm and subtle versification give his poetry "a firm delicacy and beauty of pattern."

1921

1. Bridges, Robert. Poems. In *The Daniel Press: Memorials of C. H. O. Daniel,* edited by Falconer Madan, 93–94. Oxford: The Daniel Press, 1921.

Excerpts from "Verses Written for Mrs. Daniel."

2. Bridges, Robert. Poems. In *Modern British Poetry,* edited by Louis Untermeyer, 5–7. New York: Harcourt, Brace and Co., 1921.

Reprint of 1920.4.

3. Bridges, Robert. Poem. In the Program for the Opening of the Theatre of the Royal Academy of Dramatic Art, 27 May 1921.

Contains "England will keep her dearest jewel bright."

4. Broadus, Edmund Kemper. "Robert Bridges." In *The Laureateship: A Study of the Office of Poet Laureate in England with Some Account of the Poets,* 207–18. Oxford: The Clarendon Press, 1921.

Bridges was the first poet laureate to have to write verses about the horrors of modern war. His "exotic measures" account for his general lack of popularity. He is not a slave to orthodox poetic utterances, especially those expected by the public at large. He is a poet laureate like no other, living in a time like no other.

5. Chaundy, Leslie, and Elizabeth Cox. *Bibliographies of Modern Authors, No. 1: Robert Bridges*. London: Chaundy and Co., 1921.

   A bibliography of Bridges's verse and prose publications from 1873 to 1921. "Papers [and poems] written for periodicals and not reprinted are not included." Bridges assisted in the compilation and revision of this bibliography.

6. Davis, H. L. "Robert Bridges Once More." Review of *October and Other Poems*, by Robert Bridges. *Poetry* 17 (1921): 344–45.

   Bridges's new poems are in the same manner as his earliest efforts; they are "too sweet and not willful enough."

7. Madan, Falconer. *Memorials of C. H. O. Daniel with a Bibliography of the Press, 1845–1919*. Oxford: Daniel Press, 1921.

   A full description of the Bridges volumes published by the Daniel Press.

8. Manly, John Matthews, and Edith Rickert. "Robert Bridges." In *Contemporary British Literature: Bibliographies and Study Outlines*, 27–29. New York: Harcourt, Brace and Co., 1921.

   This book contains a brief biographical sketch of Bridges, a bibliography of his major publications, and a selected bibliography of books and articles about him.

9. Mason, Lawrence. "For Students of Milton." Review of *Milton's Prosody*, by Robert Bridges. *The Literary Review*, 25 June 1921, p. 2, col. 2.

   The margin summaries, paragraph headings, and appendices are happy additions to this book, which is "indispensible to all students and lovers of Milton's poetry."

10. Nichols, Beverley. "The Poets of Oxford." *The Outlook* 127 (1921): 601.

    Although Bridges is an unpopular poet who has written many poems that will never be read, he has written some lyrics that "will live as long as the English language is spoken."

11. Olivero, Federico. "Robert Bridges." *Nuova Antologia* 298 (1921): 149–54.

12. Patmore, Coventry. "Robert Bridges." In *Courage in Politics and Other Essays, 1885–1896*, 143–50. London: Oxford University Press, 1921.

    Combined reprint of 1885.1 and 1885.2.

13. "Poet and Prosodist." Review of *Milton's Prosody*, by Robert Bridges. *Times Literary Supplement*, 14 April 1921, 240.

Bridges's genius shows the lack of understanding many modern poets have regarding prosody. Bridges composes in accentual, syllabic, and quantitative verses. His rules for stressed verse are imperfect, and an acceptance of his analysis "would involve [English] poetry in an inappropriate constraint."

14. "Poet Laureate on Forgiveness." *The Times*, 14 July 1921, 12.
    Bridges's speech at the dedication of the war memorial at Newbury urged forgiveness for former enemies.

15. Sapir, Edward. "Gerard Hopkins." Review of *Poems of Gerard Manley Hopkins*, edited by Robert Bridges. *Poetry* 18 (1921): 330–36.
    Questions Bridges's commentary on Hopkins's poetry.

16. Untermeyer, Louis. "Robert Bridges." In *Modern British Poetry*, 5. New York: Harcourt, Brace and Co., 1921.
    Reprint of 1920.14.

1922

1. Bridges, Robert. Poem. In *The British Legion Album*, compiled by E. Lonsdale Deighton, n.p. London: Cassell & Co., 1922.
   Contains a holographic copy of "Of the First B.E.F."

2. Bridges, Robert. Poem. In *Modern American and British Poetry*, edited by Louis Untermeyer, 233–34. New York: Harcourt, Brace and Co., 1922.
   This anthology contains a brief biographical headnote and the poem "Winter Nightfall."

3. Bridges, Robert. Poems. In *Modern British Poetry*, edited by Louis Untermeyer, 5–7. New York: Harcourt, Brace and Co., 1922.
   Reprint of 1920.4.

4. B[right], J[ames] W[ilson]. Review of *Milton's Prosody*, by Robert Bridges. *Modern Language Notes* 31 (1922): 316–20.
   "Mr. Bridges has again indorsed errors that pervert fundamental principles of English versification." His doctrines of rhythm and inversion are untenable.

5. Evans, E. Powys. "Modern Portraits—One: Robert Bridges." *The London Mercury* 5 (1922): 567.
   A portrait of Bridges.

6. Hearn, Lafcadio. "Robert Bridges." In *Pre-Raphaelite and Other Poets*, edited by John Erskine, 407–28. New York:

Dodd, Mead and Co., 1922.
Reprint of 1916.6.

7. Hind, C. Lewis. "Robert Bridges." In *More Authors and I,* 34–39. London: John Lane, 1922.

Although Bridges as poet laureate is a disappointment to the man in the street, he is the right kind of poet for the laureateship; he has restored dignity and learning to the office. Bridges "understands what great poetry is, even if he cannot often make it."

8. Hubbell, Jay B., and John O. Beaty. "The Sonnet." In *An Introduction to Poetry,* 282–84. New York: Macmillan, 1922.

An introductory paragraph discusses the duties of the poet laureate, the characteristics of his poetry, and then quotes "Who builds a ship" as an example of the sonnet form.

9. Jameson, R. D. "English Metrists." Review of *Milton's Prosody,* by Robert Bridges. *The New Republic* 31 (1922): 224.

Bridges's book is "a personal contribution whose statement of truth is lyrical rather than objective."

10. Omond, T. S. Review of *Milton's Prosody,* by Robert Bridges. *The Modern Language Review* 17 (1922): 90–95.

"English prosody historically considered, indeed, is evidently not a thing to which Mr. Bridges has devoted much study." Nevertheless, in this book he puts his view more consistently and intelligibly than before.

1923

1. Bridges, Robert. Poem. In *Modern American and British Poetry,* edited by Louis Untermeyer, 233–34. New York: Harcourt, Brace and Co., 1923.
Reprint of 1922.2.

2. Bridges, Robert. Poems. In *English Poetry of the Nineteenth Century,* edited by George R. Elliott and Norman Foerster, 648. New York: Macmillan, 1923.

This anthology includes "So sweet love seemed" and "Melancholia."

3. "British Poet Laureate, at 80, Coming to Michigan on Mission of Scholarship." *New York Times,* 14 September 1923, p. 21, col. 4.

Bridges will spend one semester in residence at the University of Michigan.

4. Fox, Arthur W. "Robert Bridges: Poet Laureate." *The Manchester Quarterly* 167 (1923): 135–55.

Bridges is a "true poet" whose genius is lyrical. His dramas are generally not dramatic. *Eros and Psyche* shows a "sustained beauty" and exceptional skill in metrical invention. *The Growth of Love* has finely wrought pieces but lacks in general excellence and shows little of the growth of love. He is a true nature lover and has an equally deep appreciation of music. His careful attention to the construction of his poems curtails spontaneity. "It is as a lyric poet that he will survive and deserves to survive."

5. Squire, John C. "Mr. Robert Bridges's Poetry: Lyrical Poems." In *Essays on Poetry*, 122–39. London: Hodder and Stoughton, 1923.

Reprint of 1920.13.

6. T., A. H. R. "Mr. Roger Fry's Pictures." *The Burlington Magazine* 42 (1923): 254–59.

This review of Fry's pictures praises his portrait of Bridges, which is reproduced in the review.

1924

1. "An Anthology for Schools." Review of *The Chilswell Book of English Poetry*, by Robert Bridges. *Times Literary Supplement*, 20 March 1924, 172.

With only minor exceptions, this book "expresses its author's perfect taste and scholarly nicety as well in its form as in its substance."

2. Armstrong, Spencer. "Dr. Bridges on English." Letter. In *New York Times*, 19 April 1924, p. 12, col. 6.

The Society for Pure English is to be commended for its efforts, but reform and preservation of our language begin with the teaching of English in the schools.

3. Bridges, Robert. Poem. In *Green-Kirtled Spring*, edited by N. Graham Smith, n.p. London: Elkins Mathews, 1924.

Contains "Cheddar Pinks."

4. Bridges, Robert. Poems. In *English Poetry of the Nineteenth Century*, edited by George R. Elliott and Norman Foerster, 648. New York: Macmillan, 1924.

Reprint of 1923.2.

5. Bridges, Robert. Poems. In *The Golden Treasury of Modern*

Lyrics, edited by Laurence Binyon, 193, 202, and passim. London: Macmillan, 1924.

This anthology includes "Nightingales," "When I see childhood," "London Snow," "A Passer-By," "On a Dead Child," and "Noel."

6. Bridges, Robert. Poems. In *Poems Unpublished or Difficult to Obtain Easily,* edited by Walter Muir Whitehill.

7. "England's Laureate Here." *The Literary Digest* 82 (1924): 33.

Excerpts from a newspaper article relating the circumstances of Bridges's visit to the United States.

8. "Gives Dinner to Robert Bridges." *New York Times,* 3 April 1924, p. 25, col. 4.

Hamilton Fish Armstrong gave a dinner for Bridges.

9. Kelshall, T. M. *Robert Bridges, Poet Laureate.* London: Robert Scott, 1924.

Bridges is a "master of rhythm" whose "artistically faultless" poetry is properly called "art not mere artifice." He has a "pure lyric gift" but "there is little of the romantic in the lyrics and not overmuch passion." Bridges is a poet of Beauty, Joy, and Love who ranks with Milton as a scholar-poet. "Robert Bridges is the greatest of living poets who write in English."

10. "King George Raises Five to Peerage." *New York Times,* 3 June 1924, p. 1, col. 2

Bridges was awarded the Order of Merit.

11. "A Laureate Errant: Robert Bridges's Visit to America." *Current Opinion* 76 (1924): 651.

Bridges will be at the University of Michigan on the Fellowship in Creative Art. His poetry combines the practical and the ideal. His attitude is that of a man who has thought and felt and knows that love and religion are the greatest values in human life.

12. "The Laureate on English." *New York Times,* 13 April 1924, sect. 2, p. 6, col. 2.

Bridges's poetry illustrates "a Greek reserve and strength." It is especially laudable for its "delicate exactness and beauty." The efficacy or need for The Society for Pure English is doubtful.

13. "Michigan Honors Bridges." *New York Times,* 11 June 1924, p. 21, col. 1.

Bridges was awarded an honorary Doctor of Law degree.

14. "Mr. Bridges's Thanks." *The Times,* 11 Nov. 1924, 15.

    Bridges' letter of thanks to the donors of the clavichord that was given to him on his birthday.

15. "The Poet-Laureate." *The Canadian Magazine* 63 (1924): 57–58.

    Bridges gave a written statement to reporters upon his arrival in New York. The poet laureate comes to America at the invitation of M. Leroy Burton, President of the University of Michigan, and he plans a future collaboration of British and American philologists. Reprints "I will not let thee go."

16. "Poet Laureate Shy on His Arrival Here." *New York Times,* 2 April 1924, p. 12, col. 2.

    Bridges evaded reporters' questions when he landed in New York. He handed them a statement about his arrival, which he had written in third person.

17. Pope, Virginia. "Poet Laureate Argues Here for Pure English." *New York Times,* 13 April 1924, sect. 9, p. 8, col. 1.

    One purpose of Bridges's American visit is to consolidate an American branch of The Society for Pure English. Bridges discussed the society, its aims, and its origins. He read to the interviewer some poems that he called "the best work of my life." These poems were "Cheddar Pinks," "Emily Bronte," and Com se Quando."

18. Quinn, John. *Complete Catalogue of the Library of John Quinn,* 2 vols., 1:85–90. New York: The Anderson Gallery, 1924.

    Lists sixty-nine Bridges items, including many rare and first editions.

19. Ransom, John Crowe. "The Poet Laureate." *The Literary Review* 4 (1924): 625–26.

    Bridges is a classicist who is out of time, has no relation to his age, and does not fit easily into any modern notions of poetry. Yet, his Aristotelian mind sets him free from the irregularities of modern poetry and makes him "a great poetic force."

20. Sherman, Stuart P. "Robert Bridges." In *Men of Letters of the British Isles,* edited by Theodore Spicer-Simson, 27–28. New York: William Edwin Rudge, 1924.

    Bridges is "a conservative gentleman of classical taste and fluent and accomplished versification" whose imagination "has never left the classical school." *Demeter,* however, "smothers the terror of Hades in flowers," and *Eros and*

Psyche shuns its sensuous possibilities and "sinks . . . into dreamy chanting of pagan lays." "The pallid chastity of his classicism palls our hearts."

21. "There the Resemblance Ends." *The Outlook* 136 (1924): 584–85.

    Bridges's work is "restrained, precise, and delicate," and he should be congratulated for refraining from celebrations of royal events.

22. Trevelyan, R. C. "Prosody and the Poet Laureate." *The New Statesman* 24 (1924): 296–98.

    Bridges's new verse is not really revolutionary but merely an extension of Miltonic and Keatsian experiments in blank verse. His emphasis on syllables, not stress, creates some difficulty in comprehending his ideas.

23. Watson, Maureen. "Tennyson's Successor." Letter. *New York Times,* 25 February 1924, p. 14, col. 7.

    An unidentified poet, possibly Bridges, was Prime Minister Asquith's first choice to succeed Tennyson as poet laureate in 1892.

24. Welby, T. Earl. "The Later Nineteenth Century." In *A Popular History of English Poetry,* 265–66. London: A. M. Philpot, 1924.

    Bridges will be remembered for his rich, subtle lyrics.

1925

1. Davison, Edward. "Robert Bridges, Poet Laureate of England." *The English Journal* 14 (1925): 749–60.

    Bridges is a poet's poet of "phenomenal technical mastery," "a contemporary genius [who] employs convention as well as tradition." He addresses himself to the interests of the average man, and his themes are the quieter, simpler joys of life. A strong sense of joy separates Bridges from most contemporaries. His fame will rest on his mastery of language and meter, and his ability as a landscape poet.

2. Flasdieck, Hermann M. Review of *The Society for Pure English: Tract No. 21,* by Robert Bridges. *Anglia Beiblatt* 36 (1925): 266–67.

    The avowed aims of the society have not been achieved; the results have been disappointing.

3. K[ennedy], A[rthur] G. Review of *The Society for Pure English, NS Tract No. 1,* by Robert Bridges. *American Speech* 1 (1925): 46.

Praises Bridges's stated aims for the Society for Pure English.

4. "The Laureate's *New Verse*." Review of *New Verse*, by Robert Bridges. *Times Literary Supplement*, 17 December 1925, 879.

This volume is one of Bridges's most distinguished accomplishments. The twelve-syllable line subtly adapts measure to meaning. Although this experiment shows what can rather than what should be done in English verse, Bridges's work is always valuable in that it teaches us what is meant by prosody, meter, and rhythm.

5. Review of *The Society for Pure English: Tract No. 21*, by Robert Bridges. *Times Literary Supplement*, 16 July 1925, 482.

Summarizes the main points of the tract.

6. Shanks, Edward. "Two Innovators." Review of *New Verse*, by Robert Bridges. *The Saturday Review* 140 (1925): 740–41.

Bridges and Hardy are the most innovative poets of the day, but the difficult nature of quantitative verse and the inertia of traditional stress verse will prevent the general adoption of Bridges's metrics.

7. Williams, Harold. "Poets of the Transition." In *Modern English Writers*, 29–31. London: Sidgwick and Jackson, 1925.

Reprint of 1918.8.

1926

1. Burke, Kenneth. "Idiom and Uniformity." Review of *The Society for Pure English: Tract No. 21*, by Robert Bridges. *The Dial* 80 (1926): 57–60.

The aim of the Society for Pure English seems to be against the modern current and seems to overlook the fact that the greatness of the English language derives from change and alteration.

2. Carnoy, A. Review of *The Society for Pure English: Tract No. 21*, by Robert Bridges. *Leuvensche Bijdragen* 18 (1926): 17.

Unable to translate.

3. De M., J. E. G. "The Poet Laureate's New Volume." Review of *New Verse*, by Robert Bridges. *The Contemporary Review* 129 (1926): 253–55.

This is "a fascinating volume" full of poetic experiments that enhance Bridges's reputation as a scholarly poet, but it is not recommended for younger poets.

4. Herring, Robert. "Poetry." Review of *New Verse*, by Robert

Bridges. *The London Mercury* 13 (1926): 434–35.

These poems are "earnest, gay and gracious," and full of "compact, concrete thought."

5. LeGallienne, Richard. "New Poems by Mr. Bridges and Two Younger Poets." Review of *New Verse*, by Robert Bridges. *New York Times*, 5 September 1926, sect. 3, p. 5, col. 1.

This volume contains several poems of strength and beauty that embody the "indescribable eerie nothingness" that made Bridges's early lyrics great.

6. McKerrow, R. B. Review of *The Society for Pure English: Tract No. 20,* by Robert Bridges. *Review of English Studies* 2 (1926): 115–18.

The goals of the Society for Pure English are laudable; however, the matters of pronunciation and spelling are open to question because they reflect the speech habits and pronunciation of the founders of the Society for Pure English.

1927

1. Blunden, Edmund. "The Language Test." Review of *Collected Essays, Papers, etc. of Robert Bridges,* vol. 1. *The Nation and Athenaeum* 42 (1927): 368.

This pamphlet reveals Bridges's abiding interest in printing and orthography.

2. Bridges, Robert. Poems. In *English Poetry of the Nineteenth Century,* edited by George R. Elliott and Norman Foerster, 648. New York: Macmillan, 1927.

Reprint of 1923.2.

3. Dackweiler, Charles. "Robert Bridges, Poèt Laurèat." *Humanitas* 2 (1927): 129–36.

4. "Dr. Bridges's Essays." Review of *Collected Essays, Papers, etc. of Robert Bridges,* vol. 1. *Times Literary Supplement,* 8 December 1927, 929.

Bridges's effort to introduce simplified spelling and new orthographical symbols is "not very alarming." As English spreads worldwide, a simplified spelling may more readily lead to corruption of the language rather than prevent it. Bridges's criticism is questionable.

5. "Handwriting." Review of *The Society for Pure English: Tract No. 28,* by Robert Bridges. *Times Literary Supplement,* 27 October 1927, 754.

Two classes of handwriting: conscious and deliberative, and/or hurried and careless.

6. Harriss, R. P. Review of *New Verse,* by Robert Bridges. *The South Atlantic Quarterly* 26 (1927): 216–17.

These "are the poems of a tired old man whose favorite word is still damn. . . . Happily, he need not be judged by his last days."

7. "How to Speak English by Six British Experts." *New York Times,* 2 January 1927, sect. 8, p. 5, col. 1.

A portrait of Bridges over an article on the Society for Pure English's recommended pronunciations of doubtful words.

8. "Poet Laureate is 83." *New York Times,* 25 October 1927, p. 3, col. 2.

Bridges, a poet noted for his disregard of public opinion and lack of official poetic production, is eighty-three today.

9. Review of *Collected Essays, Papers, etc. of Robert Bridges,* vol. 1. *Notes and Queries* 153 (1927): 342.

"On the whole, it looks as if the new system of printing and spelling would be as difficult to use correctly as the present one."

1928

1. Barfield, Owen. "Poetry, Verse and Prose." Review of *Collected Essays, Papers, etc. of Robert Bridges,* vols. 2 and 3. *The New Statesman* 31 (1928): 793–94.

Bridges approaches literature from the intellectual side; that is, he views literature as embodying meaning. Meaning is the result of concrete thinking and concrete knowledge, both of which are concerned with wisdom. As a result, passion or feeling in Bridges's poetry is transmuted into wisdom, thus giving his poetry a certain emotional aloofness.

2. Bridges, Robert. Poem. In *Modern American and British Poetry,* rev. and enl., edited by Louis Untermeyer, 294–95. New York: Macmillan, 1928.
Reprint of 1922.2.

3. Bridges, Robert. Poems. In *Poetry of Our Times,* edited Sharon Brown, 354–55. New York: Scott, Foresman and Co., 1928.
This anthology includes "A Passer-By" and "Winter Nightfall."

4. Brown, Sharon, "Robert Bridges." In *Poetry of Our Times*, 353. New York: Scott, Foresman and Co., 1928.

   The classical restraint of Bridges's poetry produces "admirable grace and purity but also a chaste austerity which erects a barrier, however impalpable, between poet and reader."

5. Davison, Edward. "In Praise of the Poet Laureate." *The Fortnightly Review* 130 (1928): 66–79.

   Bridges is relatively unknown because critics are unable to criticize "pure poetry," still others are suspicious of any work by a laureate, and his own interest in prosody has made him seem more a technician than a true poet. He is unusual in that he does not write out of some spiritual dissatisfaction. The clarity, simplicity, and economy of style are the culminating achievements of Bridges's verse.

6. Davison, Edward Lewis. "The Poet Laureate." In *Some Modern Poets and Other Critical Essays*, 79–110. New York: Harper and Brothers, 1928.

   Bridges's poetry shows "fewer lapses from virtual perfection than any living poet." Critics are responsible for Bridges's lack of reputation. There are three reasons for the critical silence surrounding his work: Bridges's poetry is so perfect and pure there is little critics can say; people are suspicious of an "official poet"; and Bridges's interest in experimental verse deters people from reading him. The "peculiar originality" of Bridges's work is "its dominating mood of eager delight." No poet laureate was more "a master of his art than Robert Bridges."

7. "Dr. Bridges on Free Verse." Review of *Collected Essays, Papers, etc. of Robert Bridges*, vol. 2. *The Nation and Athenaeum* 43 (1928): 830.

   Perhaps the reprinting of Bridges's essay on free verse will drive out the spirits of free verse that haunt so much of modern poetry.

8. Dr. Bridges's Essays." Review of *Collected Essays, Papers, etc. of Robert Bridges*, vol. 2. *Times Literary Supplement*, 13 September 1928, 645.

   Although the conclusions of these two essays seem pedestrian, Bridges's method of reaching them is "convincing and exhilarating." This is criticism marked by care and leisure. It is the highest and best type of criticism, the kind rarely written today.

9. Graves, Robert, and Laura Riding. "Unpopular with the Plain Reader." In *A Survey of Modernist Poetry*, 92–94. New York: Doubleday, Doran and Co., 1928.

Bridges's criticism of Hopkins is an example of criticism that rejects artistic innovations simply because they are "new" or "non-traditional."

10. Grierson, Herbert John Clifford. "The Nineties." In *Lyrical Poetry from Blake to Hardy*, 129–32. London: The Hogarth Press, 1928.

Bridges is "a poet not with a message but with a manner," and he is a welcome relief from the spasmodic poets of his day. His nature poetry is unique in that "he feels what he portrays or suggests." Bridges "sings only for those who have ears to hear."

11. Grierson, Herbert John Clifford. "The Nineties." In *Lyrical Poetry from Blake to Hardy*, 129–32. London: L. and V. Woolf, 1928.

Reprint of 1928.10.

12. Jackson, Holbrook. "Robert Bridges, George Moore, Bernard Shaw, and Printing." *The Fleuron* 4 (1928): 43–53.

Bridges's early interest in printing influenced the Daniel Press in the press's adaptation of signatures and the simplicity of design that distinguishes the press's publications. Bridges's books are always typographically sound. *The Poems of Digby Mackworth Dolben* is the best example of Bridges's interest in typography.

13. Manly, John Matthews, and Edith Rickert. "Robert Bridges." In *Contemporary British Literature: Bibliographies and Study Outlines*, 101–2. New York: Harcourt, Brace and Co., 1928.

Reprint of 1921.8 in which biographical and bibliographical material is updated.

14. Morley, Christopher. "The Bowling Green." *The Saturday Review of Literature* 4 (31 March 1928): 719.

The Society for Pure English should examine the causes for the differences between English and American handwriting. Excerpt from Bridges's "English Handwriting."

15. Price, H[arold] T. Review of *Collected Essays, Papers, etc. of Robert Bridges*, vol. 1. *Anglia Beiblatt* 39 (1928): 263–65.

Bridges's attempt to prove the Elizabethan audience negatively influenced Shakespeare is unsupported and only provokes curiosity rather than satisfying it. However, he does a great service in drawing attention to Shakespeare's inconsistent representation of character.

16. Raleigh, Sir Walter. *Letters of Sir Walter Raleigh,* 2 vols., edited by Lady Raleigh, 2:390–91. London: Methuen and Co., 1928.

    In a letter to Lady Elcho, Raleigh mentions a brief visit by a "delightfully grumpy" Robert Bridges.

17. Review of *Society for Pure English: Tract No. 30,* edited by Robert Bridges. *Englische Studien* 63 (1928–29): 413–14.

    Summarizes Bridges's essay on the pronunciation of "clothes."

18. Squire, John C. "An Attack on the Laureate." *The London Mercury* 19 (1928): 3–7.

    Defends Bridges against attacks in the newspaper. "It is probable that since English literature began no man has been so productive, or so admirably productive, as the present Poet Laureate, and it will be sheer good luck if so good a poet as Mr. Bridges ever again occupies the Laureateship."

19. "Walter Raleigh's Letters." Review of *A Selection from the Letters of Sir Walter Raleigh, 1880–1920,* edited by Lady Raleigh, with an introduction by Robert Bridges. *Times Literary Supplement,* 22 November 1928, 890.

    Bridges's introduction is "two pages of sheer gold."

20. Ward, Alfred Charles. "Poetry." In *Twentieth-Century Literature, 1901–1925,* 104–5. London: Methuen and Co., 1928.

    Bridges is chronologically a Victorian, but in form and spirit he is a man of the future. His work exhibits a "strict sense of form" and a "desire for purity of outline." "Although his poetic dramas are undramatic and involved to the point of obscurity, his lyrics are as clear as crystal—and often as cold." Feeling is "contained . . . rather than expressed" in his verse.

1929

1. "Bridges Issues a Poem on His 85th Birthday." *New York Times,* 24 October 1929, p. 20, col. 3.

    The Testament of Beauty is "a monumental poem" that is "not far short of the great work of Lucretius."

2. Bridges, Robert. Poem. In *The Legion Book,* 40–41. London:

Privately printed, 1929.
Contains "The Widow."

3. Bridges, Robert. Poems. In *Chief Modern Poets of England and America,* edited by Gerald DeWitt Sanders and John Herbert Nelson, 37–60. New York: Macmillan, 1929.

This anthology contains twenty-seven poems by Bridges, including "I will not let thee go," "A Passer-By," "London Snow," and "Nightingales." A brief biographical and bibliographical introduction is also included.

4. Bridges, Robert. Poems. In *Twentieth Century Poetry,* edited by Harold Monro, 22 and passim. London: Chatto and Windus, 1929.

This anthology includes "The Linnet," "My delight and thy delight," "The Garden House in September," and "Eros."

5. C[lerke], A. M. Review of *The Testament of Beauty,* by Robert Bridges. *The Oxford Magazine* 48 (1929–30): 446–47.

The Testament of Beauty is long, obscure, abstract, and didactic. The meter is little more than that of imaginative prose. It lacks the intensity of either *The Prelude* or *De Rerum Natura.*

6. Chapman, R. W. "Dr. Johnson, Dr. Bridges and the B.B.C." *Times Literary Supplement,* 15 August 1929, 637.

Contrary to Bridges's opinion, Dr. Johnson did not intentionally distort the pronunciation and source quotations of his dictionary. Any fault should be ascribed to "carelessness rather than craft." Neither do the errors stem from a preference for Latinisms.

7. Church, Richard. "The Laureate Epic." Review of *The Testament of Beauty,* by Robert Bridges. *The Bookman* (London) 77 (1929): 191–92.

The Testament of Beauty combines classical and romantic attitudes in depicting the individual struggle for self-realization. The verse is "a technical triumph" that can carry anything, even ideas deemed unpoetic; the poem's rhythms are paragraphic. Bridges's technique is large imagination supported by a vigorous intellect.

8. "Dr. Bridges on Keats." Review of *Collected Essays, Papers, etc. of Robert Bridges,* vol. 4. *Times Literary Supplement,* 29 August 1929, 665.

Bridges's essay on Keats is "a classic of criticism" and "a model of what a critical essay on the poetry of a great poet should be." The essay combines critical insight, a subtle power of distinction, and considered poetic judgment.

9. Grierson, Herbert John Clifford. "The Nineties." In *Lyrical Poetry of the Nineteenth Century,* 129–32. New York: Harcourt, Brace and Co., 1929.
   Reprint of 1928.10.

10. Groom, Bernard. "Some Modern Poets." In *A Literary History of England,* 365. London: Longmans, Green, 1929.
   Bridges's "unfailing refinement and devotion to the highest ideals of art" place him in the highest rank among all living scholar-bards. The "infinite metrical variety and flawless taste" which characterize his work "are apt to elude the less literate reader."

11. H., H. H. Review of *Collected Essays, Papers, etc. of Robert Bridges. The Quarterly Journal of Speech* 15 (1929): 125–26.
   Typographic and phonetic innovations are pleasant, but Bridges appears to have fulfilled only half of his stated aims.

12. Henderson, W. B. Drayton. "The Soul Returneth to the Body's Loving." Review of *The Testament of Beauty,* by Robert Bridges. *The Yale Review* 19 (1929–30): 601–3.
   The Testament of Beauty is a "meta-epic" that approaches God through "the worship of Beauty in noblest Epicureanism." It is written in "Bible English" with the prosody of *Beowulf* and *Piers Plowman.*

13. Hillebrand, Harold N. Review of *Collected Essays, Papers, etc. of Robert Bridges,* vol. 1. *Modern Language Notes* 44 (1929): 396–97.
   "The essay is interesting and gives food for thought," but Bridges's chief interest seems to lie in spelling reforms.

14. Karpf, Fritz. Review of *Society for Pure English: Tract No. 29* and *Tract No. 30. Die Neueren Sprachen* 37 (1929): 419–20.

15. Kennedy, Arthur G. Review of *Society for Pure English: Tract No. 32,* by Robert Bridges. *American Speech* 5 (1929): 169–70.
   Bridges illustrates the British tendency to shorten polysyllabic words or to lengthen the final syllable of other words.

16. Korschat, Erna. "Versuche in antiken Metren bei Robert Bridges." Ph.D. Diss, Wein, 1929.

17. "Mr. Bridges' New Poem." Review of *The Testament of Beauty,* by Robert Bridges. *New Statesman* 34 (1929): 125.

"No other living English poet . . . could have made an attempt at once so magnificent and so foolhardy." The elasticity of the loose alexandrines is suited to the subject. The simplified spelling, however, is an obstacle to "undisturbed appreciation." Bridges breaks down the self-imposed restrictions of modern poetry. Although the attempt is magnificent, the aim is doomed to failure.

18. "Poet Laureate on Radio." *New York Times,* 1 March 1929, p. 28, col. 1.

Bridges's lecture on Poetry at Magdalen College was broadcast by the BBC. He insisted on the need to educate children by teaching them to appreciate Beauty.

19. "The Poet Laureate's Bomb." *The Literary Digest* 103 (1929): 20.

Bridges may be England's last poet laureate.

20. Porter, Alan. "The Spirit of Man." Review of *The Testament of Beauty,* by Robert Bridges. *The Spectator* 143 (1929): 635–36.

The Testament of Beauty is "the greatest English poem of our time." It exhibits "an air of serenity and deep cultivation of mind" in which "idiom and cadence are perfectly matched to substance." However, Bridges lacks the "imaginative reach of Dante" and the unifying vision of the communal solidarity of all men. He preserves distances and differences.

21. "The Pronunciation of English." Review of *Society for Pure English: Tract No. 32,* by Robert Bridges *Times Literary Supplement,* 1 August 1929, 605.

Bridges's discussions form "delightful little essays, full of learning, of fine critical insight and that special quality which gives his prose so rare a distinction."

22. Read, Herbert. "Poet or Pedant?" Review of *The Testament of Beauty,* by Robert Bridges, and *Poetical Works of Robert Bridges,* 6 vols. *The Nation and Athenaeum* 46 (1929): 287–88.

Bridges lacks strong poetic instincts; he has been sustained by his "technical ability." The manner of *The Testament of Beauty* is loose alexandrines, the method is discursive and descriptive, and the matter is removed from actuality. Indeed, *The Testament of Beauty* is "too remote to comfort us."

23. Read, William A. Review of *Society for Pure English: Tract No. 30. Englische Studien* 63 (1929): 408–14.

It is doubtful the spelling and pronunciation reforms advocated by Bridges will be achieved.

24. Review of *The Testament of Beauty*, by Robert Bridges. *The Saturday Review of Literature* 6 (1929): 442–43.

An advance publication excerpt of the opening of *The Testament of Beauty*.

25. *"The Testament of Beauty."* Review of *The Testament of Beauty*, by Robert Bridges. *Times Literary Supplement*, 24 October 1929, 829–30.

The Testament of Beauty is "a gift of healing in a time of need" and the product of a "seasoned mind." It is the most adaptable, most confiding, most tranquil verse ever written. The rhythmical and lyrical equilibrium parallel the thought and structure of the poem. "No artist has written in English with a more practiced sense of the contributive value of every word and letter."

26. Thornton, James. "An Appreciation of the Poet Laureate." *The Spectator* 143 (1929): 621.

Bridges is as great a laureate as Tennyson; both are superb lyric poets and seek to unite Art with moral beauty. Although he is prone to faulty emotional emphasis, Bridges's "lyric skill is without fault." His poetic experiments account for his lack of popularity, but he should be congratulated for raising the laureateship above politics.

27. Twitchett, E. G. "The Poetry of Robert Bridges." *The London Mercury* 21 (1929): 136–45.

Bridges's early poetry conformed to the demands of the day, but since the war he has gone his own way. His theme has always been "the revelation of the joy of life." *The Growth of Love* is "a real sonnet-sequence" that foreshadows all of Bridges's other poetry. *Prometheus* and *Eros and Psyche* are perfect wholes with perfect parts. The dramas are the poorest part of Bridges's art. In *October,* the verbal life of the poems is "dimmed & dull," while *New Poems* harkens back to *Poems in Classical Prosody* and prepares the way for *The Testament of Beauty*.

28. Ward, Alfred Charles. "Poetry." In *Twentieth-Century Literature, 1901–1925,* 2d ed, 104–5. London: Methuen and Co., 1929.

Reprint of 1928.20.

29. Welby, T. Earl. "The Poet Laureate." Review of *The Testament of Beauty*, by Robert Bridges. *The Saturday Review* 148 (1929): 545–46.

The Testament of Beauty is the work of a great scholar and philosopher who reconciles Stoic and Christian doctrines; nevertheless, it is at least a partial failure because the nature of the work is unsuited to Bridges's talents. He abandons "pure song for speech" and exchanges lyric implication for direct prose statement. Bridges's usual interest in settled results is not suited to depicting the dynamic process contained in the poem.

30. Wood, H. G. "*The Testament of Beauty.*" *The Central Literary Magazine* 29 (1929–30): 263–68.

The themes of *The Testament of Beauty* are the priority of Beauty to Reason and Art to Philosophy and Science. Flexible alexandrines allow such philosophical discussion in poetry. The poem demonstrates an alliance between religion and scientific rationality.

1930

1. A., D. S. "Robert Bridges, 1844–1930." *The Pelican Record* 19 (1930): 138–39.

Personal recollection and obituary notice.

2. Abercrombie, Lascelles. "A Century of Laureates: Robert Bridges: Technique and *The Testament of Beauty.*" *The Bookman* (London) 79 (1930): 166–67.

The Testament of Beauty reveals Bridges's broad, deep intellectual and spiritual experiences, and thus debunks the notion that Bridges is merely a poet of technique, not feeling. This idea stems from the uncritical exaltation of Bridges's lyrics, which are so exquisitely wrought as to seem devoid of emotion. They are actually highly charged with emotion.

3. Aiken, Conrad. "Prose and Music." Review of *The Testament of Beauty,* by Robert Bridges. *The New Republic* 62 (1930): 164–66.

Much of Bridges's poetry commits "the cardinal sin of deadness." His unpopularity stems from poetic experiments that are "cold, dull, precious, actionless, full of affectations and archaisms, primly formal, niggardly florid." Works in the *Shorter Poems* also "combine a kind of chilly loveliness with a high degree of technical and prosodic ingenuity." *The Testament of Beauty* is Bridges's finest achievement, but in it there is "no wrestling with the dynamics of the soul, no probing of horrors or sounding of wonder; chaos has removed itself from the shores of Albion."

4. Bacon, Leonard. "The Old Lion's Voice." Review of *The Testament of Beauty,* by Robert Bridges. *The Saturday Review of Literature* 6 (1930): 913–14.

    The Testament of Beauty is "a singular work," the likes of which has not been seen in modern time. In it "splendid severity of thought goes hand in hand with a sympathy wide enough to touch and include all living." Although it lapses into prose and the spelling is bothersome, "it is extraordinary verse."

5. Binsse, H. L. "Gerard Manley Hopkins." Review of *Poems of Gerard Manley Hopkins,* edited by Robert Bridges and Charles Williams. *The Saturday Review of Literature* 7 (9 August 1930): 33–34.

    "The whole of [*The Testament of Beauty*] is a monument in prosody to [Bridges's] friendship for Gerard Hopkins."

6. Blunden, Edmund. "The Ideal Laureate." *The Nation and Athenaeum* 47 (1930): 106.

    Bridges is "a triumph of the English race" who, like Shelley, combines strength and beauty in poetry that is perpetually beautiful.

7. Boas, Cicely. "The Metre of *The Testament of Beauty.*" *The London Mercury* 22 (1930): 147–53.

    The small print, lack of capitals, unusual spelling, and loose alexandrines are hurdles that every reader must overcome. The matter of the poem is religion, philosophy, and poetry; the manner of the poem is music.

8. Boutell, H. S. "Robert (Seymour) Bridges: A Bibliographical Check List of the First Editions of His Books." *Publishers' Weekly* 117 (1930): 2650–54.

    Bibliography of first editions of Bridges's publications in verse and prose.

9. Brede, Alexander. "Studies in Contemporary Poetry: I. Robert Bridges." Ph.D. diss., Stanford University, 1930.

10. "Bridges, Poet Laureate, Is Dead." *Publishers' Weekly* 117 (1930): 2227–28.

    An obituary notice. Bridges was "known as an exponent of 'pure poetry' . . . who sought for objective beauty rather than subjective appeal." There was controversy about his tenure as poet laureate because he refused to write on demand, but *The Testament of Beauty* silenced his critics so that "he died in the midst of renewed and almost universal praise." *The Testament of Beauty* is "probably the greatest poetical work yet produced in the century."

11. Bridges, Robert. Poems. In *Modern British Poetry,* edited by Louis Untermeyer, 104–10. New York: Harcourt, Brace and Co., 1930.

    Adds an essay by Robert Hillyer (see 1930.37) and several poems, including "A Passer-By," "Awake, my heart, to be loved," and "I have loved flowers that fade."

12. Bridges, Robert. Poems. In *Poetry of the Victorian Period,* edited by George Benjamin Woods, 851–58. New York: Scott, Foresman and Co., 1930.

    This anthology includes "Elegy," "I will not let thee go." "A Passer-By," "London Snow," "Nightingales," "Pater Filio," and excerpts from *The Growth of Love.*

13. Brocklehurst, J. H. "Tract XXXII of the Society for Pure English." *Papers of the Manchester Literary Club* 16 (1930): 53–63.

    Bridges's recommendations for pronunciation are sometimes eccentric; nevertheless, he "deserves highest praise for the way he has conducted the inquiry."

14. Brown, Ivor. "The Duke of Milan." *The Saturday Review* 149 (1930): 46.

    The Humours of the Court is "pure Milanese" and "pure pastiche." It is "versified prettily" and is unexpectedly humorous.

15. Busey, Garetta. "Essay on Man." Review of *The Testament of Beauty,* by Robert Bridges. *New York Herald Tribune Book Review,* 16 February 1930, 7–8.

    The Testament of Beauty arrives at its own "not very radical conclusions" in an unrhymed hexameter verse which too often falls into the rhythm of good prose, not good verse. The simplified spelling has the effect of distracting the reader from the thought to the appearance of the poem.

16. "Buys Scott Letter and Laureate MSS." *New York Times,* 24 October 1930, p. 17, col. 1.

    Gabriel Wells purchased the manuscript of Bridges's poem "Our Lady."

17. Casson, T. E. *"The Testament of Beauty."* Review of *The Testament of Beauty,* by Robert Bridges. *The Poetry Review* 21 (1930): 85–87.

    The Testament of Beauty is similar to Dante's *Divine Comedy.* "It is a very noble poem."

18. "College Notes." *The Pelican Record* 19 (1930): 121.

    An anonymous recollection of the deceased poet laureate. "The inspiration of the poet found secure lodging in the humanity of the Man."

19. Cholmondeley, L. B. Letter. *The Times,* 6 January 1930, 8.

> Points out the parallel arguments between *The Testament of Beauty* and Akenside's "Pleasures of the Imagination."

20. D., St. Obituary notice. *St. Bartholomew's Hospital Journal* 37 (1930): 138–41.

> Six letters concerning the details of Bridges's medical career by various people who knew him.

21. de Selincourt, Ernest. *"The Testament of Beauty."* Review of *The Testament of Beauty,* by Robert Bridges. *The Hibbert Journal* 28 (1930): 416–35.

> *"The Testament of Beauty* is an imaginative exposition of the spiritual origin and destiny of man," which "reveals the manner in which by the influence of beauty man may rise to a consciousness of his spirit."

22. "Death of Mr. Robert Bridges, O.M." *The Times,* 22 April 1930, 12.

> Obituary notice.

23. Denniston, J. G., Reverend. Letter. *The Times,* 28 April 1930, 10.

> *The Yattendon Hymnal* reveals Bridges to have been "the greatest of all English hymn writers." Mrs. Bridges is responsible for the musical settings of twenty-eight of the hymns in the hymnal.

24. "Dr. Bridges and His Successor." *The Week-End Review* 1 (1930): 220–21.

> Bridges was a poetic revolutionary who went his own way, left nothing to chance, and widened the metrical range of English poetry. His reputation is bound to grow, and his best will be rated with Tennyson.

25. "Editorial Notes." *The London Mercury* 22 (1930): 96–99.

> Bridges is "one of the greatest English lyric poets and one of the most consummate of all literary artists." *The Testament of Beauty* is "the most remarkable long English philosophic poem since *The Prelude.*" Bridges has a youthful heart and mind and is always very much himself, even to the point of being eccentric. He is "the most productive old man who ever adorned our annals."

26. Elton, Oliver. "Robert Bridges." *The Pelican Record* 19 (1930): 124–28.

Bridges never became a popular poet until the publication of *The Testament of Beauty*. He "always went his own way and never made concession to public taste." *The Testament of Beauty* is a great artistic experiment similar to *The Prelude*. Although his plays contain much noble poetry, they are never likely to be popular. Bridges is a poet of happiness whose greatest achievement is in the lyric.

27. "Fifty Well-Made Books of 1929–1930." *New York Times Book Review,* 2 February 1930, p. 1, col. 1.

The Testament of Beauty was chosen as an example of the bookmaker's art because "no volume had greater dignity than the limited edition of *The Testament of Beauty.*"

28. Finley, John, Jr. "The Man of the Month: Robert Bridges." Review of *The Testament of Beauty,* by Robert Bridges. *The Atlantic Bookshelf,* April 1930, 24–26.

The Testament of Beauty represents "the gathered conclusions of [Bridges's] life concerning the development and meaning of the human soul." The poem has "an abstractness" that differentiates it from other great poems of the past. Like *Paradise Lost,* the unit of expression in *The Testament of Beauty* is the paragraph, not individual lines. The poem has an "apocalyptic force" that raises apparently unrelated facts "to a high unity of poetic vision."

29. Fischer, W. Review of *Collected Essays, Papers, etc. of Robert Bridges,* vol. 4. *Deutsche Literaturzeitung* 52 (1930): 1703–4.

Unable to translate.

30. Fletcher, James Gould. Review of *The Testament of Beauty,* by Robert Bridges. *The New Criterion* 9 (1930): 533–35.

Bridges's ability to match mood and cadence leaves an overall "impression of pure and lasting delight." The poem, however, is pedantic, "flatters the snobbish," and lacks sense. "Dr. Bridges has written a poem without structure of thought, and commonplace in range of feeling."

31. "Gerard Manley Hopkins." Review of *Poems of Gerard Manley Hopkins,* edited by Robert Bridges and Charles Williams. *Times Literary Supplement,* 25 December 1930, 1099.

The newly added poems add nothing to Hopkins's reputation, but they do show that Bridges was a superb editor of Hopkins's work.

32. Grew, Eva Mary. "Music in *The Testament of Beauty.*" *The Contemporary Review* 138 (1930): 209–17.

Bridges employs music and musical metaphors to portray the spiritual Beauty that he conceives to be the highest good in human existence.

33. Groth, Ernst. "Das Testament des englishen Poeta Laureatus." *Anglia Beiblatt* 41 (1930): 217–24.

   The Testament of Beauty attempts to solve the mystery of the purpose and meaning of life by combining scientific experience and philosophy to illustrate the idea that the highest morality and the highest beauty can be found in Christian belief.

34. Hall, William C., Rev. *"The Testament of Beauty."* *The Manchester Quarterly* 174 (1930):237–59.

   The Testament of Beauty "will stand as a landmark in our literary history." It is "the most exhaustive study of stress-rhythm" yet written and "sets the standard of a syllabic line." In addition it provides "a vehicle for poetical discourse" on scientific and philosophical subjects. It is the greatest philosophical poem yet attempted in English, but it will be regarded for its craftsmanship, poetical values, and consistency of theme. An analysis of the development of the theme concludes the essay.

35. Hall, William C., Rev. *"The Testament of Beauty."* *Papers of the Manchester Literary Club* 56 (1930): 237–59.

   See 1930.33.

36. Hillyer, Robert. "In the Pages of *The Testament of Beauty.*" *Boston Evening Transcript,* 21 February 1930, Book Section, p. 4, col. 3.

   Outlines the main themes of the poem by tracing the movement of human passions from the egocentric particular to the egalitarian universal. Bridges is "high-minded, sensitive, and wise"; *The Testament of Beauty* is "one of the great philosophical poems of the world," perhaps even "the *De Rerum Natura* of our Christian civilization."

37. Hillyer, Robert. "Robert Bridges." In *Modern British Poetry,* edited by Louis Untermeyer, 104–6. New York: Harcourt, Brace and Co., 1930.

   Bridges was a "poet's poet" who was relatively unknown until the publication of *The Testament of Beauty.* Nevertheless, he is an acknowledged master of English verse. His lack of popularity may be attributed to his use of archaic diction and syntax, lack of violent moods, too simple diction, and too delicate rhythms.

38. Hutchinson, Percy. *"The Testament of Beauty."* Review of *The Testament of Beauty*, by Robert Bridges. *New York Times*, 19 January 1930, sect. 4, pp. 1, 22, col. 1.

　　The Testament of Beauty is "somewhat lacking in lyric buoyancy" because it is metaphysical rather than emotional. Outlines the philosophy and argument of the poem.

39. "The Laureate's Play." Review of *Humours of the Court*, by Robert Bridges. *The Times*, 8 January 1930, 8.

　　Bridges borrows not only plots from past poets but manners of past ages as well. The characters are stiff, but "they have a fairy-like quality which makes their company continuously delightful and raises the play above the level of their contrivances."

40. Little, Arthur. "The Testament of Dr. Bridges." *Studies* 19 (1930): 33–44.

　　The Testament of Beauty illustrates "all that was great in Victorianism without its humbug." Yet Bridges's acceptance of evolutionary philosophy and his apparent Christianity seem incompatible and contradictory. This poem philosophically surveys human experience with a mood of calm strength. Its effect is cumulative. All modern poetry seems "raw or insignificant" beside it.

41. MacCarthy, Desmond. "Notes on the Poetry of Robert Bridges." *Life and Letters* 4 (1930): 477–84.

　　Bridges's later poems have more emotion than the earlier ones. He refined his emotions too much to capture "the true accents of passion"; thus he is a poet of joy, not love, because joy is only a part of the lover's experience. He wrote of reveries and scenes that harmonized with the life of man as a social being.

42. Magnus, Laurie. Letter. *The Times*, 23 April 1930, 13.

　　Bridges and Wordsworth were both poet laureates, both lived to be eighty, and they died one day apart.

43. Magnus, Laurie. *"The Testament of Beauty."* Review of *The Testament of Beauty*, by Robert Bridges. *The Cornhill Magazine* 68 (1930): 527–38.

　　Bridges is the first modern English poet who has not had to struggle to accept Darwin. He is a physician of the body and the mind, and has no philosophical or pragmatic doubts. As a result *The Testament of Beauty* "is testificatory rather than testamentary, the declaration of an ethical will, not the deposition of worldly goods." Bridges is a moral poet in the vein of Virgil, Dante, and Milton, who uses Darwinian science instead of legend and myth to communicate his vision.

44. Mansbridge, Albert. Letter. *The Times,* 24 April 1930, 14.

Bridges was a friend of the working man.

45. M[onroe], H[arriet]. "Bridges as a Lyrist." *Poetry* 36 (1930): 146–50.

Bridges is a laureate of the upper class, "a poet of the more decorous and gentlemanly English tradition." His early poems are incredibly naive and "graceful rather than impassioned." In them a soft, wistful beauty "almost reached a classic perfection of form and melody." Bridges's art is bookish, based on scholarship, and not the direct experience of life. It is "typical of English twentieth-century poetry."

46. "Mr. Bridges' Poem." Review of *The Testament of Beauty,* by Robert Bridges. *The London Mercury* 21 (1930): 193–94.

The Testament of Beauty is fuller of thought and feeling than *The Prelude* and "metrically full of manifestations of genius." It expresses the conclusions of a man aware of the groping of the modern age, of the age's intellectual and moral struggles. "A thousand years hence men will still read [Bridges] and learn from him."

47. "Mr. Robert Bridges, O.M." *The Times,* 22 April 1930, 17.

Although much of his poetry was too subtle and too experimental to achieve wide popularity, *The Testament of Beauty* may be the last major poem to express the spirit of an age.

48. Nichols, Wallace B. "Poets Laureate." *The Bookman* (London) 78 (1930): 168–70.

Bridges was a poet of joy who wrote from inner contentment, not turmoil, and whose two main concerns were technique and writing about life at a remove. "No poet in English ever possessed a more delicate ear than Robert Bridges." His fame will rest on his lyrics. Only his metrical experiments kept him modern. His plays are undramatic. Like his successor, Bridges was preoccupied with beauty.

49. Note. *The Saturday Review of Literature* 6 (21 June 1930): 1140.

Excerpt from *London Mercury* article on Bridges's stamina. See 1930.25.

50. P[into], V. de S[ola]. "Robert Bridges, 1844–1930." *Wessex* 1 (1930): 97–99.

51. Parker, Stanley E. Letter. *The Times,* 3 May 1930, 8.
    Explains the circumstances of Bridges's memorial to his nurse, Catherine Ashy.

52. "A Play by the Poet Laureate." *New York Times,* 26 January 1930, sect. 8, p. 1, col. 8.
    A review of a production of *The Humours of the Court,* performed by the Oxford University Dramatic Society. The play "has the authentic bloom of spring upon it."

53. "The Poet Laureate." *The Times,* 22 April 1930, 13.
    In all that he did, Bridges was ever moved by the spirit of Beauty and was its unflagging champion. He was as much a match for his age as Milton was for his own, and in time he will be recognized as a poet of such caliber as is only produced at rare intervals.

54. "Poet Laureate Dies at 85 in England." *New York Times,* 22 April 1930, p. 29, col. 1.
    An obituary notice that briefly relates Bridges's biography and quotes from *The Times* (London) editorial. See 1930.53.

55. "The Poet Laureate." *The Commonweal* 12 (1930): 4–5.
    Bridges courageously assumed the risks of individuality. Though sometimes intellectually narrow, he was culturally comprehensive. The vitality of *The Testament of Beauty* is tantamount to a medieval summa or a new book of Psalms.

56. "The Poet Laureate." *The Spectator* 144 (1930): 693.
    Bridges was a great scholar in the art of poetry. He was a student of the past and an innovator for the future. Aristocratic in manner, speech, and style, he was yet able to talk with common men without condescension.

57. "Poet Laureate's Estate, $34,640." *New York Times,* 31 July 1930, p. 11, col. 3.
    Bridges left an estate valued at $34,640.

58. "Poete-laureat." *Mercure de France* 220 (1930): 244–46.
    Obituary notice and history of the laureateship.

59. "The Poetry of Robert Bridges." *Times Literary Supplement,* 1 May 1930, 357–58.
    The freshness, resolution, sculpture, and architecture of Bridges's poetry show it is possible to believe in poetry in the modern age. His metrical experiments emancipate

others from convention. His dramas are artificial and over-studied. The sonnets of *The Growth of Love* are "too deliberately moulded," but the lyrics are his own, hard, clean, and sure. *The Testament of Beauty* is itself "a lyrical monologue," with "no pose or falsity anywhere," that reveals a mind "that has never capitulated."

60. Potter, John. "Robert Bridges (1844–1930): Medicine as a Training for Poetry?" *Oxford Medical School Gazette* 5 (1930).

61. Price, H[arold] T. Review of *Collected Essays, Papers, etc. of Robert Bridges*, vol. 3. *Anglia Beiblatt* 41 (1930): 313.

   Although first written in 1895, and in some ways superseded by modern criticism, Bridges's essay "will delight and charm, and bring new readers to Keats, so long as English is read at all."

62. Priestly, J. B. "A London Letter." *The Saturday Review of Literature* 6 (24 May 1930): 1074.

   Bridges viewed the laureateship as merely a mark of distinction, not as an official or court poet. Thus he ignored attacks on his silence.

63. Reader, Inconstant. "Preferences." Review of *The Testament of Beauty*, by Robert Bridges. *The Canadian Forum* 10 (1930): 166–68.

   The Testament of Beauty is in the oldest philosophical tradition in English poetry: Christian Platonism. "Its sole purpose is to re-affirm an old vision," not to bring new vision to the world.

64. Review of *Collected Essays, Papers, etc. of Robert Bridges*, vol. 3. *Review of English Studies* 6 (1930): 495.

   With the addition of three new phonetic symbols "the text is beginning to look slightly worrying, and suggestive of some of the more fantastic newer type."

65. Ridge, Lola. "Robert Bridges Dispenses his Hale Wisdom of Life." *New York Evening Post*, 18 January 1930, 7.

66. "Robert Bridges." *New York Times*, 23 April 1930, p. 26, col. 4.

   Bridges "made glorious his laureateship in taking leave of it and set a stately standard for his successor." *The Testament of Beauty* "lifts English literature to a parity with that of its Golden Age."

67. "Robert Bridges Cremated." *New York Times*, 27 April 1930, p. 5, col. 3.

   Bridges was cremated in secrecy; there was no public funeral service.

68. "Robert Bridges' Essays." Review of *Collected Essays, Papers, etc. of Robert Bridges,* vol. 6. *Times Literary Supplement,* 30 June 1930, 477.

    These essays on pronunciation and spelling reform reveal Bridges's "prevalent respect for the language." In his efforts to reform English, "Bridges remints the language." The essay on Emily Bronte is a bit captious, whereas the essay on Dryden and Milton shows the "scholar's jeu d'esprit."

69. Robert, R. Ellis. "Robert Bridges." *The New Statesman* 35 (1930): 80–81.

    The Testament of Beauty is unquestionably Bridges's greatest work, but the very character of its greatness will keep it from being popular. Bridges's entire life and art were in the service of Beauty, a service most potently revealed in the lyrics. Contrary to popular belief, Bridges's work exhibits deep emotion, which runs the gamut from deepest love to profoundest grief.

70. Roberts, W. Wright. "Music in Robert Bridges." *Music and Letters* 11 (1930): 341–51.

    Music was a pervading instinct that prompted Bridges's lyrical urges. He used music in his plays, sound images in his poetry, and musical terms throughout his writings. Parry, Woolridge, and Purcell were his primary musical influences. "Since Milton died, no English poet has treated the sister art with such honor."

71. Roth, Georges. "Robert Bridges." *Larousse Mensuel* 282 (August 1930): 466–67.

    As Bridges's technical ability was perfected, his poetic style became less accessible to the public. *The Growth of Love* was his most widely appreciated work. Bridges was a Ronsard who strayed among the Philistines.

72. "Royal College of Physicians." *The Times,* 25 April 1930: 7.

    The Royal College of Physicians sends condolences to the Bridges family.

73. Sasaki, Tatsu. *On the Language of Robert Bridges' Poetry.* Tokyo: Kenkyusha, 1930.

    This study is divided into three parts: the place of the adjective attribute, the intensive plural of the noun, and the infinitive and the gerund. In addition to showing the influence of archaisms, rhythm, and rhetoric on Bridges's poetry, the linguistic characteristics of the poetry reveal many of Bridges's personal characteristics.

74. Shepard, Odell. "Robert Bridges." *The Bookman* (New York) 71 (1930): 151–56.

> *The Testament of Beauty* is a *Religio Medici* of uneven quality, which, nevertheless, "shows us that we have still with us a poet of major importance." Bridges's "archaic habit of mind, indifference to fame, undemocratic attitudes, and subtle craftsmanship have prevented him from achieving wide popularity." Although sanity, health, and normality pervade his writing, he "has known too little of life's give-and-take, has had too little social criticism, and has therefore come to feel rather naively that almost any idea entering his mind gains thereby a certain dignity." His best work is *Shorter Poems*.

75. Shillito, Edward. "Robert Bridges Leaves a Testament of Beauty." Review of *The Testament of Beauty*, by Robert Bridges. *The Christian Century* 47 (1930): 652–54.

> *The Testament of Beauty* is "the last fruit of a tree which has yielded a rich store and is a most convincing defense of ideal philosophy and Christian life."

76. Shuster, George N. *"The Testament of Beauty."* Review of *The Testament of Beauty*, by Robert Bridges. *The Commonweal* 11 (1929–30): 448–49.

> *The Testament of Beauty* is a metaphysical bridge between the world of man and the world of nature that combines natural with supernatural evolution, and reconciles animal and spirit in man. "*The Testament of Beauty* is destined to become an enduring testimonial to the faith and struggle of our time."

77. Stewart, George R., Jr. Review of *The Testament of Beauty*, by Robert Bridges. *The University of California Chronicle* 32 (1930): 382–84.

> *The Testament of Beauty* is archaic and audacious. It is audacious because it involves a nonspecialist speaking out on issues that divide the specialists. The spelling, grammar, and meter of the poem are equally daring. The poem is an "honest record fitly expressed of the ideas and aspirations of one who was a great and noble man of his age."

78. Toynbee, Padget. Letter. *The Times*, 23 April 1930, 13.

> *The Times* obituary neglects to say that Bridges had two medical distinctions in addition to his academic honors.

79. Van Doren, Mark. "Big and Little Poetry." Review of *The Testament of Beauty*, by Robert Bridges. *The Virginia Quarterly Review* 6 (1930): 292–96.

Bridges is a "derivative poet" who echoes Dante, Lucretius, Milton, and Wordsworth. *The Testament of Beauty* adds nothing to the issues and ideas of Bridges's earlier poems. It is not the great poem English critics say it is because it lacks passion and the philosophy is confused. The creed is conventionally Christian.

80. Walton, Eda Lou. *"The Testament of Beauty."* Review of *The Testament of Beauty,"* by Robert Bridges. *The Nation* 130 (1930): 193–96.

The Testament of Beauty is comparable with *The Prelude* and *The Excursion.* Moral and aesthetic progress are identical, and together they point to conventional morality and religion. Religious emotion is lost because it is "freighted much too heavily with argument and philosophical jargon." The lyric passages persuade more than the argument.

81. Ward, Alfred Charles. "Poetry." In *Twentieth-Century Literature, 1901–1925,* 3d ed., 104–5. London: Methuen and Co., 1930.

Reprint of 1928.20.

82. Ward, Alfred Charles. "Robert Bridges: *The Testament of Beauty.*" In *The Nineteen-Twenties: Literature and Ideas in the Post-War Decade,* 80–86. London: Methuen and Co., 1930.

The Testament of Beauty "conceives Beauty to be the sum and summit of experience" and "identical with the wisdom of God." The "loose Alexandrines" of *The Testament of Beauty,* which are essentially "free verse controlled by a modulated echo of metrical authority," are the culmination of Bridges's attempts "to naturalize classical metres to English." In this poem Bridges "revived 'the grand manner' in English poetry" and "spoke with a voice of serene assurance for the guidance of an age of despair."

83. Warner, R. E. "The Poetry of Robert Bridges." *The Saturday Review* 149 (1930): 613.

Bridges was the finest and perhaps the last representative of the best of Oxford culture, but never was he old-fashioned. He attempted to revise and renovate English prosody but always within the English literary tradition. His later verse is more aesthetically satisfying than his earlier verse. "His muse was never young."

84. Waugh, Arthur. "Robert Bridges." *The Fortnightly Review* 133 (1930): 832–43.

Bridges, "the last of the great Victorians," always valued

discipline, duty, restraint, and self-sacrifice. He was rarely "guilty of writing for writing's sake." His belief that a love of nature leads to a love of beauty and finally to a love of love was set forth in *The Testament of Beauty*. However, the verse, spelling, and argument by analogy impede the understanding of the poem.

85. Weekley, Ernest. "English Grammar and Language." Review of *Society for Pure English: Tract No. 32*, edited by Robert Bridges. *The London Mercury* 22 (1930): 381.

    Notes some of Bridges's unusual recommendations.

86. Williams, Charles. "Introduction to the Second Edition." In *Poems of Gerard Manley Hopkins*, 2d ed., edited by Robert Bridges and Charles Williams, ix–xvi. London, New York, and Toronto: Oxford University Press, 1930.

    This edition is "a memory not only of Gerard Hopkins but also of the poet [Bridges], his friend, to whom all readers of either owe so great a devotion."

87. Williams, Charles. "Robert Bridges." In *Poetry at Present*, 18–29. Oxford: The Clarendon Press, 1930.

    An assessment of the poetical success of Bridges's lyrics. The concreteness and high quality of Bridges's verse are two main reasons for his success. The beauty of the lyrics stems from their emotional restraint; the joys are internalized and grow out of natural experience. The five characteristic aspects of Bridges's lyrics are the English landscape, man in society, Hellenism, solitude, and piety.

88. Z[abel], M[orton] D[auwen]. "The Testament of Robert Bridges." Review of *The Testament of Beauty*, by Robert Bridges. *Poetry* 36 (1930): 96–100.

    The Testament of Beauty represents the thought of a lifetime and is "a document on the highest form of individuality." It will not appeal to modern readers because it is discursive rather than intuitive. Emotion, passion, and compassion are all subdued by Bridges's studied discipline, which has chilled his inspiration. "He has not found the words or art which liberate his message, and make it the property and guide of his contemporaries."

1931

1. Arnold, Eric. "Keats, Blake, and Bridges." Letter. In *Times Literary Supplement*, 14 May 1931, 310.

The Testament of Beauty is "the clearest exposition of the poetic faith which Blake and Keats strove to express." Bridges shares a close poetic kinship with Keats.

2. Benet, William Rose. "Round about Parnassus." *The Saturday Review of Literature* 7 (25 April 1931): 780.

Bridges's proposals for phonetic spelling are "barbarous."

3. Bridges, Robert. Poems. In *Chief Modern Poets of England and America,* edited by Gerald DeWitt Sanders and John Herbert Nelson, 37–60. New York: Macmillan, 1931.

Reprint of 1929.3.

4. Bridges, Robert. Poems. In *Philosophies of Beauty from Socrates to Robert Bridges: Being the Sources of Aesthetic Theory,* edited by E. F. Carritt, 331. Oxford: Oxford University Press, 1931.

Excerpts from *The Testament of Beauty: Book II,* lines 842–47, and *Book IV,* lines 1439–41.

5. "Bridges's Shorter Poems." Review of *Shorter Poems,* by Robert Bridges. *Times Literary Supplement,* 25 June 1931, 505.

These lyrics reflect "versatility of mood and manner; an exquisite scrupulousness of workmanship rules everywhere." However, the beauty of the workmanship "is an attainment in the second degree, like an English gentleman's good horsemanship, who never becomes part of his horse, as the base Indian does." The margins are too narrow, the typeface is too small, and the poems are poorly arranged on the page.

6. Casson, T. E. *"The Testament of Beauty." The Poetry Review* 21 (1930–31): 85–86.

The Testament of Beauty is like the *Divine Comedy,* not *De Rerum Natura.* The craftsman and artist have combined in this poem.

7. Daryush, Elizabeth. "Robert Bridges's Work on the English Language." *The Society for Pure English* 35 (1931): 503–11.

Summarizes Bridges's "views on the chief problems presented by our language and literature" and "his contributions towards their solution."

8. "Dr. Bridges on Darley." Review of *Collected Essays, Papers, etc. of Robert Bridges,* vol. 4. *Times Literary Supplement,* 22 January 1931, 57.

Bridges's criticism of Darley is sometimes too harsh and even unsatisfactory; however, one must reluctantly agree with his judgment.

9. Garrod, H. W. *"The Testament of Beauty."* In *Poetry and the Criticism of Life*, 129–47. Oxford: Oxford University Press; Cambridge: Harvard University Press, 1931.

   The Testament of Beauty is "the last will and monition, upon the subject of beauty, of a life-long student of the beautiful." It has a "Chaucerian simplicity" and an "essentially English" temper. The poem was Bridges's first best seller because he "put more of nature, and less of art, into it than into any other of his compositions." It is "the only readable philosophical poem since Lucretius"; however, its power is not in its philosophy but in the life experience it reflects. Although it is slightly marred by Bridges's unwillingness, or inability, to relate Reason to Beauty, *The Testament of Beauty* is "the only great poem that has appeared in living memory."

10. Grigson, Geoffrey. "A Poet of Surprise." Review of *Poems of Gerard Manley Hopkins*, edited by Robert Bridges and Charles Williams. *The Saturday Review* 151 (1931): 237–38.

    Bridges's introduction, while at times too critical, is essential reading for understanding Hopkins's poetry and some of his poetic idiosyncracies.

11. Holst, Gustav. *A Choral Fantasia, Op. 51.* London: J. Curwen and Sons, 1931.

    Vocal score of Bridges's 1896 ode to Henry Purcell.

12. Jones, G. W. *The Message of One of England's Greatest Poets to a Printer and Printers.* [London: The Sign of the Dolphin, 1931.]

    Reproduces portions of *The Testament of Beauty* to illustrate Bridges's care for the craft of typography.

13. Larrabee, Harold Atkins. "Robert Bridges and George Santayana." *Faculty Papers of Union College* 2 (1931): 77–95.

    As a metrical innovator Bridges is "a sort of Einstein in poetry" who replaces "Newtonian" meter with "relativist" pure rhythm, a meter that allows for easier composition and reading of long philosophic poems. *The Testament of Beauty* "touches all the great themes of human life and destiny." Bridges is neither a profound nor an original thinker; he is the spokesman for a great tradition that sees beauty as the pathway to a spiritual destiny. He is "likely to remain a connoisseur's poet."

14. Magnus, Laurie. *"The Testament of Beauty."* *Essays by Members of the Royal Society of Literature* 10 (1931): 1–16.

    Reprint of 1930.43.

15. Milford, Humphry S. "Bridges's *Shorter Poems.*" Letter. *Times Literary Supplement*, 2 July 1931, 528.

    Although *Shorter Poems* was issued in two formats, the paper size was the same for both. Both editions reflect Bridges's wishes regarding the order and presentation of the poems.

16. Pearce, T. M. "The Legacy of Robert Bridges." Review of *The Testament of Beauty*, by Robert Bridges. *The New Mexico Quarterly* 1 (1931): 393–404.

    Victorian faith and optimism combine with modern scientific clear-headedness in *The Testament of Beauty* to produce a searching analysis of the impulses that move mankind. In this work Bridges's mind has distilled the cultured thought of European civilization and held the mirror of science up to nature. Nevertheless, his "philosophy is . . . deep centered in the intuitive nature of man."

17. Read, Herbert. Review of *Poems of Gerard Manley Hopkins*, edited by Robert Bridges and Charles Williams. *The New Criterion* 10 (1931): 553–54.

    Bridges understood the craftsmanship and beauty of Hopkins's verse, but a "lack of sympathy" for his poetic ideals caused Bridges to judge Hopkins's verse by a standard that Hopkins never sought to be measured by. Bridges's introductory remarks are marked by "pedantic velleity."

18. Scovell, E. J. "Robert Bridges." Review of *The Shorter Poems of Robert Bridges. New Statesman and Nation* 2 (1931): 283–84.

    Bridges's lyrics, which are primarily about love and joy, are closer to the Elizabethans in their "union of spontaneous feeling with finished, ingenious craftsmanship." His best nature poetry is akin to Wordsworth's in capturing the portentous moment and recording "the irrational motions of joy or hope or fear or sorrow, that are fired by something external, apparently trivial, not logically related."

19. Smith, Fred. "Two Testaments." *The Holborn Review* (1931): 175–79.

    Compares Davidson's *The Testament of a Man Forbid* to *The Testament of Beauty*. Whereas Davidson sinks through despair to death, Bridges rises through joy to transcendental vision.

20. Smith, Logan Pearsall. "Robert Bridges: Recollections." *The Society for Pure English* 35 (1931): 481–502.

     Relates Bridges's role in the creation and early history of the society. Includes three letters from Bridges to Smith and one from Sir Walter Raleigh to Bridges.

21. Smith, Nowell Charles. *Notes on 'The Testament of Beauty.'* London: Oxford University Press, 1931.

     This book is a paraphrase of and commentary on *The Testament of Beauty.* Although some critics feel the poem lacks a coherent philosophy, the poem is imbued with "a definitely reasoned aesthetic theory of life" and, further-more, it is the "first great didactic poem of aesthetic philosophy."

22. Sulkie, Thomas A. *"The Testament of Beauty."* Review of *The Testament of Beauty,* by Robert Bridges. *The Catholic World* 133 (1931): 422–27.

     The Testament of Beauty reverses the modern trend toward short literary works. It has "little or no lyricism," and ex-pounds the same rationalistic errors of both the nineteenth century and the modern mind. "It is the *Aeneid* of a pinch of dust into a saint"; it is not a classic. It is "a testimonial of the emptiness of a literature and a faith in matter as the prime principle of life, even a supernatural life; a testi-monial to the struggle and turmoil of a bewildered genera-tion clamped in the iron jaws of error."

23. Walton, Eda Lou. Review of *The Shorter Poems of Robert Bridges. New York Times,* 23 August 1931, sect. 4, p. 5, col. 3.

     Bridges's poetry, which seems Victorian, is English to the core. He will be remembered as a writer of perfect lyrics, not as an innovator in verse.

24. Ward, Alfred Charles. "Poetry." In *Twentieth-Century Literature, 1901–1925,* 4th ed., 104–5. London: Methuen and Co., 1931.

     Reprint of 1928.20.

25. Winters, Yvor. "Traditional Mastery: The Lyrics of Robert Bridges." Review of *The Shorter Poems of Robert Bridges. The Hound and Horn* 5 (1931–32): 321–27.

     Bridges is "the most valuable model of poetic style to appear in the language since Dryden." "No living poet is capable of such masterly writing." Bridges's technical merits have caused him to be ignored by critics. Those qualities praised in the work of Hopkins are the very qualities that make Hopkins's poetry inferior to Bridges's. The experience rendered in Hopkins is incomplete, whereas in Bridges it is complete. "It is to be hoped, for the sake of twentieth-century poetry, that [Bridges] will receive the study his own poetry merits."

26. Wolfe, Humbert. "Robert Bridges." *The English Review* 53 (1931): 79.

27. Wolfe, Humbert. "Robert Bridges." *The Literary Digest* 110 (1931): 22.

    A sonnet to Robert Bridges.

28. Z[able], M[orton] D[auwen]. "Two English Classicists." Review of *The Shorter Poems of Robert Bridges. Poetry* 39 (1931–32): 280–85.

    The lyric character of Bridges's poems is curtailed by his restrained sensibility. The poems would have profited by an "expansion and substantiation in contemporary consciousness." However, the rhetorical and archaic tendencies of the poems are justified because they are organic to the lyrics. Bridges is "one of the first modern writers in the English lyric tradition."

1932

1. Berger, Rosa. "Robert Bridges's Weltanschauung und Kunstprinzip." Ph.D. diss., Wein, 1932.

2. Boas, George. *Philosophy and Poetry.* Norton, Mass.: Wheaton College Press, 1932.

    "A philosophic poem is philosophy made concrete," and such a poem needs a central image that reflects the poet's evaluation of the universe. *The Testament of Beauty* fails as a philosophic poem because of an inherent contradiction in Bridges's image of the charioteer, which depicts man as the master of his warring passions, and Bridges's acceptance of evolutionary theory as a basis for his poem, a theory that holds that man is merely the product of his passions. Despite this, *The Testament of Beauty* is "one of the great English poems of the first quarter of the twentieth century."

3. Bridges, Robert. Poems. In *The Book of Living Verse*, edited by Louis Untermeyer, 480–81. New York: Harcourt, Brace and Co., 1932.

    This anthology includes "Nightingales," "A Passer-By," and "I love all beauteous things."

4. Bridges, Robert. Poems. In *Modern British Poetry,* edited by
   Louis Untermeyer, 3d ed., 168–72. New York: Harcourt,
   Brace and Co., 1932.

   This anthology omits the Hillyer essay (see 1930.37) and
   several poems found in previous editions.

5. Bridges, Robert. Poems. In *New Hesperides,* edited by Andrew
   Robert Ramey and Winifred Johnston, 127–29. New York:
   Thomas Nelson and Sons, 1932.

   This anthology includes "Triolet" and "Rondeau."

6. Bridges, Robert. Poems. In *Poetry of the Transition: 1850–1914,*
   edited by Thomas Marc Parrott and Willard Thorpe, 454–
   69. New York: Oxford University Press, 1932.

   This anthology includes "I love all beauteous things," "A
   Passer-By," "Elegy," "I never shall love snow again," "Pater
   Filio," "My delight and thy delight," "I will not let thee go,"
   and "I have loved flowers that fade."

7. Caldwell, James Ralston. "Beauty's Will." *The University of California Chronicle* 34 (1932): 81–86.

   The Testament of Beauty is a loosely organized restatement
   of the idea that to love and cherish beauty is to attain
   wisdom. Bridges's ideas and attitudes are reactionary, commonplace, orthodox, trite, and conventional. The Beauty in
   this poem is "a soft garment" that protects and isolates
   Bridges "from the bitter gust of life."

8. "Care-free Lines." Review of *Verses Written for Mrs. Daniel,* by
   Robert Bridges. *Times Literary Supplement,* 4 August 1932,
   554.

   Bridges's mastery of style is evident in this playful verse
   that grows out of deep friendship. Here is much "banter-
   ing, affectionate kindliness." Includes a collotype reproduc-
   tion of the original manuscript.

9. Elton, Oliver. "Robert Bridges and *The Testament of Beauty.*"
   English Association Pamphlets 83 (1932): 3–15.

   In *The Testament of Beauty* Bridges attempts "to show the
   place of Beauty in the whole economy of thought," especially as it relates to ethics, theology, and his personal
   outlook on life. The poem traces the growth of the idea of
   Beauty through four historical/biological stages. "The conception of Beauty set forth in this poem does not fit very
   clearly into the long history of philosophical speculation on
   the subject." Because Bridges's genius is lyrical and meditative rather than speculative, the personal experiences re-

lated in the poem are more poetic than the philosophical passages. Bridges's "new" poetic style accommodates the technical jargon of philosophy and "surely deserves all the honors."

10. Hughes, Mabel L. Violet. *Everyman's Testament of Beauty: A Study in The Testament of Beauty of Robert Bridges.* London: Student Christian Movement Press, 1932.

   This study examines three aspects of *The Testament of Beauty:* the teachings of the poem, its social and educational importance, and its value for literature and life. The final section of the book contains a religious service derived from lines taken from the poem. *The Testament of Beauty* is "a Greek Testament brought to its inevitable completion in the Christian faith."

11. Larrabee, Harold Atkins. "Robert Bridges and George Santayana." *The American Scholar* 1 (1932): 167–82.

   Reprint of 1931.13.

12. Long, T. S. Review of *The Testament of Beauty,* by Robert Bridges. *The Saturday Review* 38 (1932): 369–73.

13. McK[errow], R[obert] B. Review of *Collected Essays, Papers, etc. of Robert Bridges,* vol. 5. *Review of English Studies* 8 (1932): 371.

   Bridges's recommendation for the pronunciation of "the" is questionable.

14. Newbolt, Henry. "Mary Coleridge and Robert Bridges." In *My World as in My Time,* 184–91 and passim. London: Faber and Faber, 1932.

   An account of Newbolt's first two meetings with Bridges at Yattendon and Bridges's comments on both Newbolt's poetry and "the great need of modern poetry for a fresher diction and a broader freedom." Also mentioned is the role Bridges played in the publishing of Mary Coleridge's poetry.

15. Parrott, Thomas Marc, and Willard Thorpe. "Robert Bridges." In *Poetry of the Transition: 1850–1914,* 450–54. New York: Oxford University Press, 1932.

   Bridges fought to preserve "the best of the old order." All the excellencies of English poetry are distilled in his verse. "His lyric gift was as great as that of any English poet; his critical sense could match it." He was a "poet of joy," and *The Testament of Beauty* represented the culminating expression of "his store of wisdom, a perfected technique, and a love of beauty."

16. "Robert Bridges as Critic." Review of *Collected Essays, Papers, etc. of Robert Bridges*, vol. 5. *Times Literary Supplement*, 28 January 1932, 57.

These essays "attempt to persuade us to use our English voices and language as though we loved the sound of them." The criticism shows patient thought, elaborate skill and ingenuity, grace, poise, wit, intuition, judgment, and imagination. Bridges is a philosopher and artist, one devoted to method, order, and precision, who knew life at first hand.

17. Smith, Nowell Charles. *Notes on 'The Testament of Beauty.'* 2d ed. Oxford: Oxford University Press, 1932.

Essentially a reprint of 1931.21. Minor revisions and additions to the notes.

18. Stevenson, Lionel. "Contemporary Poets." In *Darwin among the Poets*, 335–43. Chicago: University of Chicago Press, 1932.

Much of Bridges's early work reveals his acquaintance with modern scientific theories. *Prometheus* has definite evolutionary implications while "Winter Delights" is a "detailed and enthusiastic survey of the whole scope of science," which draws inspiration from the past evolutionary record. It is "the first real poem of modern science." The ideas in these and other poems are brought together in *The Testament of Beauty* and clarified into a coherent whole "based solidly on the whole cycle of modern science." However, all natural processes in this poem refer back to the will of God.

19. Stonier, George W. "Gerard Manley Hopkins." Review of *Poems of Gerard Manley Hopkins*, edited by Robert Bridges and Charles Williams. *The New Statesman and Nation* n.s. 3 (1932): 836–38.

Bridges's criticism of Hopkins's sensualism and asceticism fails to see that these are the qualities that make Hopkins's poetry great.

20. "Three Friends." Review of *Three Friends*, by Robert Bridges. *Times Literary Supplement*, 17 November 1932, 855.

Though written in later life, these essays represent different periods in Bridges's life, and the reticence with which Bridges wrote them reveals more about him than about those who are honored by them.

21. van Doorn, Willem. "Die-hards: Third Group. Romancers."
    In *Of the Tribe of Homer: Being an Inquiry into the Theory and
    Practice of English Narrative Verse since 1883*, 139–43.
    Amsterdam: N. V. de Arbeiderspers, 1932.

    Bridges's strict attention to poetic form leads to gra-
    tuitous lines and stanzas that come "dangerously near to
    mere twaddle." Although his use of scientific theory is
    sometimes incongruous, his descriptions of the natural
    world are superb. The "interest" created by his poetry "is of
    the mildest kind."

22. Winters, Yvor. "T. Sturge Moore." Review of *The Poems of
    T. Sturge Moore*. *Hound and Horn* 6 (1932–33): 542–43.

    Bridges's Nero plays are the "greatest tragedy since *The
    Cenci*" and superior to anything outside of Shakespeare.
    The Christian Captives is nearly as fine, and *Achilles in Scyros* is
    "nearly as lovely as *Comus*." Bridges is "the most finished
    and original master of blank verse since Milton."

1933

1. Evans, Benjamin Ifor. "Robert Bridges and His Associates."
   In *English Poetry in the Later Nineteenth Century*, 218–43 and
   passim. London: Methuen and Co., 1933.

   Bridges was "the last of the Victorians." His experiments
   in prosody and adherence to classical forms and subjects
   produced a "fastidious" poetry that lacked imagery. *The
   Growth of Love* emphasizes the effect of love on art and life.
   The dramas are only "dubiously successful" and remain
   "poetic exercises" in which intellectual concerns supersede
   human concerns. *The Testament of Beauty* is vitiated by idiosyncratic spelling, unfamiliar meter, and a facile dismissal
   of the problem of evil. Despite this the poem depicts a
   certainty of faith combined with a serenity of mood and
   unites the poetry of the early and late nineteenth century.
   "It is with *The Testament of Beauty* that nineteenth-century
   poetry comes to an end."

2. Field, Michael. "Revisiting Cambridge." In *Works and Days:
   From the Journal of Michael Field*, edited by T. Sturge and
   D. C. Moore, 128. London: J. Murray, 1933.

   Relates a brief conversation about Bridges's poetry.

3. Hillyer, Robert. *Some Roots of English Poetry*, 9, 13. Norton,
   Mass.: Wheaton College Press, 1933.

   Bridges exhibits two necessary qualities for a poet to

write good poetry: he is at home in his world, and he weaves together the past and the present. *The Testament of Beauty* illustrates both of these characteristics.

4. Kunitz, Stanley J. "Robert Bridges." In *Authors Today and Yesterday*, 91–94. New York: H. W. Wilson Co., 1933.

   Primarily a biographical essay with an occasional critical comment.

5. Mackenzie, Compton. "The Oxford Point of View." In *Literature in My Time*, 133–36. New York: Loring and Mussey; London: Rich and Cowan, 1933.

   Bridges's article on the proper pronunciation of Latin was the most important article to appear in *The Oxford Point of View*, and his essay on Keats is "the finest piece of poetic criticism in the English language." Although Bridges was always "aloof from popularity," the popularity of *The Testament of Beauty* was due to the public's longing "for any work of literature . . . that seemed to offer a thread of guidance through the bewildering maze into which science had plunged itself and the world."

6. McKay, George L[eslie]. *A Bibliography of Robert Bridges*. New York: Columbia University Press; London: Oxford University Press, 1933.

   A primary descriptive bibliography based upon the Coykendall Collection at Columbia University. Cites Bridges's first-edition publications.

7. Megroz, R. L. "Anti-Decadence." In *Modern English Poetry, 1882–1932*, 103–5. London: Ivor Nicholson and Watson, 1933.

   Bridges "is chronologically as well as by his temper a poet of last century" whose early poetry combined Latin scholarship and "skilled imitations of classical English poetry," and avoided contemporary influences. *The Testament of Beauty* is a "prosaic and rhetorical but skillful metric exercise in un–original uplifting thought." *The Growth of Love* is too ambitious for his "definitely limited capacity for matching depth of emotion with profundity of insight or magnificence of vision." Bridges is one of those " 'nature poets' who seek not consolation or dark secrets but texts for delight."

8. Nowell–Smith, Simon. "Bibliography of Robert Bridges." Letter. *Times Literary Supplement*, 28 December 1933, 924.

   Supports Wilkinson on the issue of anonymity and *The Growth of Love* (see 1933.12).

9. Review of *Three Friends,* by Robert Bridges. *The London Quarterly and Holborn Review* 158 (1933): 271–72.

"Amusing stories, acute literary criticism, and ripe wisdom make these lives a rare treasure."

10. Southron, Jane Spence. "Three Friends of Robert Bridges." Review of *Three Friends,* by Robert Bridges. *New York Times,* 19 January 1933, sect. 5, p. 8, col. 3.

Bridges interpreted the finest tendencies of his day. These essays represent three distinct aspects or times in his life: Eton and the Oxford Movement, Oxford and the Pre-Raphaelites, and interest in language. Bridges's humanity shines through these essays.

11. Ward, Alfred Charles. "Robert Bridges: *The Testament of Beauty.*" In *The Nineteen-Twenties: Literature and Ideas in the Post-War Decade,* 2d ed., 80–86. London: Methuen and Co., 1933.

Reprint of 1930.82.

12. Wilkinson, Cyril H. "Bibliography of Robert Bridges." *Times Literary Supplement,* 28 December 1933, 924.

Corrects errors in McKay's bibliography and questions whether Bridges sought anonymity in the publication of *The Growth of Love.*

13. Williams, Charles Walter Stansby. "The Dispersal of Mist." In *Reason and Beauty in the Poetic Mind,* 173–75. Oxford: The Clarendon Press, 1933.

The Testament of Beauty does not achieve greatness because it contains no "essence of tragedy"; it fails to reconcile the discordant elements of life, a reconciliation that is the chief aim of poetry. *The Testament of Beauty* has greater amplitude but less insight than Pope's *Essay on Man.* Parts of *The Testament of Beauty* are better analyses of poetic genius than of life.

14. Williams, Charles. "Robert Bridges." In *English Critical Essays: Twentieth Century,* edited by Phyllis M. Jones, 290–301. London: Oxford University Press, 1933.

Reprint of 1930.87

1934

1. Abercrombie, Lascelles. "Bridges on Prosody." Review of *Collected Essays, Papers, etc. of Robert Bridges,* vol. 7. *The Listener* 11 (1934): 810.

The use of phonotype shows Bridges's deep reverence for the spoken word, a reverence at the root of his metrical experiments also. He could have been "the finest critic in our literature," if he had wanted to make a career of criticism.

2. Bateson, Frederick Wilse. "The Present Day." In *English Poetry and the English Language*, 127–28. Oxford: The Clarendon Press, 1934.

Bridges's poetry is less dependent on prose than that of his Victorian predecessors, but it lacks "firmness and vividness." His poems are morally didactic and undramatic. Bridges attempted to revitalize the poetic language he inherited from the Pre-Raphaelites.

3. Bridges, Robert. Poem. In *Poetry: Its Appreciation and Enjoyment*, edited by Louis Untermeyer and Carter Davidson, 240–41. New York: Harcourt, Brace and Co., 1934.

This anthology includes "London Snow."

4. "Bridges on Dryden." Review of *Collected Essays, Papers, etc. of Robert Bridges*, vol. 6. *Times Literary Supplement*, 11 January 1934, 25.

Bridges was "potentially the finest critic of his age." Perhaps he did not write more criticism because he regretted his lack of qualification, a lack he cultivated through idiosyncratic reading and prejudice. He condemned Dryden primarily because he attacked Milton.

5. Bullough, Geoffrey. "Inheritance of the Twentieth Century." In *The Trend of Modern Poetry*, 12–15. Edinburgh and London: Oliver and Boyd, 1934.

Bridges was "the last of the platonic poets," to whom beauty was "an ethical and intellectual principle." *The Testament of Beauty* is a "noble reflective poem" that "rivals Lucretius and contains more fine passages of description, reminiscence, and argument than any other poem of our day." Although his experiments with classical prosody left him "with an excessive regard for quantity," Bridges's prosodic experiments "form a definite contribution to the development of English verse."

6. Coblentz, Stanton A. "Robert Bridges and His Own Spelling." Review of *Collected Essays, Papers, etc. of Robert Bridges*, vol. 2. *New York Times*, 27 May 1934, sect. 5, p. 4, col. 2.

Bridges has much to say in these essays that is worthwhile; however, the eccentric spelling and printing are barriers to comprehension and enjoyment.

7. de Selincourt, Ernest. "Robert Bridges." In *Oxford Lectures in Poetry*, 207–32. Oxford: The Clarendon Press, 1934.

The Testament of Beauty reveals all that went to make up Bridges's "lofty, distinguished personality." His early poetry, which depicts "the theme of the joy that lives in beauty," shows how he "demanded from poetry . . . a flawless beauty of form and language." Bridges's fame rests on his lyrics, *Eros and Psyche,* and *The Testament of Beauty;* but his dramas are the poorest aspect of his work. The beauty of Bridges's verse is in its rhythmical variations, variations stimulated by his friendship with Hopkins. His "characteristic beauties of rhythm and melody" are brought to perfection in his nature poems, and he is among the finest of the English love poets. "He is essentially the poet of joy, rather than of sorrow, of attainment rather than of unsatisfied longing."

8. de Selincourt, Ernest. *"The Testament of Beauty."* In *Oxford Lectures in Poetry*, 233–56. Oxford: The Clarendon Press, 1934.

"The Testament of Beauty is an imaginative exposition of the spiritual origin and destiny of man," which "reveals the manner in which by the influence of beauty man may rise to a consciousness of his spiritual heritage." Reason may either assist or retard man's progress. The meter of the poem is "a triumph of art" and a "perfect union of sound and sense." "All this is great poetry; our century, at least, has not heard its likes before. . . . What Wordsworth did for the choicer spirits of his own time, Bridges has done for ours."

9. Hearn, Lafcadio. "Bridges." In *A History of English Literature,* 754–55. Tokyo: The Hokuseido Press, 1934.

Bridges, a classical poet with none of the faults of classicism, wrote in the midst of the romantic triumph with "a plain beauty, a simple strength, a cool, clear color, that are simply delightful." His poems on children are his best.

10. Hearn, Lafcadio. "Poems about Children." In *On Poetry*, edited by Ryuji Tanabe, et al., 16–46. Tokyo: Hokuseido Press, 1934.

"Robert Bridges is a very great poet—as great as any English poet now living, with the single exception of Swinburne." Although his poetry is "a little too fine for the common class of reader," it contains "deep and true beauty" which is only apparent after several readings. "On a Dead Child" is "unapproachable" in its pathos. "Pater Filio" and sonnet 39 from *The Growth of Love* are also mentioned.

11. Kunitz, Stanley J. "Robert Bridges." In *Authors Today and Yesterday*, 91–94. New York: H. W. Wilson Co., 1934.

Reprint of 1933.4.

12. Leslie, Shane. Review of *The Letters of Gerard Manley Hopkins to Robert Bridges,* edited by Claude Colleer Abbott. *The Saturday Review of Literature* 11 (1934–35): 449–50.

Bridges, the human counterpart and poetical counterpoint to Hopkins, "learned to write poetry to Hopkins's invisible baton."

13. "The Morality of Beauty." Review of *Collected Essays, Papers, etc. of Robert Bridges,* vol. 8. *Times Literary Supplement,* 6 September 1934, 601.

Bridges, convinced "that the good and the beautiful in human behavior are identical," always defended "complete humanity" and was "by nature incapable of admitting a division between the moral and the aesthetic and the religious."

14. Nowell-Smith, Simon. "Check List of the Works of Robert Bridges." *Book Collector's Quarterly* 16 (1934): 30–40.

Drawn up in connection with the *Cambridge Bibliography of English Literature,* this list goes beyond Mackay's bibliography by including all revised and pirated editions of Bridges's work.

15. "Poetry and Technique." Review of *Collected Essays, Papers, etc. of Robert Bridges,* vol. 7. *Times Literary Supplement,* 24 May 1934, 372.

"The critical quality of the reviews is extraordinarily high," although Bridges perhaps exaggerates the degree of consciousness with which a poet works.

16. Review of *Collected Essays, Papers, etc. of Robert Bridges,* vol. 8. *The Commonweal* 20 (1934): 626.

These critical essays are more valuable than dozens of vastly more imposing tomes.

17. Swinnerton, Frank. "Pre-War Poets." In *The Georgian Scene,* 258–60. New York: Farrar and Rinehart, 1934.

Bridges's work represents "a beautiful vein of pure poetry" that "provides an invaluable link between the old and new." Although he wrote much about "joy," it was always an abstraction and rarely seemed felt on the pulses. His poetry is "the product of genius overlaid by breeding."

1935

1. Abbott, Claude Colleer, ed. "Introduction." In *The Letters of Gerard Manley Hopkins to Robert Bridges.* Vol. 1 of *The Letters of Gerard Manley Hopkins,* xv–xlvii. London: Oxford University Press, 1935.

    This volume contains 117 letters and postcards from Hopkins to Bridges that reveal "the delicate record of a long and fruitful fellowship." Bridges's devotion to Hopkins "was exemplary throughout"; indeed, "it may safely be said that the work of no poet has ever been treated by a contemporary with greater reverence." These letters depict "the attraction and clash of two very different and finely sensitive natures. Of the two Bridges was more sure of his course." For Bridges, despite his religious differences with Hopkins, "poetry is, in itself, a religion." He is "first and always a poet." Volumes 2 and 3 contain scattered references to Bridges.

2. Bridges, Robert. Poems. In *The Golden Book of Modern English Poetry,* edited by Thomas Coldwell, 1–12. London: J. M. Dent and Sons; New York: E. P. Dutton and Co., 1935.

    This anthology includes "Nightingales," "A Passer-By," "On a Dead Child," and "London Snow."

3. Bridges, Robert. Poems. In *The Poet's Tongue,* edited by W. H. Auden and John Garrett, 128, 153–54. London: G. Bell and Sons, 1935.

    This anthology includes "Johannes Milton, Senex" and "November."

4. Gordon, George Stuart. *Poetry and the Moderns.* Inaugural Lecture, Delivered before the University of Oxford on 3 December 1934. Oxford: The Clarendon Press, 1935.

    Bridges's metrical experiments are a precursor of modernism.

5. Johnson, Wingate M. "The Physician in Literature." *Hygeia* 13 (1935): 886–87.

    Bridges is a "scholar's poet." A portrait is included.

6. Lipscomb, Herbert C. "Lucretius and *The Testament of Beauty.*" *The Classic Journal* 31 (1935–36): 77–88.

Cites close moral, aesthetic, and philosophical parallels between Bridges and Lucretius.

7. Millet, Frederick B. "Robert (Seymour) Bridges." In *Contemporary British Literature,* 150–54. New York: Harcourt, Brace and Co., 1935.

    Essentially a reprint that updates the biographical and bibliographical material of previous editions.

8. Stonier, George W. "Books in General." Review of *The Letters of Gerard Manley Hopkins to Robert Bridges,* edited by Claude Colleer Abbott. *The New Statesman and Nation* 9 (1935): 108.

    Contrary to Bridges's opinion, religion did not stifle Hopkins's poetry. Hopkins developed his poetry despite his friendship with Bridges. The relationship of the two poets was a struggle between the genius of Hopkins and the talent of Bridges.

1936

1. Beach, Joseph Warren. "Victorian Afterglow." In *The Concept of Nature in Nineteenth-Century English Poetry,* 524–28. New York: Macmillan, 1936.

    Bridges's poetry is filled with "scientific lore" and is "written with a mild, genial idiosyncracy of thought and expression" which makes it seem "curiously antedilluvian." *Poems in Classical Prosody* and *The Testament of Beauty* are "poetry in form only" whose major weakness is Bridges's vague definition of Beauty. He fails "to make more than a plausible synthesis of his evolutionary positivism and his religious-platonic cult of Eternal Essences." Bridges's effort to be scientific was "betrayed by the loyalty he felt he owed to poetry."

2. Bridges, Robert. Poems. In *Modern British Poetry,* edited by Louis Untermeyer, 104–10. New York: Harcourt, Brace and Co., 1936.

    Reprint of 1930.11.

3. Bridges, Robert. Poems. In *The Oxford Book of Modern Verse, 1892–1935,* edited by W. B. Yeats, 10–17. Oxford: The Clarendon Press, 1936.

    Includes "On a Dead Child," and "Nightingales."

4. Bridges, Robert. Poems. In *Poetry of the Transition: 1850–1914,* edited by Thomas Marc Parrott and Willard Thorpe, 454–69. New York: Oxford University Press, 1936.

    Reprint of 1932.6.

5. Grew, Eva Mary. "*The Testament of Beauty:* A Study of Musical Passages." *The British Musician and Musical News* 13 (1936): 127–20, 154–56, 182–84, 202–4; 14 (1937), 9–10, 35–36.

   Examines the role of music in *The Testament of Beauty.* Bridges's comments on music in the poem "are a glossary to what has been determined concerning this art during the past two thousand and more years."

6. Guerard, Albert, Jr. "Robert Bridges." *The Virginia Quarterly Review* 12 (1926): 354–67.

   Bridges wrote mature poetry from the first. His short lyrics exhibit form and convention, technical excellence, and an avoidance of strained originality. A sense of beauty pervades all. He is without peer as a landscape poet. He has a wider range of feeling, meters, and language than Hopkins, Eliot, or Pound. Bridges is "a more important experimenter than any poet of our time." The Nero plays and *Achilles* deserve a permanent place in English literature. *The Growth of Love* is a miniature *Testament of Beauty.* "Bridges has more to teach us concerning our present literary failings than any writer of the century."

7. Houston, Percy Hazen, and Charles W. Cooper. "Literature of the Last Generation." In *Main Currents of English Literature,* 429. New York: F. S. Crofts and Co., 1936.

   Bridges is "distinguished for purity of form and for his gentle and graceful lyrics." His fame will rest on *The Testament of Beauty.*

8. Jack, Peter Monro. "The Collected Poems of Robert Bridges." Review of *Poetical Works of Robert Bridges,* vol. 2. *New York Times,* 28 June 1936, sect. 6, p. 2, col. 2.

   This second edition adds *October* and *New Verse.* The new poems enhance Bridges's reputation.

9. Parrott, Thomas Marc, and Willard Thorpe. "Robert Bridges." In *Poetry of the Transition: 1850–1914,* 450–54. New York: Oxford University Press, 1936.

   Reprint of 1932.15.

10. "A Poet's Social Vision: Robert Bridges on Democracy and Education." Review of *Collected Essays, Papers, etc. of Robert Bridges,* vol. 10. *Times Literary Supplement,* 26 December 1936, 1065.

    This last volume of Bridges's collected essays represents a prose commentary on *The Testament of Beauty,* and reveals "an authentic Platonist" who ignored the problems of modern industrial society.

11. Read, Herbert. "Gerard Manley Hopkins." In *In Defence of Shelley and Other Essays*, 111–44. London and Toronto: William Heinemann, 1936.

   Despite the fact that Bridges first edited and published Hopkins's poetry, he had no sympathy with Hopkins's poetic ideals and probably did not actually understand the theory of sprung rhythm. The introduction to the 1918 edition of Hopkins's poetry is marked by "pedantic velleity," as though Bridges were dealing with a poet of only minor interest. Bridges's character is marked by pedantry, lack of perception, and conceit, a conceit illustrated by his destruction of his letters to Hopkins to protect his self-image.

12. "Robert Bridges as Music Critic." Review of *The Collected Essays, Papers, etc., of Robert Bridges,* vol. 3. *Times Literary Supplement,* 1 February 1936, 91.

   Bridges writes with unexpected powers of analysis and scholarship while adhering to a clear and consistent aesthetic.

13. Spender, Stephen. "The Sheltered Muse." Review of *Collected Essays, Papers, etc. of Robert Bridges,* vol. 10. *The London Mercury* 35 (1936–37): 334–36.

   "Bridges was a considerable poet" whose writings were "profoundly and continuously affected." He was an "individualist cut off from the life of his time" who imposed an egocentric philosophy on the world around him.

14. Trevanian, Michael (pseud.). "Bridges: *Shorter Poems* (1890)." *Bibliographical Notes and Queries* 2, no. 7 (October 1936): 3.

   Suggests a later printing for *Shorter Poems* (1890).

15. Ward, Alfred Charles. "Poetry." In *Twentieth-Century Literature, 1901–1925,* 6th ed., 104–5. London: Methuen and Co., 1936.

   Reprint of 1928.20.

16. Yeats, W. B. "Introduction." In *The Oxford Book of Modern Verse,* edited by W. B. Yeats, xvii–xviii. Oxford: The Clarendon Press, 1936.

   Bridges seemed "a patron saint" of early aestheticism. His lyric poetry had a new cadence of restrained emotion, a poetry felt more on the nerves than in the blood.

1937

1. Brandl, Leopold. "Robert Bridges' 'Das Vermachtnis der Schonheit.'" *Germanische-Romanische Monatsschrift* 25 (1937): 34–50.

   The theme that runs throughout all of Bridges's writings is the idea that beauty is the motivating goal and purpose of man and culture.

2. Bridges, Robert. Poems. In *British Poetry of the Eighteen-Nineties,* edited by Donald Davidson, 234–43. New York: Doubleday, Doran and Co., 1937.

   Ten poems by Bridges, including "A Passer-By," "London Snow," "Winter Nightfall," "Nightingales," and "I love all beauteous things."

3. Buckley, G. *"The Testament of Beauty." The Parents' Review* 48 (1937): 18–36.

   The Testament of Beauty's inherent weakness is its combination of poetry and philosophy because they arrive at Truth in antithetical ways. Nevertheless, Bridges is a craftsman whose lyrics are "reflective and architectural" and reveal his peculiar virtue of originality. *The Testament of Beauty* is "the first great didactic poem of aesthetic philosophy" and will achieve the permanence of "the great unread."

4. Bush, Douglas. "Robert Bridges (1844–1930)." In *Mythology and the Romantic Tradition in English Poetry,* 433–43. Cambridge: Harvard University Press, 1937.

   A discussion of *Eros and Psyche, Prometheus, The Return of Ulysses, Achilles in Scyros,* and *Demeter.* These works are "the sometimes beautiful mistakes of a born lyricist." Although Bridges intended all of the dramas, except for *Nero,* for stage production, "it is impossible to consider as acting dramas works so defective in stagecraft and characterization." They reveal Bridges's attitude toward life and art long before *The Testament of Beauty* was written. Bridges's quiet classicism and faith in Reason have caused critics who value "gross and violent stimulants" to misjudge his work. He is "academic and traditional in the good as well as the bad sense."

5. Cock, A. A. "Robert Bridges and *The Testament of Beauty* with some References to Gerard Manley Hopkins." *France-Grande-Bretagne,* April 1937, 92–96.

6. Davidson, Donald. "Robert Bridges." In *British Poetry of the*

Eighteen-Nineties, 233–34. New York: Doubleday, Doran and Co., 1937.

There is a "pronounced and consistent interest in classical themes and modes" throughout Bridges's career. Although *Shorter Poems* and *New Poems* are nearer in mood and manner to the 1890s in their adherence to a well-defined aesthetic ideal, Bridges was apart from the tragic generation of the Aesthetes. He experimented within the limits of tradition and was "one of the greatest and most learned of English prosodists."

7. Del Re, Arundell. "Bridges, Plato and the 'Doctrine of Ideas.'" In *The Testament of Beauty*, 155–68. Tokyo: Hokuseido Press, 1937.

Summarizes Plato's "Doctrine of Ideas" and shows their influence on the ideas in *The Testament of Beauty*, with side references to Aristotle. *The Testament of Beauty*, "taken as a whole, might be considered as an extension of Plato's allegory of the cave."

8. Del Re, Arundell. "Commentary." In *The Testament of Beauty*, by Robert Bridges, 81–152. Tokyo: Hokuseido Press, 1937.

Discussion of the philosophical and aesthetic issues alluded to and raised by the poem.

9. Del Re, Arundell. "Preface." In *The Testament of Beauty*, iii–xv. Tokyo: Hokuseido Press, 1937.

Bridges, a "stylist in the truest sense of the word," and one of the most allusive modern poets, ranks with Virgil, Lucretius, and Dante in his ability to link science and philosophy. *The Testament of Beauty*, which is "one of the greatest poems of its kind in Western literature," presents the conclusions reached after critically analyzing man's evolutionary awareness of Beauty through the three aspects of Ethic, Selfhood, and Breed.

10. Hillyer, Robert. "A Laureate's Prose." Review of *Collected Essays, Papers, etc. of Robert Bridges*, vol. 10. *The Saturday Review of Literature* 15 (1937): 16.

The "nervous scream of the italic typography" and the "freakish spelling" are regrettable distractions. The comments on poetry and technique are made by "one of the greatest masters of the art," and reveal a philosophy grounded in experience.

11. Meissner, P. Review of *Poetical Works of Robert Bridges*. *Deutsche Literaturzeitung* 58 (1937): 536–37.

Bridges's strong sense of poetic form may seem un-English; however, his desire to enrich the English language and thus renew the English character is in a long British tradition running from Milton to Arnold.

12. Nowell-Smith, Simon H. "Bridges: *Poems, 1873.*" *Bibliographical Notes and Queries* 2, no. 8 (February 1937): 5.

Suggests more copies of *Poems* (1873) in circulation than commonly supposed.

13. Smith, N[owell] C[harles]. "Bridges, Robert Seymour." *The Dictionary of National Biography, 1922–1930*. edited by J. R. H. Weaver, 115–19. Oxford: The Clarendon Press, 1937.

Biographical sketch.

14. Ward, Alfred Charles. "Robert Bridges: *The Testament of Beauty.*" In *The Nineteen-Twenties: Literature and Ideas in the Post-War Decade*, 3d ed., 80–86. London: Methuen and Co., 1937.

Reprint of 1930.82.

15. Weygandt, Cornelius. "The Old Main Line." In *The Time of Yeats*, 670–77. New York: D. Appleton-Century Co., 1937.

Bridges knew his limits, and the greatness of his work represents "an accomplishment in lyric poetry, narrow in range, but of impeccable artistry, and of a new beauty." He lacks passion, not just the passion of love but any passionate feeling at all. "There are not many 'readings of life' in Bridges." His plays are "untheatrical," but it is by his lyrics that his reputation stands or falls.

16. Winters, Yvor. "Poetic Convention." In *Primitivism and Decadence: A Study of American Experimental Poetry*, 139–41. New York: Arrow Editions, 1937.

Bridges's prosodic theory overlooks the variation of accents and fails to differentiate between accentual-syllabic and syllabic meters; therefore, the meter of *The Testament of Beauty* fails on two counts: there is no limit to the variability of accent in any given line and no established norm for the basis of variation. Despite this, Bridges's adherence to recognized poetic convention and tradition makes him "a finer poet and a saner man" than either Pound or Eliot.

17. Winters, Yvor. "Robert Bridges and Elizabeth Daryush." *The American Review* 8 (1937): 353–67.

Bridges and Hardy are the two most impressive poets since Milton. Of the two, Bridges has greater intellectual scope, artistic diversity, complexity, and richness. He was able "to imbue a simple expository statement of a complex theme with a rich association of feeling, yet with an utterly pure and unmannered style." Unlike Daryush, Bridges's poetry is impersonal, balanced, and intellectual.

18. Winters, Yvor. "Traditional Mastery: The Lyrics of Robert Bridges." In *Literary Opinion in America,* edited by Morton Dauwen Zabel, 237–45. New York: Harper and Brothers, 1937.

Reprint of 1931.25.

1938

1. Batho, Edith Clara, and Bonamy Dobree. "Poetry." In *The Victorians and After, 1830–1914.* Vol. 4 of *Introductions to English and American Literature,* edited by Bonamy Dobree, 70–71 and passim. London: The Cresset Press; New York: Robert M. McBride and Co., 1938.

Although Bridges "lacked the imaginative leap" to transform experience into poetry, he injected a necessary scholarly quality into English poetry. His best work is his lyrics, the best of which are found in *Shorter Poems.* Bridges's work sums up the preceding literary tradition and carries it to its conclusion. His later works are marred by "a somewhat crabbed philosophy."

2. Bridges, Robert. Poem. In *A New Anthology of Modern Poetry,* edited by Selden Rodman, 67. New York: Random House, 1938.

This anthology includes "Johannes Milton, Senex."

3. Bridges, Robert. Poem. In *Understanding Poetry,* edited by Cleanth Brooks and Robert Penn Warren, 198. New York: Henry Holt and Co., 1938.

This anthology contains "Nightingales."

4. Brooks, Cleanth, and Robert Penn Warren. "Nightingales." In *Understanding Poetry,* 198–200. New York: Henry Holt and Co., 1938.

An interpretation of "Nightingales."

5. Guerard, Albert J., Jr. "A Study of the Poetry of Robert Bridges." Ph.D. diss., Stanford University, 1938.

6. Heywood, Terence. "Hopkins and Bridges on Trees." *The Poetry Review* 29–30 (1938–39): 213–18.

Bridges is more eclectic in his use of trees than Words-

worth, but like Wordsworth, spiritual elation and response
to nature are the tenor of much of his tree imagery.

7. Howgate, George W. "In America." In *George Santayana*, 289–
   91. Philadelphia: University of Pennsylvania Press;
   London: Oxford University Press, 1938.

   Bridges's *The Testament of Beauty* shares with Santayana's
   The Life of Reason an evolutionary view of Reason; however,
   Bridges goes further and posits a teleological view of the
   evolutionary process, one that "justifies man's religious in-
   sights." "Bridges's rationalism is brought into line with what
   a good Anglican might expect of his poet laureate."

8. Kunitz, Stanley J. "Robert Bridges." In *Authors Today and Yesterday*, 91–94. New York: H. W. Wilson Co., 1938.

   Reprint of 1933.4.

9. Lahey, G. F., S.J. *Gerard Manley Hopkins*, 16–18. London, New
   York, and Toronto: Oxford University Press, 1938.

   Bridges withheld the publication of Hopkins's poems in
   order to wait for a fit audience for his friend's verse, and it
   is "intolerable that his understanding and sympathy for his
   friend should be questioned."

10. Langdon-Brown, Walter. "Robert Bridges: The Poet of Evolu-
    tion." In *Thus We Are Men*, 152–71. London: Kegan Paul,
    Trench, Trubner and Co., 1938.

    Bridges is "the poet of emergent evolution" who "wished
    his poetry to express the philosophy he acquired from
    natural science in general and from medicine in par-
    ticular." He is "a poet's poet" whose depth and beauty of
    thought appeal to the "ordinary" reader. His broadcast
    Lecture on Poetry is the most succinct statement of his phi-
    losophy. *The Testament of Beauty* is "the rich flowering of a
    generous, cultivated mind which brings a wealth of consola-
    tion and calm to a distraught age."

11. Oberdieck, Wilhelm. "Die Weltanschauung des *Testament of
    Beauty* von Robert Bridges." Ph.D. diss., Gottingen, 1938.

12. Palmer, Herbert. "Robert Bridges and Some Others." In *Post-
    Victorian Poetry*, 53–61. London: J. M. Dent and Sons, 1938.

    Unlike Housman and Hardy, Bridges advanced in poetic
    technique and lost little in poetic content or vision. His best
    volumes of poetry are *October* and *New Verse*. Although
    Bridges emphasized the necessity of discovering new
    rhythms, he was inclined to exaggerate the importance of
    form. His knowledge of Greek and Latin prosody makes

him "possibly the most Greek of all our poets." "Though Bridges was lacking in lyrical passion, as also in sudden inspiration and fluency, he made up for nearly everything by his intellectual ardor, his vision, his sensitiveness, his diligent concentration, and his metrical learning."

13. Rodman, Selden. "Biographical Notes." In *A New Anthology of Modern Poetry,* 416–17. New York: Random House, 1938.

The bulk of Bridges's work is pedantic and patterned on classical models. His lyrics and *The Testament of Beauty* are distinguished by "conventional, pietistic subject-matter." Bridges discovered Hopkins but did not understand his genius.

1939

1. Binyon, Laurence. "Gerard Hopkins and His Influence." *The University of Toronto Quarterly* 8 (1939): 264–70.

Bridges is to be credited for gradually introducing Hopkins's poetry to the public. Although less revolutionary, Bridges was Hopkins's disciple and was the first to accustom English ears to the rhythms of the new prosody.

2. Bridges, Robert. Poem. In *The New Modern American and British Poetry,* edited by Louis Untermeyer, 288–89. New York: Harcourt, Brace and Co., 1939.

Includes "Winter Nightfall."

3. Eaker, J. Gordon. "Robert Bridges' Concept of Nature." *Publications of the Modern Language Association* 54 (1939): 1181–97.

Bridges reconciles the natural order with the moral order in nature. Beauty in nature is the vehicle by which man, with his use of reason, comes to an understanding or awareness of the reality of goodness or God. "How the Reason learned to choose the best [in nature] is the subject of *The Testament of Beauty.*"

4. Elton, Oliver. "Robert Bridges and *The Testament of Beauty.*" In *Essays and Addresses,* 70–91. London: Edward Arnold and Co., 1939.

Reprint of 1932.9

5. Jackson, Holbrook. "Robert Bridges." In *The Printing of Books,* 99–108. New York: Scribners, 1939.

Although not a printing reformer or revivalist, Bridges's interest in printing influenced the Daniel Press and Oxford

University Press's use of Fell type. His beautiful typographic designs are an invitation to read and to be read correctly. In general, Bridges let simple yet gracious type act as the medium between himself and the reader. The notable exception, however, is *The Yattendon Hymnal* (1899). The most satisfying of all the books which came under his typographical influence is *The Poems of Digby Mackworth Dolben* (1911).

1940

1. Bradley, Henry. Letters. In *Correspondence of Robert Bridges and Henry Bradley, 1900–1923*. Oxford: The Clarendon Press, 1940.

    Forty-nine letters and postcards to Bridges, mostly on technical philological matters.

2. "Bridges—Bradley." *Times Literary Supplement,* 22 June 1940, 297.

    The Bodleian Library announces the acquisition of the correspondence between Bridges and Bradley.

3. Bridges, Robert. Poem. In *Types of English Poetry,* edited by Rudolf Kork and Clara Marburg Kirk, 477–78. New York: Macmillan, 1940.

    Includes "I will not let thee go."

4. Bridges, Robert. Poems. In *English Poetry of the Nineteenth Century,* edited by George R. Elliott and Norman Foerster, 648. New York: Macmillan, 1940.

    Reprint of 1923.2.

5. Daiches, David. "Hardy–Housman–Hopkins." In *Poetry and the Modern World: A Study of Poetry in English between 1900– 1939,* 22–23. Chicago: University of Chicago Press, 1940.

    Bridges is "a scholarly and cultured poet whose work combines ethical interests with a connoisseur's mild experimentations in language." Although his technical experiments are not of great importance, the body of his work is important because it represents "the graceful petering-out of an important tradition in English poetry—the Neo-Platonic tradition."

6. Evans, Benjamin Ifor. "Towards the Twentieth Century: Gerard Manley Hopkins and T. S. Eliot." In *Tradition and Romanticism: Studies in English Poetry from Chaucer to W. B.*

Yeats, 187–92. London: Methuen and Co.; New York: Longmans, Green and Co., 1940.

A discussion of Hopkins's poetry and poetic theories that draws upon Hopkins's letters to Bridges to reveal Bridges's limited sympathy for Hopkins's experiments.

7. Green, Andrew J. "Robert Bridges: Studies in His Work and Thought to 1904." Ph.D. diss., University of Michigan, 1940.

8. Guerard, Albert, Jr. "The Dates of Some of Robert Bridges' Lyrics." *Modern Language Notes* 55 (1940): 199–200.

Fixes the dates of composition for fifty-eight poems in manuscript form, and transcribes and dates the composition of the fifty-three poems in *Poems* (1873).

9. Morgan, Charles. "The End of the Turmoil: *The Spirit of Man.*" Review of *The Spirit of Man,* by Robert Bridges. *The Spectator* 164 (1940): 807.

Bridges saw and understood the continuity of the German philosophy, which has led their civilization twice in a generation to wage war in Europe. *The Spirit of Man* "is a manual of civilization as we understand and hope to live it."

10. Nowell-Smith, Simon. Review of *Correspondence of Robert Bridges and Henry Bradley, 1900–1923. English* 3 (1940–41): 138.

The letters show "Bridges, the poet, of magnificent presence, willful, but of sound and penetrating judgment, self-assured but eager for sympathy."

11. Review of *Correspondence of Robert Bridges and Henry Bradley. Notes and Queries* 179 (1940): 53–54.

Bridges sought and valued Bradley's opinion.

12. "Robert Bridges and Henry Bradley." Review of *Correspondence of Robert Bridges and Henry Bradley, 1900–1923. Times Literary Supplement,* 22 June 1940, 304.

Reveals much about Bridges's prejudices about some contemporaries, and also much about his later poems and his experiments in quantitative verse.

13. Smith, Nowell Charles. *Notes on the Testament of Beauty.* 3d ed. Oxford: Oxford University Press, 1940.

Reprint of 1931.21.

14. Ward, Alfred Charles. "Poetry." In *Twentieth-Century Literature, 1901–1940,* 7th ed., rev. and enl., 139–42. London: Methuen and Co.; New York: Longmans, Green and Co., 1940.

Essentially a reprint of 1928.20 that updates material on Bridges and includes a discussion of *The Testament of Beauty* taken from Ward's *The Nineteen-Twenties* (see 1930.82).

1941

1. Adams, Charles M. "Robert Bridges' First Edition." *American Notes and Queries* 1, no. 3 (June 1941): 40–41.
   Wonders how many copies of *Poems* (1873) exist.

2. Bridges, Robert. Poem. In *Reading Poems: An Introduction to Critical Study,* edited by Wright Thomas and Stuart Gerry Brown, 82. New York: Oxford University Press, 1941.
   Includes "Nightingales."

3. Bridges, Robert. Poems. In *The Viking Book of Poetry of the English-Speaking World,* 2 vols., edited by Richard Aldington, 2:1063–65. New York: The Viking Press, 1941.
   Includes "Pater Filio," "I love all beauteous things," and "On a Dead Child."

4. Cecil, David, Lord. *The English Poets,* 44–45. London: Adprint, 1941.
   Compares Bridges and Yeats. Bridges began as a smooth lyricist writing in a traditional manner. He ended his career as a philosophic poet writing in an austere, experimental manner in *The Testament of Beauty.* His view of life was based on a belief in the absolute value of art and the worship of serene beauty.

5. Fleming, Thomas P. "Bibliographical Note on Bridges' 'A Case of Thickening Cranial Bones, 1879.'" *Papers of the Bibliographical Society of America* 35 (1941): 161.
   Cites an article by Bridges not recorded in McKay's bibliography.

6. Green, Andrew J. "Bridges' Odes for Music." *Sewanee Review* 49 (1941): 30–38.
   "A Hymn to Nature" and "Ode to Music" are "symphonic" poems that epitomize Bridges's philosophy and depict music as "one of the chief avenues of artistic beauty by which man attains spiritual redemption." The poems were "conceived in music and exist in music"; their verse and movement follow an internal conceptualized symphony.

7. Holmes, Oliver Wendell. Letters. In *Holmes-Pollock Letters,* 2 vols., edited by Mark DeWolfe Howe, 2:261–64. Cambridge: Harvard University Press, 1941.

Holmes objects to "the faint rhythms" and archaisms of *The Testament of Beauty* and feels the poem depicts "the Cosmos arranged to suit polite English taste."

8. Mackay, James. "The Religion of Robert Bridges." *The Expository Times* (1941): 300–3.

The religious view found in *The Testament of Beauty* combines Platonism and Christianity.

9. M., D. "Bridges: *Poems, 1873*." *Bibliographical Notes and Queries* 2, no. 11 (June 1941): 3.

The Pickering and Company catalog of 1878 lists Bridges's *Poems* (1873), and copies of the volume were still on hand when Pickering was purchased by Thomas Chatto in 1886.

10. Pollock, Sir Frederick. Letters. In *Holmes-Pollock Letters*, 2 vols., edited by Mark DeWolfe Howe, 2:261–64. Cambridge: Harvard University Press, 1941.

The Testament of Beauty is "the only great philosophical poem . . . in the English language." There is nothing like it as far back as Lucretius's *De Rerum Natura* for an intimate knowledge and love of nature, and the combination of scientific training and the humanity of a scholar.

1942

1. Bridges, Robert. Poems. In *Modern British Poetry*, edited by Louis Untermeyer, 54–60. New York: Harcourt, Brace and Co., 1942.

Reprint of 1930.11.

2. Bridges, Robert. Poems. In *A Treasury of Great Poems*, edited by Louis Untermeyer, 381–83. New York: Simon and Schuster, 1942.

This anthology includes "Nightingales" and "London Snow."

3. Fox, Adam. "English Landscape in Robert Bridges." *English* 4 (1942): 74–79.

Bridges communicates moods in his poetry by accurately describing particular landscapes. His early poems are more detached; he often uses rivers and clouds to objectify human emotions. In his later poems the landscape serves more as background, and there is a keener focus on flowers.

4. Guerard, Albert Joseph, Jr. *Robert Bridges: A Study of Tradi-*

tionalism in Poetry. Cambridge: Harvard University Press, 1942.

Bridges is "one of the most impressive as well as one of the most serious poets of the last hundred years." His poetry can be divided into three classes: lyric poetry, dramatic poetry, and philosophical poetry. The discussion of the lyrics outlines Bridges's concept of love, sense of taste, and view of life. After tracing the publishing history, critical reception, and literary influences on the lyrics, Guerard praises Bridges's "masterly control of the material," which sets him apart from his contemporaries and places him in the classical tradition. The primary virtue of Bridges's historical dramas lies in their character development. The discussion of the philosophical poetry focuses on *The Testament of Beauty.*

5. Tindall, William York. "The Robert Bridges Collection." *Columbia University Quarterly* 33 (1942): 154–58.

Frederick Coykendall donated his Robert Bridges collection to the Columbia University Library. This collection is the basis of McKay's *Bibliography of Robert Bridges* (see 1933.6). Bridges is as Victorian as Hardy and Arnold and as modern as Eliot. As a modern classicist and Neoplatonist, Bridges has "hidden the wasteland" from view and imposed an illusion of order upon the world, but this is a natural response to the times.

6. Untermeyer, Louis. "Robert Bridges." In *A Treasury of Great Poems,* 381. New York: Simon and Schuster, 1942.

Although Bridges's ideas were direct and his emotions were simple, he remained unpopular because his preoccupation with meter led him to write verses too subtle for wide appreciation. He was a "cold classicist" who wrote poetry that was characterized by "serenity," "fastidiousness," and "a persistently sweet strain of music."

7. Ward, Alfred Charles. "Poetry." In *Twentieth-Century Literature, 1901–1940,* 139–42. 8th ed. London: Methuen and Co., Ltd., 1942.

Reprint of 1940.14.

1943

1. Bevan, Bryan. "The Poetry of Robert Bridges." *The Poetry Review* 34 (1943): 235–38.

Bridges's chief qualities as a poet are his refined taste, classicism, sense of beauty, and joy in Nature. The plays have "great dramatic power." *The Growth of Love* is extremely mature and exhibits a Keatsian religion of love. In *Shorter Poems,* love is less elusive. *October* and *New Verse* reflect Bridges's growing interest in language and experimentation. *The Testament of Beauty* is a reasoned aesthetic of life and a rare example of a great didactic poem. Bridges's reputation will grow, but he will never be universally popular.

2. Church, Richard. "Robert Bridges." In *British Authors: A Twentieth-Century Gallery with Fifty-Three Portraits,* 15–17. London: Longmans, Green and Co., 1943.

    Bridges was "a kind of English literary figure which changing social conditions tend to make more and more rare." His "austere, water-clear verse had an appeal only to the few," and his views of the economic inequalities of society were "picturesque, rather than deeply felt."

3. Clough, H. Charles. "The 'Unpopularity' of Robert Bridges." *The Poetry Review* 34 (1943): 318–19.

    Lists fourteen reasons for Bridges's unpopularity.

4. "Experiment and Discipline." *Times Literary Supplement,* 28 August 1943, 415.

    Bridges's limited success experimenting with quantitative verse laid the foundation for *The Testament of Beauty.*

5. Hone, Joseph. "Dramatis Personae: Lady Gregory." In *W. B. Yeats, 1865–1939,* 141–44 and passim. New York and London: Macmillan, 1943.

    Bridges, who was one of the "few men whom Yeats liked for themselves alone," admired Yeats's gift of poetry and humor. Yeats wanted to produce Bridges's plays.

6. Hutchinson, F. E. "Bridges's Classical Prosody." Letter. *Times Literary Supplement,* 11 September 1943, 444.

    Supports Nowell-Smith's claim that the date for Bridges's recorded experimentation in quantitative verse should be moved up.

7. Nowell–Smith, Simon. "Bridges's Classical Prosody: *New Verse* and Variants." *Times Literary Supplement,* 28 August 1943, 410.

    Letters from Henry Bradley and poems in the Muirhead manuscript establish 1901–5 as the earliest date of Bridges's recorded experimentation in quantitative verse.

8. Nowell–Smith, Simon. "Thoughts on Laurence Binyon's Poetry." *English* 4 (1943): 143–46.

    Bridges introduced Binyon to Hopkins's poetry during a

visit to Yattendon. Bridges is more adventurous in prosody and more objective in subject matter than Binyon.

9. R., B. "Andrew Lang on Robert Bridges." *Notes and Queries* 185 (1943): 376–77.

Credits Lang with being "the first to salute the poetry of Robert Bridges."

1944

1. Green, Andrew J. "Robert Bridges and the Spiritual Animal." *The Philosophical Review* 53 (1944): 286–95.

Examines the philosophical coherence of Bridges's attempt to reconcile naturalism and idealism, a reconciliation that "appears as a potpourri, not as an integration, of philosophy." *The Testament of Beauty* falls short of being an organic and whole poem. Any judgment of Bridges as a poet must be conditioned by a corresponding judgment of him as a thinker. "Bridges will be esteemed for his lyrical and critical gifts, and for the beauty of certain aspects of his thought, not for the coherence and acceptability of his philosophy."

2. Knopf, Kamilla. "Robert Bridges und die englische Sprache." *Anglia* 67–68 (1944): 353–448.

3. Looker, Samuel J. "Andrew Lang and Robert Bridges." *Notes and Queries* 186 (1944): 57.

Quotes from Sir Algernon West's *Private Diaries* to show that others besides Lang were early enthusiasts of Bridges's poetry.

4. Price, Fannie. "G. M. Hopkins on Robert Bridges." *Notes and Queries* 186 (1944): 49.

Quotes a letter from Hopkins to Bridges encouraging Bridges in his work.

5. "Robert Bridges." *Times Literary Supplement*, 28 October 1944, 523.

Bridges has had a wide and sustained influence in literature, criticism, lexicography, handwriting, and vocabulary sound. He was a promoter of "whatever was eternally beautiful," and his style exhibited a similar "timelessness and permanence."

6. "Robert Bridges: A Centenary Criticism." *Times Literary Supplement*, 28 October 1944, 524.

Bridges was poetically mature from the start; all of his

poems were of an even quality. He was an innovator within tradition. *The Testament of Beauty,* his longest and metrically most adventurous poem, shows his mastery of invention.

7. Thompson, Edward. *Robert Bridges: 1844–1930.* London: Oxford University Press, 1944.

This critical study omits "all that is biographical, unless it illustrates the poet's personality or work, or comes under the head of essential outline and framework." Thompson praises the *Shorter Poems* (1890) for their organic unity of theme and their metrical and rhythmical innovations, "the triumphant marriage of speech-rhythms with traditional forms." Bridges's dramas and poems on classical themes exhibit technical skill and beauty but lack of genuine emotion and significant philosophical content. The concluding discussion of *The Testament of Beauty* likens it to *The Prelude.* In general Bridges's poetry is to be applauded for its simplicity and clarity of description but faulted for a lack of compassion and intellectual depth: "if Bridges had possessed more intellectual curiosity and had acknowledged a wider range of ideas, even heretical and subversive ideas, as being at least of interest, he would have been a still greater poet."

1945

1. Bridges, Robert. Poems. In *Poems of Our Time,* edited by Richard Church and Mildred Bozman, 63–65. London: J. M. Dent and Sons, 1945.

Includes "Flycatchers" and "Cheddar Pinks."

2. Bridges, Robert. Poems. In *Poet Physicians,* edited by Mary Lou McDonough, 91–93. Springfield, Il.: Charles C. Thomas; Toronto: The Ryerson Press, 1945.

Includes "Fortunatus Nimium," "On a Dead Child," and "When death to either shall come."

3. Bridges, Robert. Poems. In *Poet to Poet,* edited by Houston Petersen and William S. Lynch, 44–45. New York: Prentice-Hall, 1945.

Includes excerpts from *The Testament of Beauty.*

4. Church, Richard. "The Chemistry of Time." *The Fortnightly Review* 163 (1945): 194–200.

Bridges is a disturbing paradox, disturbing because, although he espouses the brotherhood of man, his attitudes are distinctly undemocratic.

5. McDonough, Mary Lou. "Robert Bridges." In *Poet Physicians*, 91. Springfield, Il.: Charles C Thomas; Toronto: The Ryerson Press, 1945.

   A biographical sketch emphasizing Bridges's medical career.

1946

1. Bridges, Robert. Poem. In *Collected English Verse*, edited by Margaret Bottrall and Ronald Bottrall, 495–96. London: Sidgwick and Jackson, 1946.

   Includes "A Passer-By."

2. Bridges, Robert. Poems. In *A Little Treasury of Modern Poetry*, edited by Oscar Williams, 106 and passim. New York: Charles S. Scribner's Sons, 1946.

   Includes "The idle life I lead," "I hear a linnet courting," "Nightingales," and "A Passer-By."

3. Gordon, George Stuart. "Gerard Manley Hopkins and Robert Bridges." In *The Discipline of Letters*, 168–84. Oxford: The Clarendon Press, 1946.

   Hopkins's fame derives from Bridges's "patient and understanding loyalty," but Hopkins's Catholicism "was a barrier which by its nature would never be wholly removed." As a result "the range of their friendship, though never the force of their affection, was proportionately restricted." They were brought together by poetry. "Nothing is more notable in Robert Bridges's long life than his care for his friends while living and for their memory when dead."

4. Gordon, George Stuart. *Robert Bridges*. The Rede Lecture, 1931. Cambridge: Cambridge University Press, 1946.

   Examines the importance of Bridges's formative years and focuses on the autobiographical aspects of his literary and artistic evolution. Bridges's reading at Eton and Oxford, especially his reading of Ovidian elegies, influenced his sense of craftsmanship, form, language, and control. This classical influence largely accounts for the apparent lack of emotion in Bridges's poetry. The absolute unity of meaning and form is the characteristic attribute of all of Bridges's work. From his work as a linguist and grammarian to his work as a poet, "no man was more steadily true to himself."

5. Grierson, Herbert John C., and J. C. Smith. "The Nineties."

In *A Critical History of English Poetry,* 512–16. New York: Oxford University Press, 1946.

Bridges was a conscious and careful artist who wrote in the classical tradition and sought to restore a sense of the quantity of syllables to English poetry. He wrote about the value of love, moments in Nature, human joy and sorrow, and Beauty. *The Testament of Beauty,* which illustrates Bridges's faith in Beauty as "the inspiring and guiding force in human progress," is comparable with *De Rerum Natura* but lacks Lucretius's "deeper strain of feeling."

6. Laird, John. "Robert Bridges and *The Testament of Beauty.*" In *Philosophical Incursions into English Literature,* 205–23. Cambridge: Cambridge University Press, 1946.

    The Testament of Beauty deals with the spiritual habitat of the human soul. Although unevenly argued, "there is grandeur in the philosophy of the *Testament,* and an approach to greatness in much of its poetry."

7. Sassoon, Siegfried. *Siegfried's Journey, 1916–1920,* 140–43. New York: Viking Press, 1946.

    Recounts Sassoon's first meeting with Bridges. He found Bridges in "one of his grumpiest moods" and judged him to be "proud, self-conscious, and often aggressively intolerant; but in his writings [Bridges] showed splendid control of self and spirit, undeviating devotion to his art, and the gracious purity of one who 'uttered nothing base.'"

8. Stauffer, Donald Alfred. "Poetry is Concret." In *The Nature of Poetry,* 136–38. New York: W. W. Norton and Co., 1946.

    Cites a description of an English garden in a passage from *The Testament of Beauty* to show how Bridges directly presents the flower odors by dwelling on the physical description and sight of the flowers, hoping to revive the odor in the mind of the reader.

1947

1. Jackson, Holbrook. "Robert Bridges." In *The Printing of Books,* 99–108. London: Cassell, 1947.

    Reprint of 1939.5.

2. M., M. "The First Poems of Robert Bridges." *More Books,* 6th ser., 22 (1947): 70.

    A recently acquired edition of *Poems* (1873) contained a letter from Bridges to Elkins Mathews requesting a copy of

Laurence Binyon's new book of verse, probably *The Praise of Life*.

3. Nowell–Smith, Simon. "The Phonotypes of Robert Bridges." *Alphabet and Image* 5 (1947): 30–42.

Bridges's difficulty in employing classical meters in English prosody led him to develop phonetic fonts. His use of old fonts to print English in a more phonetic type reflects his dual habit of mind: traditional and innovative. Traces Bridges's interest in phonetic fonts.

4. Stauffer, Donald A. "Poetry as Symbolic Thinking." *The Saturday Review of Literature* 30.12 (22 March 1947): 9–10.

Poetry welds philosophy and concrete particulars into poetic vision. *The Testament of Beauty* fails because it is "too much of a philosophical argument to which illustrations are fitted."

5. Tindall, William York. "Right." In *Forces in Modern British Literature, 1885–1946*, 104–5. New York: Alfred A. Knopf, 1947.

Bridges, a poet steeped in classicism, "produced poems of almost incredible emptiness." Although the Platonism of *The Testament of Beauty* ignores the problem of evil and turns its back on modern life, the poem itself gives "suitable expression to the humanism of the middle class."

1948

1. Bridges, Robert. Poems. In *The Golden Book of English Poetry*, edited by Thomas Caldwell, 1–12. London: J. M. Dent and Sons; New York: E. P. Dutton and Co., 1948.
   Reprint of 1935.2.

2. Chew, Samuel C. "Other Late-Victorian Poets." In *A Literary History of England*, edited by Albert Baugh et al., 1538–40. New York and London: Appleton-Century Crofts, 1948.

The best of Bridges's art is "gay," and the lyrics found in *Shorter Poems* represent his best work. The dramas are wasted effort. Although *The Testament of Beauty*, which was the final result of his metrical experimentation and Hopkins's influence, initially received a popular public reception, the modern reassessment of the poem has been less enthusiastic.

3. Church, Richard. "Robert Bridges." In *British Authors: A Twentieth-Century Gallery with Fifty-Three Portraits*, New ed., 15–

17. London: Longmans, Green and Co., Ltd., 1948.
      Reprint of 1943.2.

4. Gardner, W. H. "Introduction to the Third Edition." In *Poems of Gerard Manley Hopkins*, 3d ed., xii–xxvi. London: Oxford University Press, 1948.
      Approves Bridges's handling of Hopkins's poetry but questions some of his critical judgments about the verse.

5. Marchand, Leslie A. "The Symington Collection." *The Journal of the Rutgers University Library* 12 (1948): 1–15.
      The Symington Collection contains several manuscript letters of Bridges.

6. Nowell–Smith, Simon. "A Poet in Walton Street." In *Essays Mainly on the Nineteenth Century*, edited by G. F. J. Cumberlege, 58–71. London, New York, and Toronto: Oxford University Press, 1948.
      An account of the printing history of Bridges's work and his long association with the Oxford University Press.

7. Patmore, Derek. "Coventry Patmore and Robert Bridges: Some Letters." *The Fortnightly Review* 169 (1948): 196–204.
      Seven letters from Bridges to Patmore on subjects ranging from publishing and reviews to works in progress, with special mention of *Prometheus, Eros and Psyche, Nero,* and *Ulysses.* The letters show Bridges as a struggling poet.

8. Routh, Harold Victor. "The Crisis in English Poetry and Its Would-Be Reformers." In *English Literature and Ideas in the Twentieth Century*, 109–11. New York: Longmans, Green and Co., 1948.
      Bridges's output was "sustained and prolific," his odes and lyrics being the most notable aspect of his work. *The Testament of Beauty* is "one of the most revealing and characteristic documents of the twentieth century," but it is marred by digressions, discontinuities, archaisms, and idiosyncratic spelling.

9. Thompson, Francis. "Mr. Bridges and Metre." In *Literary Criticisms*, edited by Terence L. Connolly, 289–91. New York: E. P. Dutton, 1948.
      Reprint of 1902.9.

10. Winters, Yvor. "A Foreword." In *Elizabeth Daryush: Selected Poems*, ix–xiv. New York: The Swallow Press and William Morrow and Co., 1948.
      "Dr. Bridges was one of the greatest of all the English poets and one of the most remarkable of English metrists,"

but he never fully succeeded with his syllabic meter. The twelve-syllable line of *The Testament of Beauty* is "awkwardly long," primarily because of Bridges's scheme of elision for the eye and his doing away with rhyme. This resulted in the disappearance of the syllabic pattern in the poem. The poem's rhythm is achieved by "a more or less regular but unplanned pattern of accents."

11. Winters, Yvor. "The Poetry of Gerard Manley Hopkins." *The Hudson Review* 1 (1948): 455–76.

    Bridges's "Low Barometer" is superior to poems by Donne and Hopkins because it is a generalized description of a common human experience. It is general yet precise and has "the dignity of conviction."

1949

1. Bridges, Robert. Poems. In *The London Book of English Verse,* edited by Herbert Read and Bonamy Dobree, 379–81. New York: Macmillan, 1949.

    This anthology includes "London Snow" and "After the Gale."

2. Bullough, Geoffrey. "Inheritance of the Twentieth Century." In *The Trend of Modern Poetry,* 12–15. Edinburgh and London: Oliver and Boyd, 1949.

    Reprint of 1934.5.

3. Cooke, John D., and Lionel Stevenson. "Robert Bridges." In *English Literature of the Victorian Period,* 197–99. New York: Appleton–Century–Crofts, 1949.

    Although he was not widely known when he became poet laureate, Bridges's personal integrity and the quiet beauty of his poems won him gradual respect. His poems can be divided into two categories: lyrics of simple language and easy grace, and learned and philosophical poems with symbolic references to modern topics.

4. Del Re, Arundell. "Introductory Note." In *The Testament of Beauty,* iii–vi. Tokyo: Hokuseido Press, 1949.

    For post-war Japan, the message of *The Testament of Beauty* has special significance, especially because of the historical importance of the concept of Beauty in Japanese culture.

5. Graves, Robert. "The Unpopularity of Modernist Poetry." In *The Common Asphodel: Collected Essays on Poetry, 1922–1949,* 100–101 and passim. London: Hamilton, 1949.

Bridges rejects Hopkins and others like him for "a daring which makes the poet socially rather than artistically objectionable."

6. Rusche, Ina Maria. "Studien uber den Lyriker Robert Bridges und seine Zeit." Ph.D. diss., Freie, 1949.

7. Stewart, J. I. M. "Falstaff on Boar's Hill." In *Character and Motive in Shakespeare: Some Recent Appraisals Examined,* 11–39. London: Longmans, Green, 1949.

    Bridges's analysis of Shakespeare's art and the influence of the audience is naive. "Bridges, a poet incapable of popular appeal or of drawing strength from a common life around him, sees Shakespeare as straitened and degraded by concessions and compromises, where there is, in fact, very often true dramatic insight and energy" in the dramatist's use of obscenity and coarseness.

8. Tennyson, Charles. "1862–1863." In *Alfred Tennyson,* 344–45. New York: Macmillan, 1949.

    Relates the story of Bridges's mistake regarding a picture of Tennyson, which he believed the latter had sent to him.

1950

1. Baines, Arnold H. J. "Robert Bridges: A Source." *Notes and Queries* 195 (1950): 478.

    A song by James Newton is a possible source for Bridges's "Anniversary."

2. Bateson, Frederick W. "The Primacy of Meaning." In *English Poetry: A Critical Introduction,* 13–14. London: Longmans, Green and Co., 1950.

    Cites Bridges's essay on "Poetic Diction" (1923) as an example of the prevalence of romantic poetic theory, specifically the discarding of meaning, which is at the root of modern poetic theory.

3. Batho, Edith Clara, and Bonamy Dobree. "Poetry." In *The Victorians and After, 1830–1914.* Vol. 4 of *Introductions to English Literature,* 2d ed., rev., edited by Bonamy Dobree, 69, 241–42. London: The Cresset Press, 1950.

    Reprint of 1938.1. Updates the scholarship on Bridges.

4. Beach, Joseph Warren. "Turn of the Century." In *A History of English Literature,* edited by Hardin Craig, 590. New York: Oxford University Press, 1950.

    Bridges's metrical innovations enlarged the scope of

modern poetry. *The Testament of Beauty* is "an interesting philosophical experiment," but it is not embraced by contemporary thinkers. "Bridges' poetry has charm and subtlety, but very low poetic intensity."

5. Bridges, Robert. Poem. In *Poems in English: 1530–1940*, edited by David Daiches and William Charvat, 573. New York: The Ronald Press Co., 1950.

    This anthology contains "London Snow."

6. Bridges, Robert. Poems. In *Poems of Our Time*, edited by Richard Church and Mildred Bozman, 63–65. London: J. M. Dent and Sons, 1950.

    Reprint of 1945.1.

7. Bridges, Robert. Poems. In *Understanding Poetry*, edited by Cleanth Brooks and Robert Penn Warren, 94, 559. New York: Henry Holt and Co., 1950.

    This anthology includes "Nightingales" and "Low Barometer."

8. Brooks, Cleanth, and Robert Penn Warren. "Nightingales." In *Understanding Poetry*, 95–97. New York: Henry Holt and Co., 1950.

    Reprint of 1938.4.

9. Bush, Douglas. "Modern Science and Modern Poetry." In *Science and English Poetry: A Historical Sketch, 1590–1950*, 156–57. New York: Oxford University Press, 1950.

    The Testament of Beauty, "though it was the most ambitious successor to *In Memoriam* . . . can hardly sustain the parallel or remain an equivalent landmark in modern poetry" because "the facts of human nature seem too readily submissive to the harmonious moulds of ideal reason and beauty." It is "a piece of aloof, archaic, and often beautiful unreality."

10. Charney, Maurice. "A Bibliographical Study of Hopkins' Criticism, 1918–1949." *Thought* 25 (1950): 297–326.

    Much Hopkins criticism has come about in an effort to defend Hopkins against the three criticisms made by Bridges in the introduction to *Poems of Gerard Manley Hopkins*. Bridges criticized Hopkins's extravagant style, obscurity of meaning, and religious overtones.

11. Gordon, George Stuart. "Robert Bridges." In *Lives of Authors*, 185–202. London: Chatto and Windus, 1950.

    See 1946.4.

12. Grierson, Herbert John Clifford. "The Nineties." In *Lyrical*

Poetry of the Nineteenth Century, 129–32. London: The Hogarth Press, 1950.

   Reprint of 1928.10.

13. Heath–Stubbs, John. "Beyond Aestheticism." In *The Darkling Plain,* 181–88. London: Eyre and Spottiswoode, 1950.

   Although Bridges avoided modern influences, much of his poetry bears the characteristic marks of the Aesthetic movement. His early poetry is "entirely decorative and melodious in character." *The Testament of Beauty* depicts reality through the æsthetic experience; the whole argument of the poem evolves from man's response to Beauty. It is not a great philosophical poem because it is founded upon a limited conception of Beauty. Bridges's poetry shows no consciousness of the "abysses of passion and evil which surround man" and is "thin and unreal" when read against the background of modern Europe. It is the quintessential example of what happened to the English literary tradition in the twentieth century.

14. Hillyer, Robert. "Diction." In *First Principles in Verse,* 14. Boston: The Writer, 1950.

   Quotes "The evening darkens over" as an example of diction that rises to a dramatic climax. "London Snow" is one of the few great poems in terza rima in English.

15. Treneer, Anne. "The Criticism of Gerard Manley Hopkins." In *Penguin New Writing, No. 40,* edited by John Lehmann, 98–115. Harmondsworth, England: Penguin Books, 1950.

   Compares reading habits, poetic theories, literary judgments, and mutual influences of Bridges and Hopkins. Bridges had better critical judgment than Hopkins and was "an altogether more dispassionate critic."

1951

1. Batho, Edith Clara, and Bonamy Dobree. "Poetry." In *The Victorians and After, 1830–1914.* Vol. 4 of *Introductions to English Literature,* 2d ed., rev., edited by Bonamy Dobree, 69, 241–42. New York: Dover Publications, 1951.

   Reprint of 1938.1. Updates scholarship on Bridges.

2. Bridges, Robert. Poems. In *Modern Poetry: American and British,* edited by Kimon Friar and John Malcolm Brinnin, 22–26. New York: Appleton-Century-Crofts, 1951.

   Includes "Poor Poll," "Nightingales," and "The storm is over."

3. Cohen, J. M. "The Road Not Taken: A Study in the Poetry of Robert Bridges." *The Cambridge Journal* 4 (1951): 555–64.

Bridges will be remembered as a romantic poet with poetic roots in the Elizabethan age, his childhood, the English landscape, and marriage. Poems on other subjects in experimental meters lack emotion. Despite his apparent classicism, he "had no vital link with the classical past." His poetic peaks, the lyrics and the later poems (excepting *The Testament of Beauty*), owe their greatness to Bridges's romantic aesthetic founded on Beauty and Platonism.

4. Patmore, Coventry. Letter. In "Three Poets Discuss New Verse Forms," by Derek Patmore. *The Month* n.s. 6 (1951): 74.

In a letter to Hopkins, Patmore compliments the "pure style" and "high finish" of Bridges's *Prometheus*.

5. Patmore, Derek. "Three Poets Discuss New Verse Forms." *The Month* n.s. 6 (1951): 69–78.

Letters of Bridges, Hopkins, and Patmore regarding experiments in verse. Includes three letters from Bridges to Patmore. Poetic experiments of Victorian poets like these prepared the way for modern English poetry.

6. Pinto, Vivian de Sola. "Hopkins and Bridges." In *Crisis in English Poetry, 1880–1940*, 59–84. London: Hutchinson's University Library, 1951.

Bridges is "not a poet of the modern crisis" but rather the "last authentic example of the aristocratic Victorian artist in verse." His early lyrics are remarkable for their "fastidious delicacy of form" and avoidance of modern influences. Bridges is an explorer of neither the inner life nor the outer life but rather "an exquisite craftsman in verse with a peculiar gift for verbal melody." He is "a remarkable prosodist" whose contribution to new English poetry is as an experimenter in metrical forms.

7. Ransom, John Crowe. "The Poetry of 1900–1950." *The Kenyon Review* 13 (1951): 452.

Bridges is only a minor poet of our time.

8. Raymond, William O. "'The Mind's Internal Heaven' in Poetry." *University of Toronto Quarterly* 20 (1951): 215–32.

Bridges is a Neoplatonist for whom physical beauty exists to lead man to the perception of spirit. Although he is a discerning critic, his critique of Keats's "Ode to a Nightingale" is "wide of the mark."

9. Ward, Alfred Charles. "Poetry." In *Twentieth-Century Literature, 1901–1940,* 11th ed., 139–42. London: Methuen and Co., 1951.

   A reprint of 1940.14.

10. Wright, Elizabeth Cox. *Metaphor, Sound, and Meaning in Bridges' The Testament of Beauty.* Philadelphia: University of Pennsylvania Press, 1951.

   Calling *The Testament of Beauty* "an adventure of the mind, a consideration of all the experience [Bridges] knew," this study attempts to determine the degree and character of aesthetic unity and its subtle, indirectly expressed meanings in Bridges's last poem. Close studies of poetics, narrative voices, imagery, metaphors, and thematic structure reveal the closely knit unity and total coherence of *The Testament of Beauty.*

1952

1. Bridges, Robert. Poem. In *An Approach to Literature,* edited by Cleanth Brooks, et al., 313. New York: Appleton-Century-Crofts, 1952.

   This anthology includes "A Passer-By."

2. Bridges, Robert. Poems. In *The London Book of English Verse,* edited by Herbert Read and Bonamy Dobree, 370, 379–81. New York: Macmillan, 1952.

   A reprint of 1949.1 that adds "Low Barometer."

3. Bush, Douglas. "The Modern Period." In *English Poetry: The Main Currents from Chaucer to the Present,* 193–94. New York and London: Oxford University Press, 1952.

   The Testament of Beauty, although "an ambitious attempt to fuse naturalism with idealism, was not a satisfying affirmative *De Rerum Natura* for our age." The poem failed because its "aloof serenity and preciosity . . . seemed to belong to a noble but not quite real world."

4. Clark, Bruce B. "The English Sonnet Sequence, 1850–1900." Ph.D. diss., University of Utah, 1952.

5. Martin, Robert B. "Coventry Patmore." *The Princeton University Library Chronicle* 14 (1952): 48.

   Princeton recently acquired nine letters from Bridges to Coventry Patmore.

1953

1. Bridges, Robert. Poems. In *Poetry and Life: An Introduction to Poetry,* edited by Clyde S. Kilby, 228–29, 369–70. New York: Odyssey Press, 1953.

    This anthology includes "My delight and thy delight" and "Triolet."

2. "Bridges the Poet: The Master of an Idea." *Times Literary Supplement,* 26 June 1953, 405–6.

    Bridges has been a victim of his own success. The consistent quality and smoothness of his verses have led critics to dismiss him. He should be remembered because he was a whole man of balanced facilities whose temperament was classical and whose range of attainment was wide. Bridges was a poet of "high and sustained talent."

3. Connolly, Cyril. "The Bard of Boar's Hill." *The Sunday Times,* 11 January 1953, 5.

    No poet seems so consistently without inspiration as Bridges. *The Testament of Beauty* is a "swansong of Victorian integrity, Edwardian learning, and Georgian questioning." His shorter poems contain "lovely things."

4. De la Mare, Walter. "The Poetry of Robert Bridges." In *Private View,* 108–13. London: Faber and Faber, 1953.

    Reprint of 1913.8.

5. De la Mare, Walter. *"The Spirit of Man."* In *Private View,* 185–93. London: Faber and Faber, 1953.

    Reprint of 1916.3.

6. Fraser, G. S. "Books in General." Review of *Poetical Works of Robert Bridges. The New Statesman and Nation* n.s. 46 (1953): 424–25.

    Bridges was a more adventurous and more widely ranging technical innovator than Hopkins, but he was also less successful. Although he was "a triumphant craftsman," he is ignored today because the academic ideal of humanism that he represents seems too remote for today's world.

7. Hughes, Mabel L. Violet. "The Philosophy of Neighborliness." *The London Quarterly,* 6th ser., 22 (1953): 123–29.

    Links Bridges and Plotinus as "fellow thinkers" by tracing similar themes and philosophies in *The Testament of Beauty* and *The Enneads.*

8. Hughes, Mabel L. Violet. "The Philosophy of Neigh-

borliness." *The London Quarterly and Holborn Review* 178
(1953): 123–29.
See 1953.7.

9. Kellog, George A. "Bridges' Milton's Prosody and Renaissance
Metrical Theory." *Publications of the Modern Language Association* 68 (1953): 268–85.

After examining Bridges's theory of syllabic verse in the
light of Renaissance theories of syllabic verse and other
sources of poetical theory that Milton might have known, it
seems that Bridges's criticism of Milton's prosody is accurate.

10. Read, Herbert. "The True Voice of Feeling: Keats." In *The
True Voice of Feeling*, 62–73. London: Faber and Faber,
1953.

Bridges's criticism of *Hyperion* shows how little he understood the organic nature of Romantic style and how incorrect he was to attribute the "failure" of the poem to faulty
organization. Bridges's own poetry is the lifeless and inorganic experiments of an "essentially academic" mind. *The
Testament of Beauty* is "a grotesque failure," which "deforms
the natural rhythm of speech and produces no compensating intensity of inscape.

11. Santayana, George. *My Host the World.* Vol. 3 of *The Background of My Life*, 80–84. New York: Charles Scribner's
Sons, 1953.

Recounts a weekend visit at Bridges's home and Santayana's friendship with the poet laureate during his tenure
at Oxford. Santayana denies he influenced Bridges's philosophy and doubts Bridges even understood it.

12. Ward, Alfred Charles. "Poetry." In *Twentieth-Century Literature,
1901–1940*, 139–42. London: Methuen and Co., 1953.
Reprint of 1940.14.

1954

1. Hopkins, Kenneth. "Robert Bridges." In *The Poets Laureate*,
178–84. London: The Pitman Press, 1954.

Gives biographical sketch, early poetic tastes, and publishing history of Bridges's work. *Shorter Poems* (1873) "contained perfect, imperishable lyrics." *The Testament of Beauty*
was "the crown to a career given wholly to poetry." Bridges
wished to be remembered by his work, and his work "is a
monument that will not perish."

2. Price, J. B. "Robert Bridges." *The Contemporary Review* 185 (1954): 290–94.

   The odes and lyrics are the best of Bridges's work. "Among living poets none has a name more to be held in honour for the rare and delicate beauty of his work, for the respect he has shown for his art, and for the light he has thrown upon the laws and secrets of English versification." He is a passionate writer, but it is passion without heat.

3. Yeats, William Butler. *The Letters of W. B. Yeats*, edited by Allan Wade. London: Rupert Hart-Davis, 1954.

   Three letters from Yeats to Bridges and a letter of condolence to Mrs. Bridges on the death of her husband.

1955

1. Bridges, Robert. Poems. In *Exploring Poetry*, edited by M. L. Rosenthal and A. J. M. Smith, 183. New York: Macmillan, 1955.

   Includes "Eros," "I love all beauteous things," "Nightingales," "Screaming Tarn," and "The hill pines were sighing."

2. Bridges, Robert. Poems. In *Poetry of the Victorian Period*, edited by George Benjamin Woods and Jerome Hamilton Buckley, 851–58. New York: Scott, Foresman and Co., 1955.

   Reprint of 1930.12.

3. Bridges, Robert. Poems. In *Robert Bridges: Poetry and Prose*, edited by John Sparrow, 2–103. Oxford: The Clarendon Press, 1955.

   This book includes selections from Bridges's entire literary corpus, from *Poems* (1873) to *The Testament of Beauty*. It also contains excerpts from his prose writings and excerpts of critical assessments of his work by various critics.

4. Bridges, Robert. Poems. In *Six Centuries of Great Poetry*, edited by Robert Penn Warren and Albert Erskine, 468–74. New York: Dell Publishing Co., 1955.

   This anthology includes "A Passer-By," "On a Dead Child," "The Evening Darkens Over," "Winter Nightfall," and "Low Barometer."

5. Bridges, Robert. Poems. In *A Treasury of Great Poems*, edited by Louis Untermeyer, 381–83. New York: Simon and Schuster, 1955.

   Reprint of 1942.2.

6. Carritt, E. F. "Robert Bridges." Letter. *New Statesman and Nation* 50 (1955): 543.

   Bridges's poetry is comparable to Wyatt's.

7. Groom, Bernard. "Thompson and Bridges." In *The Diction of Poetry from Spenser to Bridges*, 266–76. Toronto: University of Toronto Press, 1955.

   Phrase and rhythm are "selected with unhurried and scrupulous care" in Bridges's poetry, but the poetry remains aloof and too remote to interpret satisfactorily the harsher side of the modern world. Bridges's finest work is found in *Shorter Poems* (1890) and *New Verse* (1925). His poetic gifts include his mastery of musical meters and syllables, his response to natural beauty, and his love of words. He sought to harmonize the rhythms of verse with the cadences of speech, but in *The Testament of Beauty* the speech rhythms overcame metrical regularity. Although much of his poetry lacks passion and power, Bridges "reset" the Spenserian tradition of English poetry in its rightful course and infused it with new vigor.

8. Hennecke, Hans. *Gedichte von Shakespeare bis Ezra Pound*, 154–55. Wiesbaden, 1955.

9. O'Gorman, Ned. "The Poet Revealed to His Friends." Review of *The Letters of Gerard Manley Hopkins to Robert Bridges*, edited by Claude Colleer Abbott. *The Commonweal* 62 (1955): 403–4.

   Compared with Hopkins, Bridges was not an original poet. Their friendship was strengthened by their disparate personalities.

10. Reeves, James. "Too Little of a Blackguard." *The New Statesman and Nation* n.s. 50 (1955): 516.

    Bridges pursued a single-minded search for beauty through decorum, manners, order, and form. His work lacks passion and inspiration.

11. Rosenthal, M. L., and A. J. M. Smith. "The Life and Truth of Poetry." In *Exploring Poetry*, 183–85. New York: Macmillan, 1955.

    An analysis of the paradoxical language of "Eros" and how it reveals the paradoxical nature of love.

12. Santayana, George. Letters. In *The Letters of George Santayana*, edited by Daniel Cory, 156 and passim. New York: Charles Scribner's Sons, 1955.

Ten letters to Bridges on topics ranging from religion and philosophy to *The Testament of Beauty.*

13. Sparrow, John. "Introduction." In *Robert Bridges: Poetry and Prose,* edited by John Sparrow, vii–xvii. Oxford: The Clarendon Press, 1955.

Bridges links the Victorian and the modern ages. He was an innovator who sought change within the tradition of English literature. His life, career, and aesthetics are parallel to Tennyson's in many ways. "His true gift was lyrical," and he probably wrote more fine lyrics than any other English poet. He should be congratulated for giving Hopkins to the literary world. *The Testament of Beauty* will be remembered for its poetry and beauty, not its philosophy and wisdom. Bridges spoke with "the voice of a noble human being and a true poet, and such voices do not die."

14. Trevelyan, R[obert] C[alverley]. *XXI Letters: A Correspondence between Robert Bridges and R. C. Trevelyan.* Stanford Dingley: Mill House Press, 1955.

15. Untermeyer, Louis. "Robert Bridges." In *A Treasury of Great Poems,* 381. New York: Simon and Schuster, 1955.
Reprint of 1942.6.

1956

1. Bridges, Robert. Poems. In *A Treasury of Great Poems,* edited by Louis Untermeyer, 982–83. New York: Simon and Schuster, 1956.

This anthology includes "Nightingales" and "London Snow."

2. Brown, T. J. "English Literary Autographs, XX: Robert Bridges, 1844–1930." *The Book Collector* 5 (1956): 369.

Bridges was "a poet and . . . a connoisseur of handwriting." Reprints the fair copy of "Pax Hominibus Bonae Voluntatis."

3. Gregory, Horace. "Graceful Stoic." Review of *Robert Bridges: Poetry and Prose,* edited by John Sparrow. *The Saturday Review* 39 (1956): 26.

Bridges was "a lyric poet of very nearly the first order" whose lyrics recall Campion, Spenser, and Gray, and are superior to those of Housman. He was an original poet who sometimes wore his art too consciously and was limited in his vision.

4. Hudson, William Henry. "The Age of Hardy." In *An Outline History of English Literature,* 273–74. London: G. Bell and Sons, 1956.

   Bridges enriched English love poetry; he was not passionless. Except for the "loose alexandrines" of *The Testament of Beauty,* most of his experiments with classical meters failed.

5. Pick, John. "Gerard Manley Hopkins." In *The Victorian Poets: A Guide to Research,* edited by Frederick E. Faverty, 196–227. Cambridge: Harvard University Press, 1956.

   A bibliographical/critical essay that touches on Bridges's relationship with Hopkins, his role in influencing Hopkins's poetry, and, after Hopkins's death, his role in spreading Hopkins's reputation.

6. Stevenson, Lionel. "The Later Victorian Poets." In *The Victorian Poets: A Guide to Research,* edited by Frederick E. Faverty, 242–45. Cambridge: Harvard University Press, 1956.

   A bibliographical/critical essay on Bridges's life and work. The truest picture of Bridges's life can be derived from an examination of his relationship with other literary figures.

7. Tindall, William York. "Right." In *Forces in Modern British Literature, 1885–1946,* 84–86. New York: Random House, 1956.

   Reprint of 1947.5.

8. Untermeyer, Louis. "Robert Bridges." In *A Treasury of Great Poems,* 981–83. New York: Simon and Schuster, 1956.

   Reprint of 1942.6.

9. Ward, Alfred Charles. "Poetry." In *Twentieth-Century Literature, 1901–1950,* 143–46. London: Methuen and Co., 1956.

   Reprint of 1940.14.

1957

1. Bridges, Robert. Poem. In *English Love Poems,* edited by John Betjeman and Geoffrey Taylor, 155–56. London: Faber and Faber, 1957.

2. Nowell–Smith, Simon. "Bridges, Hopkins and Dr. Daniel." *Times Literary Supplement,* 13 December 1957, 764.

   The evidence in six letters to Dr. Daniel and two to Hopkins's mother indicates Bridges twice attempted to publish Hopkins's poetry before 1918.

3. Ward, Alfred Charles. "Poetry." In *Twentieth-Century Literature, 1901–1950,* 12th ed. 143–56. New York: Barnes and Noble, 1957.
   Reprint of 1956.9.
4. Winters, Yvor. "The Poetry of Gerard Manley Hopkins." In *The Function of Criticism,* 101–56. Denver, Col.: Alan Swallow, 1957.
   Reprint of 1948.11.

1958

1. Aiken, Conrad. "Bridges, Robert." In *Reviewer's ABC: Collected Criticism of Conrad Aiken from 1916 to the Present,* 141–43. New York: Meridian, 1958.
   Reprint of 1930.3.
2. Beum, Robert. "Syllabic Verse in English." *The Prairie Schooner* 31 (1957–58): 259–75.
   Syllabic verse has the virtue of being flexible. Bridges was the first English poet who approached syllabic verse as a serious alternative to traditional meter. The exhaustion of traditional meter and the need to incorporate the polysyllabic diction of science into poetry led him to experiment. The preface to *New Verse* is the best explanation of the technique used in *The Testament of Beauty.* Bridges proclaimed syllabic verse as a panacea for modern poetry.
3. Bridges, Robert. Poem. In *The Atlantic Book of British and American Poetry,* edited by Dame Edith Sitwell, 757. Boston and Toronto: Little, Brown and Co., 1958.
   Includes "Nightingales."
4. Bridges, Robert. Poems. In *The Viking Book of Poetry of the English-Speaking World,* 2 vols., edited by Richard Aldington, 2:1063–65. New York: The Viking Press, 1958.
   Reprint of 1941.3.
5. Clark, Alexander P. "The Manuscript Collections of the Princeton University Library." *The Princeton University Library Chronicle* 19 (1958): 168.
   The collection contains letters from Coventry Patmore to Bridges.
6. Green, David Bonnell. "A New Letter of Robert Bridges to Coventry Patmore." *Modern Philology* 55 (1958): 198–99.
   This letter reveals Bridges's deep political conservatism and shows the deep nature of his friendship for Hopkins.

7. Ward, Alfred Charles. "Post-Victorian Verse and Prose." In *English Literature: Chaucer to Bernard Shaw,* 723–24. London: Longmans, Green and Co., 1958.

A classicist in form and a romantic in feeling, Bridges looks back to the cultural past of literature and scholarship. Although the poetic dramas are failures, *The Growth of Love, Eros and Psyche,* and the short lyrics guarantee him a high place in English poetry.

1959

1. Bridges, Robert. Poem. In *Collected English Verse,* edited by Margaret and Ronald Bottrall, 495–96. London: Sidgwick and Jackson, 1959.

Reprint of 1946.1.

2. Bridges, Robert. Poems. In *Victorian Poetry: Clough to Kipling,* edited by Arthur J. Carr, 329–32. New York: Rinehart and Co., 1959.

This anthology includes "Nightingales," "My delight and thy delight," "Pater Filio," and "Eros."

3. Corke, Hilary. "A Housecarl in Loyola's Menie." Review of *The Journals and Papers of Gerard Manley Hopkins,* edited by Humphrey House. *Encounter* 12, no. 5 (1959): 63–67.

The idea that Bridges suppressed Hopkins's work does not stand up under scrutiny. Bridges's method of handling Hopkins's poetry was "the best one possible." The journals indicate Bridges "represented for [Hopkins] the principle of temptation, irreligion, [Bridges] was the Devil's advocate if not the Devil."

4. Hopkins, Gerard Manley. *The Journals and Papers of Gerard Manley Hopkins,* edited by Humphrey House and Graham Storey, 159. London: Oxford University Press, 1959.

Hopkins notes Bridges's graduation from Oxford and his trip abroad.

5. Nowell–Smith, Simon. "Housman Inscriptions." *Times Literary Supplement,* 6 November 1959, 643.

Two letters from Bridges to Housman regarding a Latin inscription for Bridges's edition of Hopkins's poems.

6. Stewart, J. I. M. "Falstaff on Boar's Hill." In *Character and Motive in Shakespeare: Some Recent Appraisals Examined,* 11-39. New York: Barnes and Noble, 1959.

Reprint of 1949.7.

7. Storey, Graham. "Preface." In *The Journals and Papers of Gerard Manley Hopkins,* edited by Humphrey House and Graham Storey, ix–xxxii. London: Oxford University Press, 1959.

Discusses Bridges's role in the acquisition, collating, and editing of Hopkins's manuscripts.

8. Ward, Alfred Charles. "Poetry." In *Twentieth-Century Literature, 1901–1940,* 143–56. New York: Barnes and Noble, 1959.

Reprint of 1940.14.

1960

1. Altick, Richard D. "Four Victorian Poets and an Exploding Island." *Victorian Studies* 3 (1960): 249–60.

Bridges's allusion to the spectacular sunsets seen after the eruption of Krakatoa appears in *Eros and Psyche.* Hopkins wondered if Bridges had written the passage after reading Hopkins's own description of a Krakatoa sunset. Bridges "reduced the unearthly splendors of the Krakatoa sunsets to the artistic level of stage scenery."

2. Bridges, Robert. Poem. In *Poetry: Its Power and Wisdom,* edited by Francis X. Connolly, 185. New York: Charles Scribner's Sons, 1960.

Includes "When first we met."

3. Bridges, Robert. Poems. In *Understanding Poetry,* edited by Cleanth Brooks and Robert Penn Warren, 100, 498–99. New York: Holt, Rinehart and Winston, 1960.

Reprint of 1950.7.

4. Brooks, Cleanth, and Robert Penn Warren. "Nightingales." In *Understanding Poetry,* 100–2. New York: Holt, Rinehart and Winston, 1960.

Reprint of 1938.4.

5. Hillyer, Robert. "The Elements of Verse." In *In Pursuit of Poetry,* 74–76. New York: McGraw-Hill Book Co., 1960.

"Bridges was one of the greatest technicians in the history of English poetry." In the study of prosody he had "no superior in all the range of poetry in the English language." Bridges's use of archaisms and his defiance of other conventions of modern speech are impediments to comprehension, but the effort to overcome these impediments is small compared to the reward.

6. Ritz, Jean-George. *Robert Bridges and Gerard Hopkins, 1863–1889: A Literary Friendship.* London: Oxford University Press, 1960.

Examines the letters of Bridges and Hopkins and attempts to assess how fairly Bridges has been judged regarding his friendship with Hopkins. The study is divided into two parts. The first analyzes Bridges's personality as it is revealed in his poems, essays, memoirs, and reminiscences. The second part of the study examines the correspondence of the two poets in an effort to glean further evidence of Bridges's character and to determine the nature of his relationship with Hopkins. Evaluating the influence each exerted on the other, it appears Hopkins gave Bridges the necessary impetus to experiment with poetic rhythms and that he broadened Bridges's literary and moral views. Bridges, on the other hand, gave Hopkins more control over his eccentric poetics and, most important, greater self-confidence. Bridges, the classicist who sought always to balance his emotions, was the dearest and closest friend of Hopkins, the romantic who passionately expressed the extremes of emotion.

1961

1. Bateson, Frederick Wilse. "The Present Day." In *English Poetry and the English Language,* 127–28. New York: Russell and Russell, 1961.

   Reprint of 1934.2.

2. In Bateson, Frederick W. "The Primacy of Meaning." In *English Poetry: A Critical Introduction,* 13–14. New York: Longmans, Green and Co., 1961.

   Reprint of 1950.2.

3. Gardner, W. H. "Bridges's Debt to Hopkins." *Times Literary Supplement,* 18 August 1961, 549.

   A letter from Hopkins to Bridges dated 1868 shows that the two poets had discussed sprung rhythm before 1872; therefore, "Poor withered rose and dry" is Bridges's earliest extant attempt at sprung rhythm.

4. Mackenzie, Norman. "Bridges's Debt to Hopkins." *Times Literary Supplement,* 1 September 1961, 588.

   Doubts Hopkins's influence on Bridges's "Poor withered rose and dry."

5. Nowell-Smith, Simon. "Bridges's Debt to Hopkins." *Times Literary Supplement,* 12 May 1961, 293.

   Doubts Bridges wrote "Poor withered rose and dry" (1872) in "new prosody" since Bridges and Hopkins were estranged at the time, and Hopkins had not formulated his ideas regarding sprung rhythm.

6. Reeves, James. "The Later Nineteenth Century." In *A Short History of English Poetry: 1340–1940,* 201. London: J. M. Dent, 1961.

   Bridges wrote "lyrical and reflective poetry" that "seldom betrayed any passion."

7. Ritz, Jean-George. "Bridges's Debt to Hopkins." *Times Literary Supplement,* 30 June 1961, 408.

   Bridges and Hopkins discussed new prosody prior to 1872, and "Poor withered rose and dry" represents Bridges's first conscious attempt to write a poem in Hopkins's style.

8. Tillotson, Geoffrey. "Bridges's Debt to Hopkins. *Times Literary Supplement,* 30 June 1961, 408.

   "Poor withered rose and dry" is not written in sprung rhythm.

9. Yeats, William Butler. "The Return of Ulysses." In *Essays and Introductions,* 198–202. New York: Macmillan, 1961.

   Reprint of 1897.1.

1962

1. Berg, Sister Mary Gretchen. *The Prosodic Structure of Robert Bridges' "Neo-Miltonic Syllabics."* Washington, D.C.: The Catholic University of America Press, 1962.

   This book "consists of a descriptive analysis of an adequate sample of the 'Neo-Miltonics' and demonstrates that Bridges' thinking on the verse was generally true." Bridges's theory is gleaned from three primary sources: his statements on general prosodic theory; his analysis of Milton's verse in successive editions of Milton's Prosody; and his specific statements about neo-Miltonic syllabics. "Misconceptions inherent in Bridges' prosodic theory and his failure to distinguish properly between the ends of descriptive and preceptive prosody in his analysis of verse rhythm must be taken into account in interpreting his statements on the 'Neo-Miltonics.'" The failure of critics and interpreters to take this into account has led to "unwarranted" conclusions about Bridges's theory of poetry.

2. Bridges, Robert. Poem. In *Lyric Verse,* edited by Edwin Rakow, 16. New York: Odyssey Press, 1962.

   Includes "Triolet."

3. Bridges, Robert. Poem. In *Poetry: A Critical and Historical Intro-duction,* edited by Irving Ribner and Harry Morris, 413–14. Chicago: Scott, Foresman and Co., 1962.
   Includes "Cheddar Pinks."

4. Fairchild, Hoxie Neale. "Old Wine, Old Bottles." In *Religious Trends in English Poetry:* Vol. 5, *1880–1920,* 26–33. New York and London: Columbia University Press, 1962.
   "Within the whole period of this volume, [Bridges] is doubtless the best poet of his well-bred, inky-blooded kind," although his poetry "does very little to stretch our experience in any fresh direction." "A Passer-By," "London Snow," and "Nightingales" "verge on greatness," but on the whole "Bridges is a noble bore." *The Testament of Beauty* is philosophically explicit whereas the short lyrics tend to be vague. The poem reveals the tensions and contradictions inherent in uniting Platonism with evolution. His "romantic impulses" are "curbed by a rather thin-blooded dread of agitation." Throughout his life he thought of himself as a Christian; however, a close inspection of his poetry reveals ambiguities. He subordinates religion to ethics; therefore, "since his mind is more ethical than religious, his Platonism is more authentic than his Christianity."

5. Laird, John. "Robert Bridges and *The Testament of Beauty.*" In *Philosophical Incursions into English Literature,* 205–23. New York: Russell and Russell, 1962.
   Reprint of 1946.6.

6. Nowell–Smith, Simon. "Bibliographical Notes and Queries: Note 189, Mosher and Bridges." *The Book Collector* 11 (1962): 482–83.
   Macmillan, not Mosher, first published Bridges in America when the company published *Humours of the Court* in 1893, one year before Mosher's pirated edition of *The Growth of Love.*

7. Reeves, James. "The Later Nineteenth Century." In *A Short History of English Poetry: 1340–1940,* 201. New York: E. P. Dutton and Co., 1962.
   Reprint of 1961.6.

8. Sparrow, John Hanbury Argus. *Robert Bridges.* Writers and Their Work, No. 147. London: Longmans, Green and Co., 1962.
   Bridges "is surely the author of the largest body of entirely beautiful poetry in the language." He ranks with

Pindar, Spenser, Keats, and Shelley; and his idea of beauty and the aim of his poetry, coupled with his use of poetic diction, archaic words, and literary forms, distinguish him from the majority of modern poets. Bridges's best poetry is found in his lyrics and short verse.

9. Van Trump, James D., and Arthur P. Ziegler, Jr. "Thomas Bird Mosher: Publisher and Pirate." *The Book Collector* 11 (1962): 310.

"Mosher . . . printed the first American edition of Robert Bridges." See 1962.6.

1963

1. Agajanian, Shaakeh. "Victorian Love Sonnet: A Study in Aesthetic Metaphysics and Morphology." Ph.D. diss., New York University, 1963.

2. Cohen, J. M. "Bridges, Robert." In *The Concise Encyclopedia of English and American Poets and Poetry,* edited by Stephen Spender and Donald Hall, 59–60. New York: Hawthorn Books, 1963.

Bridges's best work is in his lyrics although he never reveals the cause of his grief. *The Growth of Love* disguises the story of the poet's love; "On a Dead Child" is "coldly rhetorical," and "London Snow" is purely visual. The shorter lyrics and an occasional passage from *The Testament of Beauty* are all that command modern attention.

3. Freeman, John. "Windsor Area." In *Literature and Locality: The Literary Topography of Britain and Ireland,* 62. London: Cassell and Co., 1963.

Discusses aspects of Bridges's biography as they relate to Eton, Walmer, Oxford, and Boar's Hill.

4. Garrod, H. W. *"The Testament of Beauty."* In *Poetry and the Criticism of Life,* 129–47. New York: Russell and Russell, 1963.

Reprint of 1931.9.

1964

1. Beum, Robert. "Profundity Revisited: Bridges and His Critics." *The Dalhousie Review* 44 (1964): 172–79.

Bridges has been ignored by modern critics because erudition, critical intelligence, and delicate beauty are not valued by an age that finds profundity only in anxiety. "Bridges is not . . . completely unprofound."

2. Bridges, Robert. Poem. In *An Approach to Literature,* edited by Cleanth Brooks, et al., 311. New York: Appleton-Century-Crofts, 1964.
   Reprint of 1952.1.

3. Day, Martin S. "Robert Seymour Bridges." In *History of English Literature, 1837 to the Present,* 307–8. Garden City, N.Y.: Doubleday, 1964.
   A "poet's poet," Bridges is master of the serene classic style in English and "one of the most important experimenters and students of English prosody."

4. Gross, H. S. "Robert Bridges." *Sound and Form in Modern Poetry: A Study of Prosody from Thomas Hardy to Robert Lowell,* 55–63. Ann Arbor: University of Michigan Press, 1964.
   Although Bridges is "as conscious a prosodist as Tennyson," he and Hopkins make the mistake of applying foot scansion to what is not foot-measured meter, thereby producing meter that is "more interesting than useful." The loose alexandrines of *The Testament of Beauty* are "unreadable." In Bridges's work feeling and rhythm move at low intensity, and his poetic achievement rests on his lyrics in traditional meter.

5. Trousson, Raymond. *Le Theme de Promethee dans la litterature europeene,* 2 vols., 2:415. Geneva: Librairiee Droz, 1964.
   Bridges's *Prometheus* seeks to reconcile science and God—Prometheus is the founder of science, and Zeus is the founder of religion. All characters are good; there is no sense of struggle between good and evil.

6. Ward, Alfred Charles. "Poetry." In *Twentieth-Century Literature, 1901–1960,* 143–46. London: Methuen and Co., New York: Barnes and Noble, 1964.
   Essentially a reprint of 1940.14. Updates the scholarship on Bridges through 1960.

1965

1. Bridges, Robert. Poems. In *Poetry of the Victorian Period,* edited by George Benjamin Woods and Jerome Hamilton Buckley, 861–68. New York: Scott, Foresman and Co., 1965.
   Reprint of 1930.12.

2. Guerard, Albert, Jr. *Robert Bridges: A Study of Traditionalism in Poetry.* New York: Russell and Russell, 1965.
   Reprint of 1942.4.

3. Woodhouse, A. S. P. "The Victorian Age: 1840–1900." In *The*

Poet and His Faith: Religion and Poetry in England from Spenser to Eliot and Auden, 251–55. Chicago and London: University of Chicago Press, 1965.

There is a sharp contrast between Bridges and Hopkins; Bridges's taste is classical, his expression reserved, and his religion Anglican. *The Testament of Beauty* is more Victorian than modern and harkens back to Shaftsbury and Wordsworth. It "is at once an essay on man, and essentially, though not exclusively, a religious poem." It is simultaneously an eclectic and profoundly original "series of meditations on nature and the life of man."

1966

1. Bateson, Frederick W. "The Primacy of Meaning." In *English Poetry: A Critical Introduction,* 11. New York: Barnes and Noble; London: Longmans, Green and Co., 1966.
   Reprint of 1950.2.

2. Beach, Joseph Warren. "Victorian Afterglow." In *The Concept of Nature in Nineteenth-Century English Poetry,* 524–28. New York: Russell and Russell, 1966.
   Reprint of 1936.1.

3. Dumbleton, William Albert. "The Literary Relationship of Robert Bridges to Gerard Manley Hopkins, 1889–1930. Ph.D. diss., University of Pennsylvania, 1966.

4. Evans, Benjamin Ifor. "Robert Bridges and His Associates." In *English Poetry in the Later Nineteenth Century,* 243–67. New York: Barnes and Noble, 1966.
   Reprint of 1933.1.

5. Grigg, John. "Forgotten Poet." *The Guardian,* 31 March 1966, 24.
   Bridges is undeservedly overlooked.

6. McKay, George L[eslie]. *A Bibliography of Robert Bridges.* New York: Columbia University Press and AMS Press, 1966.
   Reprint of 1933.6.

7. Stewart, J. I. M. "Falstaff on Boar's Hill." In *Character and Motive in Shakespeare: Some Recent Appraisals Examined,* 11–39. New York: Barnes and Noble, 1966.
   Reprint of 1949.6.

8. Ward, Alfred Charles. "Poetry." In *Twentieth-Century Literature, 1901–1960,* 14th ed., 143–46. London: Methuen and Co., 1966.
   Reprint of 1964.6.

1967

1. Bridges, Robert. Poem. In *An Approach to Literature,* edited by
   Cleanth Brooks, et al., 311. New York: Appleton-Century-
   Crofts, 1967.
     Reprint of 1952.1.

2. Chew, Samuel C. "Other Late-Victorian Poets." In *A Literary
   History of England,* edited by Albert Baugh, et al., 1538–40.
   New York: Appleton-Century-Crofts, 1967.
     Reprint of 1948.2.

3. Gardner, W. H. "Introduction to the Fourth Edition." In *The
   Poems of Gerard Manley Hopkins,* edited by W. H. Gardner
   and Norman Mackenzie, xiii–xxxviii. London: Oxford
   University Press, 1967.
     Bridges's friendship sustained Hopkins's poetic activity
   and kept his poetic eccentricities in check.

4. Guhathakurta, J. "The Use of Classical Myths in the Plays of
   Swinburne, Bridges, Sturge Moore, and T. S. Eliot." Ph.D.
   diss., London—Kings, 1967.

5. Kable, William S. *The Ewelme Collection of Robert Bridges.* Columbia, S.C.: University of South Carolina Press, 1967.
     A descriptive, annotated bibliography of primary and
   secondary Bridges material given to the University by Simon Nowell-Smith.

6. Mackenzie, Norman H. "Foreword on the Revised Text and
   Chronological Rearrangement of the Poems." In *The Poems
   of Gerard Manley Hopkins,* xxxix–lxvi. London: Oxford University Press, 1967.
     Although he made several errors, Bridges was a "scru-
   pulously accurate editor" who selected Hopkins's poems to
   maximize their public appeal. "All students and editors of
   Hopkins owe an immense debt to Robert Bridges."

7. Morison, Stanley. "Robert Bridges." In *John Fell, the University
   Press and the Fell Types,* 205–9. Oxford: The Clarendon
   Press, 1967.
     Recounts Bridges's first introduction to Fell type at the
   Daniel Press and the subsequent printing of *The Yattendon
   Hymnal* in Fell type by the Oxford University Press.

8. Owen, B. Evan. "Robert (Seymour) Bridges." In *Encyclopedia
   of World Literature in the 20th Century: A–F.* Vol. 1 of *Encyclopedia of World Literature in the 20th Century,* edited by Wolf-
   gang Bernard Fleischmann, 173–74. New York: Frederick
   Ungar Publishing Co., 1967.

A biographical/bibliographical essay. Although Bridges belonged to none of the literary movements of his day, he is a link between the Romantics and their Pre-Raphaelite off-shoot and the modernist movement.

9. Rivers, James C. "Astronomy and Physics in British and American poetry, 1920–1960." Ph.D. diss., University of South Carolina, 1967.

10. Temple, Ruth Z., and Martin Tucker. "Bridges, Robert." In *A Library of Literary Criticism: Modern British Literature*, vol. 1, 120–24. New York: Frederick Ungar, 1967.

Selections from eight critical commentaries on Bridges.

11. Warren, Thomas Herbert. "Robert Bridges." In *Robert Bridges and Contemporary Poets*. Vol. 7 of *The Poets and Poetry of the Nineteenth Century*, edited by Alfred Henry Miles, 113–24. New York: AMS Press, 1967.

Reprint of 1906.3.

1968

1. Aiken, Conrad. "Prose and Music." *Collected Criticism*, 141–43. London: Oxford University Press, 1968.

Reprint of 1930.3.

2. Bridges, Robert. Poems. In *English Poetry in Transition, 1880–1920*, edited by John M. Monro, 59–67. New York: Pegasus, 1968.

This anthology includes "London Snow," "Nightingales," "Peace Ode," and "Christmas, 1917."

3. Bridges, Robert. Poems. In *Poetry: An Introduction*, edited by William G. Lane, 328–29. New York: D. C. Heath and Co., 1968.

This anthology includes "On a Dead Child."

4. Monro, John M. "Robert Bridges." In *English Poetry in Transition, 1880–1920*, 59. New York: Pegasus, 1968.

Bridges is in the tradition of Arnold and Tennyson. His conservative, middle-class Victorianism "should not blind us to his numerous experiments in English prosody."

5. Patmore, Coventry. "Robert Bridges." In *Courage in Politics and Other Essays, 1885–1896*, 143–50. Freeport, N.Y.: Books for Libraries Press, 1968.

Reprint of 1921.12.

6. Pick, John. "Gerard Manley Hopkins." In *The Victorian Poets: A Guide to Research*, 2d ed., edited by Frederick E. Faverty, 318–51. Cambridge: Harvard University Press, 1968.

Essentially a reprint of 1956.05. Updates scholarship through 1966.

7. Stevenson, Lionel. "The Later Victorian Poets." In *The Victorian Poets: A Guide to Research,* 2d ed., edited by Frederick E. Faverty, 375–79. Cambridge: Harvard University Press, 1968.

Essentially a reprint of 1956.6. Updates scholarship through 1966.

8. Tennyson, Charles. "1862–1863." In *Alfred Tennyson,* 344–45. Hamden, Conn.: Archon Books, 1968.

Reprint of 1949.8.

9. Yeats, William Butler. "The Return of Ulysses." In *Essays and Introductions,* 198–202. New York: Collier Books, 1968.

Reprint of 1897.1.

1969

1. Bridges, Robert. Poem. In *Collected English Verse,* edited by Margaret Bottrall and Ronald Bottrall, 495–96. Freeport, N.Y.: Books for Libraries Press, 1969.

Reprint of 1946.1.

2. Bridges, Robert. Poems. In *Quest for Reality: An Anthology of Short Poems in English,* edited by Yvor Winters and Kenneth Fields, 107–10. Chicago: The Swallow Press, 1969.

Includes "Dejection," "Low Barometer," and "Eros."

3. Bullough, Geoffrey. "Inheritance of the Twentieth Century." In *The Trend of Modern Poetry,* 12–15. Folcroft, Penn.: Folcroft Press, 1969.

Reprint of 1934.5.

4. Grierson, Herbert John Clifford. "The Nineties." In *Lyrical Poetry from Blake to Hardy,* 129–32. Folcroft, Penn.: Folcroft Press, 1969.

Reprint of 1928.11.

5. Hind, C. Lewis. "Robert Bridges." In *More Authors and I,* 34–39. Folcroft, Penn.: Books for Libraries Press, 1969.

Reprint of 1922.7.

6. Jones, A. R. "Gerard Manley Hopkins: Victorian." In *The Major Victorian Poets: Reconsiderations,* edited by Isobel Armstrong, 299. London: Routledge and Kegan Paul, 1969.

Bridges's "Preface to Notes" (1918) reveals how "remarkably unsympathetic" Bridges was to Hopkins's poetry and how he "undervalued" his friendship.

7. Stanford, Donald E. "Classicism and the Modern Poet." *The Southern Review* n.s. 5 (1969): 475–500.

   In politics, religion, and poetry, Bridges, E. A. Robinson, and Yvor Winters are the true classicists of modern poetry, not Hulme, Pound, and Eliot.

8. White, Norman, and Tom Dunne. "A Hopkins Discovery." *Library* 24 (1969): 56–58.

   Extract of a letter from Bridges to Hopkins's mother, Mrs. Kate Hopkins.

9. Wiley, Paul L., and Howard Orel. "Robert Seymour Bridges." In *British Poetry, 1880–1920: Edwardian Voices,* 323–25. New York: Appleton-Century-Crofts, 1969.

10. Winters, Yvor, and Kenneth Fields, eds. "Introduction." In *Quest for Reality: An Anthology of Short Poems in English,* 1–9. Chicago: The Swallow Press, 1969.

    The poets selected for this anthology write poetry exhibiting "a high degree of concentration which aims at understanding and revealing the particular subject as fully as possible." Although Bridges's poetry is flawed by his "incurable predilection for stereotyped romantic diction," he remains among the finest poets in the language.

1970

1. Barker, Nicholas. *The Printer and the Poet.* Cambridge: Cambridge University Press, 1970.

   This book traces the planning and printing of *The Tapestry,* a selection of poems from *New Verse.* Includes ten letters from Stanley Morison to Bridges.

2. Bremer, R. "Hopkins' Use of the Word 'combs' in 'To R.B.'" *English Studies* 51 (1970): 144–48.

   Hopkins's use of the word "combs" in "To R. B." was a conscious use that fit the sound and sense patterns of the poem better than "Moulds," which Bridges later substituted in *Poems of Gerard Manley Hopkins.*

3. Bridges, Robert. Poems. In *Exploring Literature,* edited by Lynn Altenbernd, 402–4. New York: Macmillan, 1970.

   Includes "Elegy" and "London Snow."

4. Colin, Armand. "Robert Bridges." In *Histoire de la litterature anglaise de Victoria a Elisabeth II,* 2 vols., 2:197–98. Paris: Armand Colin, 1970.

   Bridges was primarily a prosodist, nourished by the classics and tradition, with a strong sense of music in verse. His great period of poetic production was from 1885 to 1916. He was barely capable of understanding or appreciating the genius of Hopkins.

5. Gervals, Claude. "The Victorian Love Sonnet Sequence." Ph.D. diss., Toronto, 1970.

6. Gordon, George S. *Robert Bridges.* The Rede Lecture. Folcroft, Penn.: Folcroft, 1970.
   Reprint of 1946.4.

7. Graves, Robert. "The Unpopularity of Modernist Poetry." In *The Common Asphodel: Collected Essays on Poetry, 1922–1949,* 100–101 and passim. New York: Haskell House, 1970.
   Reprint of 1949.5.

8. Grierson, Herbert John Clifford. "The Nineties." In *Lyrical Poetry of the Nineteenth Century,* 129–32. New York: AMS, 1970.
   Reprint of 1929.09.

9. Jackson, Holbrook. "Robert Bridges." In *The Printing of Books,* 99–108. Freeport, N.Y.: Books for Libraries Press, 1970.
   Reprint of 1939.5.

10. Robson, W. W. "Poetry in the Early Twentieth Century." In *Modern English Literature,* 60–61. London, Oxford, and New York: Oxford University Press, 1970.
    Compared with Yeats and Hopkins, "Bridges seems too comfortable and sheltered for a great poet." Despite this, a certain body of his work will stand the test of time. *The Testament of Beauty* "gives the impression of senile rambling." In it Bridges "thinks in verse rather than poetically." His prose writings are the best of his work and the criticism is "full of interest."

11. Tindall, William York. "Right." In *Forces in Modern British Literature, 1885–1946,* 104–5. Freeport, N.Y.: Books for Libraries Press, 1970.
    Reprint of 1947.5.

12. Williams, Charles Walter Stansby. "The Dispersal of Mist." In *Reason and Beauty in the Poetic Mind,* 173–75. Oxford: The Clarendon Press, 1970.
    Reprint of 1933.13.

13. Young, Francis Brett. *Robert Bridges: A Critical Study.* New York: Haskell House, 1970.
    Reprint of 1914.12.

1971

1. Butler, Samuel. Letters. In "Robert Bridges On His Poems and Plays," by Donald E. Stanford. *Philological Quarterly* 50 (1971): 284–90.

   Three letters to Bridges with comments on some of the latter's poems and plays.

2. Grierson, Herbert John Clifford. "The Nineties." In *Lyrical Poetry from Blake to Hardy,* 129–32. St. Claire Shores, Mich.: Scholarly Press, 1971.

   Reprint of 1928.11.

3. Peck, John. "Bridges' *Nero* and the Closet Tradition." *The Journal of English Literary History* 38 (1971): 591–615.

   Bridges's Nero plays illustrate basic conventions of closet drama and offer "an implicit, extended critique of romantic tragedy." The hero is an innocent victim of circumstance with extreme sensibilities. Bridges employs dramatic irony to depict the stated and implied motives of the hero. The plays portray the drama of moral maneuvering in a corrupt world.

4. Stanford, Donald E. "Robert Bridges and Samuel Butler on Shakespeare's Sonnets: An Exchange of Letters." *Shakespeare Quarterly* 22 (1971): 329–35.

   An exchange of letters between Bridges and Butler regarding Butler's criticism of Shakespeare's sonnets.

5. Stanford, Donald E. "Robert Bridges and the Free Verse Rebellion." *The Journal of Modern Literature* 2 (1971): 19–32.

   Bridges's work in accentual verse, classical meters, neo-Miltonic syllabics, and "loose alexandrines" is evidence of his long-standing opposition to conventional meters. He was "'a keen experimenter' who at the same time wished to preserve 'the traditional and characteristic beauties of our language.'"

6. Stanford, Donald E. "Robert Bridges on His Poems and Plays: Unpublished Letters by Robert Bridges to Samuel Butler." *Philological Quarterly* 50 (1971): 281–91.

   Eight letters exchanged between Bridges and Butler that show Bridges's perception of his own work and Butler's polite but restrained enthusiasm for it.

1972

1. Barker, Nicholas. *Stanley Morison,* 252–66. Cambridge: Harvard University Press, 1972.

Describes the first meeting between Morison and Bridges, and their subsequent work on *The Tapestry* and *The Testament of Beauty.*

2. Bridges, Robert. Poems. In *The New Oxford Book of English Verse,* 1250–1950, edited by Helen Gardner, 772–76. New York and London: Oxford University Press, 1972.

   This anthology includes "London Snow," "On a Dead Child," "Awake, my heart, to be loved," and "Eros."

3. Bridges, Robert. Poems. In *Poetry of the Transition: 1850–1914,* edited by Thomas Marc Parrott and Willard Thorpe, 454–69. Miami, Fla.: Royale House, 1972.

   Reprint of 1932.6.

4. Byard, Herbert. "Robert Bridges: Church Musician." *Music and Letters* 53 (1972): 44–55.

   Bridges was a middle-of-the-road Anglican all of his life. His work with hymns reveals that he was more an adaptor than a translator. Although his main interest lay in psalm singing, his work with hymns influenced all succeeding Anglican hymnals.

5. Dilligan, Robert J. "*Ibant Obscuri:* Robert Bridges' Experiment in English Quantitative Verse." *Style* 6 (1972): 38–65.

   Bridges is a tributary in the confluence of the "main streams of prosodic innovation in the nineteenth century." A computer transcription and scansion of *Ibant Obscuri* "shows beyond a doubt that there is a sense in which quantitative verse may be written in English and seen as a viable medium for lengthy poems."

6. Dumbleton, William A. "Bridges and the Hopkins MSS: 1889–1930." *Thought* 47 (1972): 428–46.

   Examines Bridges's aesthetic approach to Hopkins's poetry. Bridges sought to salvage in Hopkins's poetry that which he thought most salvageable, the metrical system, which he then experimented with. His refusal to give the manuscript to Father Keating in 1909 and then delaying publication for nine years points to Bridges's enormous pride. "We cannot judge Bridges as a fair, adequate or thorough critic of any range, for he was not."

7. Forster, Leonard. "Three Evening Hymns: Gerhardt, Claudius and Bridges." In *Deutung and Dedeutung: Studies in German and Comparative Literature Presented to Karl-Werner Maurer,* edited by Brigitte Schludermann et al., 327–35. The Hague: Mouton, 1972.

   Bridges's hymn "The duteous day now closes" is a piece

of nineteenth-century nature worship with few overt Christian elements and seems closer in spirit to Claudius than to Gerhardt. Bridges concentrates on the æsthetic, not the theological, aspects of the beauty of God's creation. The hymn is beautiful but lacks doctrinal and symbolic strength.

8. Morison, Stanley. Letters. In *Stanley Morison,* edited by Nicolas Barker, 252–66. Cambridge: Harvard University Press, 1972.

   Six letters and excerpts of letters from Morison to Bridges, primarily regarding the printing of Bridges's work.

9. Parrott, Thomas Marc, and Willard Thorpe. "Robert Bridges." In *Poetry of the Transition: 1850–1914,* 450–54. Miami, Fla.: Royale House, 1972.
   Reprint of 1932.15.

10. Williams, Harold. "Poets of the Transition." In *Modern English Writers,* 29–31. New York: Kennikat Press, 1972.
    Reprint of 1918.8.

1973

1. Bateson, Frederick Wilse. "The Present Day." In *English Poetry and the English Language,* 3d ed., 95–96. Oxford: The Clarendon Press, 1973.
   Reprint of 1934.2.

2. Bridges, Robert. Poems. In *The Oxford Anthology of English Literature: 1800 to the Present.* Vol. 2 of *The Oxford Anthology of English Literature,* edited by Frank Kermode and John Hollander, 2028–29. New York: Oxford University Press, 1973.

   This anthology includes "A Passer-By," "London Snow," and "Nightingales."

3. Bridges, Robert. Poems. In *The Oxford Book of Twentieth-Century English Verse,* edited by Philip Larkin, 26–34. Oxford: The Clarendon Press, 1973.

   This anthology includes "A Passer-By," "London Snow," "April 1885," "Poor Poll," and an excerpt from *The Testament of Beauty.*

4. Bridges, Robert. Poems. In *The Range of Literature,* 3d ed., edited by Elizabeth W. Schneider, et al., 479–80. New York: D. Van Nostrand Co., 1973.

   This anthology includes "November," "Nightingales," and "Triolet."

5. Kermode, Frank, and John Hollander. "Robert Bridges." In *The Oxford Anthology of English Literature: 1800 to the Present.* Vol. 2 of *The Oxford Anthology of English Literature,* edited by Frank Kermode and John Hollander, 2027–28. New York: Oxford University Press, 1973.

    Bridges's greatest achievements are his lyrics and his "loose accentual meters." His work is imbued with "true classical learning."

6. Lauterbach, Edward, and W. Eugene Davis. "Robert Bridges." In *The Transitional Age: British Literature, 1880–1920,* 103–5. Troy, N.Y.: Whitson Publishing Co., 1973.

    A selected bibliography of primary and secondary sources. Bridges's poetry is most popular among "people who value form more than content, finish more than feeling." His poetry "lacks passion and drama."

7. Seymour-Smith, Martin. "British Literature." In *Guide to Modern World Literature,* 211–12. London: Wolfe Publishing, 1973.

    Bridges was a conservative innovator who "wrote not one single good poem." "All his poetry, especially the long philosophical *Testament of Beauty* (1929), is marred by artificiality, lack of feeling . . . and unintelligent conservatism." He deserves credit for "dimly recognizing the genius of Hopkins."

8. Stall, Lindon. "Robert Bridges and the Laws of English Stressed Verse." *The Agenda* 2 (1973): 96–108.

    Summarizes Bridges's laws of English stressed verse as formulated in *Milton's Prosody* and evaluates the use of these laws in "London Snow," "On a Dead Child," and "Nightingales."

9. Trevelyan, R[obert] C[alverley]. *XXI Letters: A Correspondence between Robert Bridges and R. C. Trevelyan.* Folcroft, Penn.: Folcroft Library Editions, 1973.

    Reprint of 1955.14.

10. Winters, Yvor. "Traditional Mastery: The Lyrics of Robert Bridges." In *The Uncollected Essays and Reviews of Yvor Winters,* edited by Francis Murphy, 127–35. Chicago: Swallow Press, 1973.

    Reprint of 1931.25.

1974

1. Bridges, Robert. Poems. In *100 British Poets,* edited by Selden
   Rodman, 254–56. New York: The New American Library,
   1974.
     This anthology includes "The Philosopher to His Mis-
   tress" and "Johannes Milton, Senex."

2. Bridges, Robert. Poems. In *Robert Bridges: Selected Poems,* edited by Donald E. Stanford. Cheshire, England: The Carcanet Press, 1974.
     This collection contains fifty-seven poems and excerpts
   of poems by Bridges. All major poems from his earliest
   work to *The Testament of Beauty* are included.

3. Bullough, Geoffrey. "Inheritance of the Twentieth Century."
   In *The Trend of Modern Poetry,* 12–15. Folcroft, Penn.:
   Folcroft Press, 1974.
     Reprint of 1934.5.

4. Chaundy, Leslie, and Elizabeth Cox. *Robert Bridges: Bibliographies of Modern Authors, No. 1.* Folcroft, Penn.: Folcroft Library Editions, 1974.
     Reprint of 1921.5.

5. Holst, Gustav. *A Choral Fantasia, Op. 51.* London: Curwen-
   Faber, 1974.
     Reprint of 1931.11.

6. Spender, Stephen. "The Persona of Robert Bridges." In *Love-
   Hate Relations: English and American Sensibilities,* 163–70.
   New York: Random House, 1974.
     Bridges is exceptional among contemporary English
   poets for his extremely critical and wide-ranging mind. His
   poetry is marked by classical influences and impersonality;
   it is a "flame of ice." Unfortunately, "he carried the idea of
   objectification to the point of petrification."

7. Stanford, Donald E. "Introduction." In *Robert Bridges: Selected
   Poems,* 9–23. Cheshire, England: The Carcanet Press, 1974.
     A biographical/bibliographical essay that includes discus-
   sions of Bridges's life, his relationship with Hopkins, his
   poetic theory, and the types of meter he wrote. Distinguishes four metrical styles employed by Bridges, cites
   poems that exemplify each style, and briefly analyzes several of them.

8. Trevelyan, R[obert] C[alverley]. *XXI Letters: A Correspondence
   between Robert Bridges and R. C. Trevelyan.* Folcroft, Penn.:

Folcroft Library Editions, 1974.
  Reprint of 1955.14.

1975

1. Bridges, Robert. Poem. In *An Approach to Literature,* edited by
   Cleanth Brooks, et al., 429. Englewood Cliffs, N.J.: Prentice-Hall, 1975.
     Reprint of 1952.1.
2. Bridges, Robert. Poems. In *Introduction to Literature: Poems,*
   edited by Lynn Altenbernd and Leslie L. Lewis, 607–10.
   New York: Macmillan, 1975.
     This anthology includes "Elegy," "London Snow," "Night-
   ingales," "Awake, my heart, to be loved," "So sweet love
   seemed," and "Eros."
3. Trevelyan, R[obert] C[alverley]. *XXI Letters: A Correspondence
   between Robert Bridges and R. C. Trevelyan.* Norwood, Penn.:
   Norwood Editions, 1975.
     Reprint of 1955.14.
4. Ward, Alfred Charles. "Robert Bridges: *The Testament of
   Beauty.*" In *The Nineteen-Twenties: Literature and Ideas in the
   Post-War Decade,* 80–86. Folcroft, Penn.: The Folcroft Library, 1975.
     Reprint of 1930.82.
5. Ward, Alfred Charles. "Robert Bridges: *The Testament of
   Beauty.*" In *The Nineteen-Twenties: Literature and Ideas in the
   Post-War Decade,* 80–86. Norwood, Penn.: Norwood Edi-
   tions, 1975.
     Reprint of 1930.82.

1976

1. Bridges, Robert. Poem. In *Understanding Poetry,* edited by
   Cleanth Brooks and Robert Penn Warren, 366. New York:
   Holt, Rinehart and Winston, 1976.
     Reprint of 1938.3.
2. Bridges, Robert. Poems. In *Philosophies of Beauty from Socrates
   to Robert Bridges: Being the Sources of Aesthetic Theory,* edited
   by E. F. Carritt, 331. Westport, Conn.: Greenwood Press,
   1976.
     Reprint of 1931.4.
3. Dunne, Tom. "Introduction." In *Gerard Manley Hopkins: A
   Comprehensive Bibliography,* edited by Tom Dunne, xvii–xix.
   Oxford: The Clarendon Press, 1976.

"Bridges was both shrewd and perceptive in waiting until 1918 before publishing Hopkins's collected poems." His Preface, which has stirred such controversy, seems intended to disarm the critics.

4. Mackenzie, Norman H. "Forensic Document Techniques Applied to Literary Manuscripts." *The Bodleian Library Record* 9 (1976): 234–40.

Describes the use of the Infra-red Image Converter to distinguish between editorial alterations made by Hopkins in his poetic manuscripts and those alterations made by Bridges.

5. Mackenzie, Norman H. "Hopkins, Robert Bridges, and the Modern Editor."

In *Editing British and American Literature, 1880–1920*, edited by Eric W. Domville, 9–30. New York: Garland Publishing, 1976.

Discusses the use of the Infra-red Image Converter in determining the correct text of Hopkins's poetry. Given his limited tools, Bridges is to be commended for the job he did in attempting to fix the text of Hopkins's manuscripts. Bridges was "a poetic safe deposit box for Hopkins's poetry.

6. Perkins, David. "Craftsman of the Beautiful and the Agreeable." In *A History of Modern Poetry: From the 1890s to the High Modernist Mode,* 171–77. Cambridge: Harvard University Press, 1976.

Bridges is the "gruff chieftain of the tribe of Beauty," who wrote traditional poetry. His work is characterized by his "detachment, self discipline, conscious intention, and scrupulous respect for the medium." His significance in literary history is "as a representative of his time rather than as a powerfully creative influence."

7. Seymour-Smith, Martin. "Robert Bridges." In *Who's Who in Twentieth-Century Literature,* 56. New York: Holt, Rinehart and Winston, 1976.

Bridges "never achieved poetic power" because the artist in him was "muted by innate conformism."

8. Trevelyan, R[obert] C[alverley]. *XXI Letters: A Correspondence between Robert Bridges and R. C. Trevelyan.* Norwood, Penn.: Norwood Editions, 1976.

Reprint of 1955.14.

1977

1. Finneran, Richard J., ed. *The Correspondence of Robert Bridges and W. B. Yeats.* London: Macmillan, 1977.

   In addition to the letters, this volume also contains three appendixes: the first is an edited version of Yeats's "Mr. Robert Bridges" (see chapter 3, 1897.1), and the last two list the respective books in the libraries of the two men. Although Bridges and Yeats had fundamentally different backgrounds, temperaments, and aesthetics, the letters reveal a friendship "founded on a deep and mutual respect for the art and craft of poetry."

2. Haas, Rudolf. "'London Snow': Asthetische Uberblendung sozialer Motive." In *Theorie and Praxis der Interpretation,* 173–77. Berlin: Erich Schmidt Verlag, 1977.

   Unlike Swift and Blake's poetry, which combines satire and social criticism, Bridges's "London Snow" expresses only a mood, like a Turner watercolor. Like the falling snow, aesthetic concerns overlay the sociological.

3. Holst, Gustav. *A Choral Fantasia, Op. 51.* London: Ernst Eulenburg, 1977.

   Reprint of 1974.5 with an introductory note by Imogen Holst.

4. Yeats, William Butler. Letters. In *The Correspondence of Robert Bridges and W. B. Yeats,* edited by Richard J. Finneran. London: Macmillan, 1977.

   Fifteen letters from Yeats to Bridges.

1978

1. Clark, Leonard. "Poetry and Children." *Children's Literature in Education* 9 (1978): 129–30.

   Bridges is right to complain, as he does in the preface to *The Chilswell Book of English Poetry,* that children should not be raised on inferior poetry and then be expected to outgrow poor poetry for superior poetry.

2. Stanford, Donald E. *In the Classic Mode: The Achievement of Robert Bridges.* Newark: University of Delaware Press, 1978.

   Classifies, defines, and illustrates Bridges's major experiments in prosody, with special attention to William Johnson Stone's influence on Bridges's development of quantitative verse. Bridges is "one of the great lyric poets in English" and it is on those poems treating universal themes "that

Bridges's reputation as a major poet must eventually rest." As a dramatist, "Bridges's best plays . . . hold a distinguished place in the history of poetic drama, comparable, certainly, to the plays of Yeats and Eliot." His criticism is "beautifully written, challenging, and perceptive." It has "stood up well over the years" and reveals "a coherent set of critical principles."

3. Ward, Alfred Charles. "Robert Bridges: *The Testament of Beauty.*" In *The Nineteen-Twenties: Literature and Ideas in the Post-War Decade,* 80–86. Philadelphia: R. West, 1978.
Reprint of 1930.82.

1979

1. Bean, John C. "Making The Daimonic Personal: Britomart and Louis Assault in *The Faerie Queen.*" *Modern Language Quarterly* 40 (1979): 246–47.
Bridges's "Eros" is a revealing gloss on Spenser's House of Busyrane.

2. Fiske, Francis. "Correspondent Breeze: The Course of a Romantic Metaphor." *Renascence* 32 (1979): 3–12.
Bridges's "Low Barometer" metaphorically describes the withdrawal of Spirit from the modern world and the unleashing of the demonic forces in human nature.

3. Godman, Peter. "Robert Bridges on English Quantitative Verse: An Unpublished Letter." *Notes and Queries* n.s. 26 (1979): 335–36.
This letter "offers an insight into contemporary reactions to Bridges's experiment in English quantitative verse and provides evidence of the poet's considered opinion of *Ibant Obscuri.*"

4. Lange, Donald J. "George Darley: Some Re-Appraisals." *Durham University Journal* 72 (1979): 61–66.
Bridges's interpretation of Darley's "Nepenthe" is inadequate compared with Edward H. Synge's interpretation of the poem.

5. Press, John. "Robert Bridges." In *Great Writers of the English Language: Poets,* edited by James Vinson and D. L. Kirkpatrick, 137–40. New York: St. Martin's Press, 1979.
Bridges's technical accomplishments never faltered. Although modern readers detect a certain coldness and aloofness, his verse belies an emotional and technical range that is wider than is commonly believed.

1980

1. Joyce, Audry B. "The Dramas of Robert Bridges: A Critical Study." Ph.D. diss., University of South Florida, 1980.
2. Lees-Milne, James. "Bakhtiari and Foreign Office, 1927." In *Harold Nicolson: A Biography, 1886–1929*. Vol. 1 of *Harold Nicolson: A Biography*, 309–10. London: Chatto and Windus, 1980.

   Relates the story of an overnight visit by Nicolson at Bridges's home.

1981

1. Bridges, Robert. Poem. In *The Harper Anthology of Poetry*, edited by John Frederick Nims, 449–50. New York: Harper and Row, 1981.

   This anthology includes "The evening darkens over."
2. F[raser], G. S. "Bridges, Robert (Seymour) (1844–1930)." In *The Avenel Companion to English and American Literature*, edited by David Daiches, Malcomb Bradbury, and Eric Mottram, 63. New York: Avenel Books, 1981.

   "Standing aside from most of the main currents of change in his age, [Bridges] is a poet whose technical mastery and honesty of thought and feeling may win him new admirers if a neo-conservative trend in poetic taste sets in."
3. Russel, Nick. "Robert Bridges (1844–1930)." In *Poets by Appointment: Britain's Laureates*, 159–71. Poole, Great Britain: Blandford Press, 1981.

   The oldest poet, besides Wordsworth, to become laureate, Bridges is remembered primarily for being Hopkins's first editor. Bridges's poetry "bought technical excellence at the expense of emotional content." Contains six poems, mostly war poems, including "The Western Front" and "Der Tag."

1982

1. (Anderson, Emily Ann.) "Robert Seymour Bridges (1844–1930)." In *English Poetry, 1900–1950: A Guide to Information Sources*, 71–76. Detroit: Gale Research Co., 1982.

   A bibliographic checklist of twenty-eight primary and twenty-seven secondary source materials. The secondary sources are annotated.

2. Bradshaw, Graham. "Donne's Challenge to the Prosodists."
   Essays in Criticism 32 (1982): 338.

   Bridges's metrical analyses of Shakespeare and Milton
   are inaccurate; his "book-keeping instinct leads him into a
   fanciful fiddling of the main metrical account."

4. Bridges, Robert. Poems. In *Everyman's Book of Victorian Verse*,
   edited by J. R. Watson, 264, 281. London: J. M. Dent and
   Sons, 1982.

   Contains "Elegy" and "London Snow."

5. "Bridges, Robert Seymour, 1844–1930." In *Makers of Nineteenth Century Culture, 1800–1914*, edited by Justin Wintle,
   70–71. London: Routledge & Kegan Paul, 1982.

   The circumstances of Bridges's life and poetic career
   have created a false impression of literary dilettantism. His
   greatest achievement lies in his short lyrics; and, although
   he is more influenced by old masters than by contemporaries, he is far from being a wholly traditional poet. "He
   speaks to a 'fit audience though few.'"

6. Hamilton, Lee Templin. "Robert Bridges: An Annotated Bibliography." Ph.D. diss., Louisiana State University, 1982.

7. Harris, Daniel. *Inspiration Unbidden: The "Terrible Sonnets" of
   Gerard Manley Hopkins*, 7–8, passim. Berkeley: University of
   California Press, 1982.

   Bridges's oversight in not commenting more fully on
   Hopkins's manuscripts and accepting the order of the "Ter-
   rible Sonnets" has shaped and often misled modern
   Hopkins scholarship. Bridges's theological hostility led
   Hopkins to mask his true intent in his sonnets.

1983

1. Hasan, Iqbal. *Robert Bridges: A Critical Study of his Poetry,
   Masques, and Plays*. Aligarh, India: Printwell Publications,
   1983.

2. Litzinger, Boyd. "Two Notes on 'The Wreck of the Deutschland.'" *Victorian Poetry* 21 (1983): 191–95.

   Bridges's gloss of "shire" for "shore" in stanza 34 of "The
   Wreck of the Deutschland" is incorrect. Hopkins intended
   "shore."

3. Phillips, C. L. "A Critical Study of Robert Bridges's *Testament
   of Beauty* and Its Relation to His Intellectual Development."
   Ph.D. diss., University of Cambridge, 1983.

4. Sparrow, John. "Robert Bridges." In *British Writers*. Vol. 6, *Thomas Hardy to Wilfred Owen,* edited by Ian Scott-Kilvert, 71–83. New York: Charles Scribner's Sons, 1983.

   Reprint of 1962.8.

5. Stanford, Donald E. "Introduction." In *The Selected Letters of Robert Bridges,* edited by Donald C. Stanford, 1:19–73. Newark: University of Delaware Press, 1983.

   The nineteen sections of the introduction discuss Bridges's letters and relationships with various correspondents: Lionel Muirhead, G. M. Hopkins, Henry Newbolt, Henry Bradley, Samuel Butler, Edmund Gosse, G. K. Chesterton, G. B. Shaw, A. E. Housman, W. B. Yeats, and others.

6. Stanford, Donald E. "Robert Bridges." In *Dictionary of Literary Biography*. Vol. 19, *British Poets, 1880–1914,* edited by Donald E. Stanford, 40–56. Detroit: Gale Research Company, 1983.

   Bridges, "one of the dominant figures of late Victorian and early twentieth-century British poetry," made his major contribution to literature in the form of short lyrics on traditional subjects. His abiding concern was with mastery of poetic form, not personal expression. Includes a brief bibliography of primary and secondary source materials.

7. Stanford, Donald E. "Robert Bridges, Poet-Typographer." *Fine Print* 9, no. 1 (1983): 7–9.

   Bridges's life-long interest in typography "had a significant effect on the history of printing in the twentieth century."

1984

1. Fike, Francis. "Robert Seymour Bridges: A Bibliography of Secondary Sources, 1874–1981." *Bulletin of Bibliography* 41 (1984): 207–15.

   "A pioneer of syllabic verse, [Bridges] has had considerable influence on the subsequent development of poetry." A bibliography of slightly more than 300 primary and secondary sources on Bridges, including a handful of reviews of secondary materials.

2. Handley-Taylor, Geoffrey. "Crown of Laurels." Letter. *The Times,* 20 July 1984, 11.

   Corrects chronological error of Woolf's letter (see

1984.3) and argues the anecdote refers to John Masefield, not Bridges.

3. Woolf, Harry E. L. "Crown of Laurels." Letter. *The Times,* 14 July 1984, 9.

Recalls Bridges refusing to write a poem celebrating the coronation of King George IV.

1985

1. Stanford, Donald E. "Bridges and Hopkins: The Problem of Influence." In *Hopkins among the Poets,* edited by Richard F. Giles, 1–6. Hamilton, Ontario: The International Hopkins Association, 1985.

Although Bridges and Hopkins shared an interest in sprung rhythm, and Bridges even credits Hopkins with originating the technique, Hopkins's overall influence on Bridges's verses is limited.

1986

1. Laborde, Robert P. "The Poet-Physician: Medicine's Impact on the Lives and Works of John Keats and Robert Bridges." *The Pharos* 49 (1986): 8–11.

Bridges and Keats "are prime examples of the ongoing integral relationship between the healing art of medicine and the creative art of literature."

1987

1. Fletcher, Ian. "Introduction." In *British Poetry and Prose, 1870–1905,* edited by Ian Fletcher, xlii–xliii. Oxford: Oxford University Press, 1987.

Bridges delayed publication of Hopkins's poems out of concern for "his friend's reputation and the Hopkins family's ease of mind." Bridges sought only to credit Hopkins's genius.

1988

1. Bridges, Robert. Poems. In *The Norton Anthology of Modern Poetry,* edited by Richard Ellmann and Robert O'Clair, 108–12. New York: W. W. Norton and Co., 1988.

Includes "London Snow" and "Low Barometer."

2. Ellmann, Richard, and Robert O'Clair. "Robert Bridges." In

The Norton Anthology of Modern Poetry, edited by Richard Ellmann and Robert O'Clair, 108–9. 2d ed. New York: W. W. Norton and Co., 1988.

Bridges "is a poet conspicuous for his exalted utterance" and his indifference to acclaim. He is poetically conservative, emphasizing technique and sounding a note of self-possession. "There is a quite impressiveness about his life and work."

3. Phillips, C. L. "Robert Bridges and the First Edition of Gerard Manley Hopkins's Poems." *Studies in the Literary Imagination* 1 (1988): 7–21.

Although Bridges and Hopkins disagreed about the purposes of sprung rhythm, the prime criteria for assessing poetry, the use of rhymes and religious allusions, and other basic questions of meter, their differences had little effect on Bridges's editing and publishing of Hopkins's poetry. An examination of the personal circumstances of the two poets and a comparison of the manner in which Bridges dealt with the poetry of other friends indicate Bridges was consistent in his handling of Hopkins, and his edition of Hopkins's poetry "should be seen as editorially exceptionally good for 1918 and its editorial note accepted as a harsh but valid part of the history of the revolution that occurred in modern literary taste."

INDEXES

Each of the following three indexes reflects a particular aspect of the bibliography. Index A contains all of the primary works by Bridges which are found in the first two chapters of the bibliography. Index B lists anthologies which contain selections from Bridges's poetry, and Index C cites other secondary source materials.

INDEX A:
WORKS BY ROBERT BRIDGES

INDEX B:
ANTHOLOGIES

INDEX C:
SECONDARY SOURCE MATERIALS